My Lunches with Orson

My Lunches with Orson

Conversations between

Henry Jaglom and Orson Welles

Edited and with an Introduction by

Peter Biskind

Metropolitan Books
Henry Holt and Company
New York

Metropolitan Books
Henry Holt and Company, LLC
Publishers since 1866
175 Fifth Avenue
New York, New York 10010
www.henryholt.com

Metropolitan Books® and ® are registered trademarks of Henry Holt and Company,
LLC.

Library of Congress Cataloging-in-Publication data

Jaglom, Henry, 1939–
  My lunches with Orson : conversations between Henry Jaglom and Orson Welles /
edited by Peter Biskind.—First edition.
        pages cm
  ISBN 978-0-8050-9725-2 (hardback)
  1. Jaglom, Henry, 1939—Anecdotes.   2. Welles, Orson, 1915–1985—Anecdotes.
3. Motion picture producers and directors—United States—Anecdotes.   I. Welles,
Orson, 1915–1985.   II. Biskind, Peter.   III. Title.
  PN1998.3.J276A5 2013
  791.4302'33092—dc23   2013000291

Henry Holt books are available for special promotions and premiums. For details contact:
Director, Special Markets.

Designed by Meryl Sussman Levavi

Photos courtesy of Rainbow Film Company

Printed in the United States of America

10 9 8 7 6 5 4 3 2

For Steve Bloom

Contents

My Lunches
with Orson

Introduction

How Henry Met Orson
by Peter Biskind

ORSON WELLES has long been regarded as one of the greatest film-makers of all time, more specifically, the most gifted of a long line of gifted Hollywood mavericks that started with D. W. Griffith, or perhaps Erich von Stroheim. Today, his *Citizen Kane*, over seventy years after it was released in 1941, still finds a place on every Ten Best list. It topped the British Film Institute's *Sight & Sound* maga-zine's survey for fifty years in a row, only to be toppled in 2012 by Alfred Hitchcock's *Vertigo*, a picture that Welles despised.

But we all know lists and such mean next to nothing in our awards-obsessed, rankings-ridden culture, and there's a much easier and infinitely more pleasurable way to judge the stature of Welles and his films: just watch them, starting with *Citizen Kane*. The opening, a dark and doomy shot of the massive iron gates of Xan-adu capped by a gigantic K, with the Transylvanian ruins of Kane's folly looming above and behind it, grabs our attention, but at the same time warns us that there is more going on than meets the eye, so to speak, because it's all too much, drama shading into melo-drama, undermining itself with irony and camp.

Welles had a genius for the dramatic; he was a master of shock and awe long before they were turned to other, considerably less noble ends, but at the same time he was a skilled miniaturist who worked just as easily on a small canvas with lightness and subtlety. Above all, it was his wizardry with time, space, and light, along with the exquisite tension between his furious, operatic imagination and the elegant, meticulous design and execution of the film— the deep focus, extreme camera angles, striking dissolves, ingenious transitions—that make it crackle with electricity. After *Kane*, movies were never the same. When asked to describe Welles's influence, Jean-Luc Godard remarked, simply, "Everyone will always owe him everything."

Welles was not only a director, but a producer, a skilled actor and screenwriter, and a prolific author of essays, plays, stories, even a newspaper column. More often than not, he wore several of these hats at once, making him a veritable Bartholomew Cubbins of the arts. One finds oneself reaching in vain for adjectives adequate to describe him. As considerable as his gifts were, he himself was more than the sum of his parts, his own greatest production, a commanding, larger-than-life figure of equatorial girth who in later years sported a beard of biblical proportions that made him every casting director's first choice for deities and gurus of all sorts, from Jor-El (Marlon Brando eventually got the role) to God.

George Orson Welles was born on May 6, 1915, in Kenosha, Wisconsin. His parents, Richard Welles, an inventor, and Beatrice Ives, a pianist, artist, and suffragette, were a mismatched couple with a stormy marriage. Eventually, they separated, and his mother, who raised him, died at an early age. Dr. Maurice "Dadda" Bernstein, Beatrice's close friend and rumored lover, became his guardian.

Welles was fiercely precocious. Even as a child, he read widely, showed a keen interest in music, and even became an amateur magician. He finished high school in two years, and got a scholarship to Harvard. He had a prodigious intellect, and was on intimate terms with the great literature of the Western canon, able to recite lengthy swatches of prose and poetry. But he preferred experience to book learning, and persuaded Dadda Bernstein to send him on a walking tour of Ireland when he was only sixteen. Aided by raw talent and boyish good looks—he was over six feet tall, with blond hair and a face like a baby with a little snub nose that always embarrassed him—he talked his way into a small part in a play at the Gate Theatre in Dublin, run by Hilton Edwards and Micheál Mac Liammóir, that started him on his way.

Returning to the States, he soared through New York's theater world and was dubbed "the boy wonder" before he was out of his teens. In 1936, Welles was hired by the Federal Theatre. Fascinated by modernist figures like Max Reinhardt and Bertolt Brecht, he was unafraid to surprise the classics by putting them in contemporary settings, like his triumphant so-called "Voodoo" *Macbeth*, that he produced that year when he was only twenty-one, with an all-black cast. Although he venerated the classics, no text was so sacrosanct that Welles wouldn't or couldn't have his way with it. The following year, he produced his "Blackshirt" *Julius Caesar*, which he turned into an allegory of fascism. (He played Brutus.)

Although he never swallowed the Stalinist line, Welles breathed the heady fervor of those Popular Front years. He considered himself a New Deal liberal, and later would brush up against President Franklin D. Roosevelt, who used him in various ways, taking full advantage of his rhetorical and oratorical skills, most famously his booming voice that sounded like the rumble of not-so-distant thunder.

In between *Macbeth* and *Caesar*, Welles created a scandal with Marc Blitzstein's operetta *The Cradle Will Rock* in 1937. The feds padlocked the doors of the theater where it was set to open, apparently because FDR and/or his advisors feared that its full-throated defense of unions in general and striking workers at Republic Steel in particular (ten were shot by Chicago police in the so-called Memorial Day Massacre), would provoke their enemies in Congress to further slash funding for the Federal Theatre and its parent, the Works Progress Administration. On June 16, 1937, amid a firestorm of press, hundreds of ticket holders marched twenty blocks to New York's Venice Theatre, where they were treated to a bare-bones production in which Blitzstein played the piano on stage while the cast, scattered about the audience, performed the songs. That same year, Welles founded the Mercury Theatre, another successful enterprise. It seemed that he could do no wrong. Three days after his twenty-third birthday, on May 9, 1938, *TIME* magazine put him on the cover.

Controversy—welcome and unwelcome—continued to dog Welles's footsteps. After creating a name for himself in radio, most famously playing Lamont Cranston, or "the Shadow," in the series of the same name, he was given his own show on CBS. His Halloween broadcast on October 30, 1938, adapted from H. G. Wells's *War of the Worlds*, panicked millions of Americans with its urgent, you-are-there style coverage of a Martian invasion, although the target of the ostensible attack, not Washington, D.C., not New York City, but Grover's Mill, New Jersey, should have given listeners pause.

Two years later, the new head of RKO, George Schaefer, gave Welles an unprecedented two-film contract with final cut that shocked and angered the industry. Welles embarked on *Citizen Kane*, which he wrote (with Herman J. Mankiewicz), directed, and headlined. The picture earned him the enmity of news baron William Randolph Hearst, on whose life it was loosely based, and whose *petit nom d'amour* for his lover Marion Davies's nether part—Rosebud—the picture made famous, although, to be sure, there are other claimants to that particular honor.

Kane premiered on May Day, 1941, when Welles was all of twenty-five years old. Hearst made a feverish attempt to block the release of the movie. According to Hearst columnist Louella Parsons in her autobiography, several studio heads, including L. B. Mayer and Jack Warner refused to book the picture in their theaters. Hearst also threatened to decline ads from RKO. Schaefer held fast, but Hearst did manage to force *Kane* into smaller, independent, and therefore less profitable venues, damaging the box office. In the last analysis, though, *Kane* was just too sophisticated for a mass audience, and RKO lost an estimated $150,000 on the picture.

Before Welles started his next movie, the studio insisted that he sign a new contract that revoked his final cut. *The Magnificent Ambersons* (1942) was based on a novel by Booth Tarkington. Production proceeded relatively smoothly, but after he completed part of a rough cut of *Ambersons*, America entered World War II, and Welles abruptly left for Brazil at the behest of President Roosevelt on a goodwill mission, leaving that cut in the hands of editor Robert Wise to finish according to his instructions, to be delivered via phone calls and telegrams. Wise was then to carry it down to Rio for the director to polish. Welles agreed to do yet another film, *It's All True*, in Brazil, at the same time he was busy sampling the pleasures afforded by Rio's louche lifestyle, for which he confessed more than a passing interest. The war interfered with his plans to polish the film in Brazil himself, and his idyll turned to ashes when unbeknown to him, the studio sneak-previewed *Ambersons* at the Fox Theater in Pomona, California, on March 17, 1942. The screening turned into a fiasco when a flock of ticket holders walked out, leaving scathing comments on the cards. Running scared, RKO slashed 45 minutes out of Welles's original 132-minute cut, without consulting him. Then as now, unhappy endings were taboo, so the studio took it upon itself to shoot a new, happier one. What was supposed to be a dark saga of the rise and fall of a wealthy family, left behind by an America forever changed by industrialization, was turned into an inane, maudlin, and totally preposterous tale of reconciliation. The film flopped.

Welles never entirely recovered his footing. With his directing career sidelined, he found work as an actor, performing in pictures such as *Journey into Fear* (1943), *Jane Eyre* (1943), and *The Stranger* (1946), much of which he unofficially directed, while pursuing an active social life. He eventually married three times—to Virginia Nicholson, Rita Hayworth, and Paola Mori—and fathered three daughters, one by each wife. Welles spent the last twenty-four years of his life with Oja Kodar, a stunning Croatian-Hungarian artist, actress, and collaborator, twenty-six years his junior, although he never divorced Mori. He couldn't have been an easy man to live with, considering his roving eye and what Nicholson called his "crushing ego."

Hayworth, the former Margarita Carmen Cansino, was, of course, one of the brightest stars of the forties and early fifties, so much so that the crew of the *Enola Gay* is rumored to have used her pinup decal as "nose art" for either the bomber or its payload, Little Boy, before dropping it on Hiroshima. Welles whimsically fell in love with her, so the story goes, when he saw her picture on the cover of *LIFE* magazine, and then and there decided to marry her. Which he did, only to discover that she was, with much justification, insanely jealous, as well as morbidly insecure and depressed. After a few turbulent years, she kicked him out, married Prince Aly Khan, and gave birth to a daughter, Yasmin. Before the divorce was finalized, Hayworth and Welles did a movie together, *The Lady from Shanghai* (1947).

The Lady from Shanghai does not, of course, take place in Shanghai, nor is the femme fatale Hayworth plays exactly a lady. It is classic film noir with an absurdly intricate plot featuring a dizzying array of twists and turns. The picture ends with a justly celebrated face-off between Welles and Hayworth in the Magic Mirror Maze, inside a fun house. And like *Ambersons*, it was mutilated by the studio.

Welles followed up *The Lady from Shanghai* with one of his most successful turns in front of the camera, in *The Third Man*, which won the Palme d'Or at the 1949 Cannes Film Festival. Directed by Carol Reed, in part from a script by Graham Greene, it is a dark and moody specimen of its kind, shot on actual locations in rubble-strewn, postwar Vienna. An unremittingly grim picture, it is notable not only for the location work, but for Welles's diamond-hard performance as a contemptible black marketeer named Harry Lime who makes his living stealing, diluting, and selling penicillin. It also boasts of a wonderful set piece on Vienna's outsized Ferris wheel, the *Wiener Riesenrad*; a climactic manhunt in the city's sewers, anticipating Andrzej Wajda's *Kanal* by nearly a decade; and a distinctive score, performed exclusively on the zither.

His last studio movie, *Touch of Evil* (1958), was also recut. It is too much of a mixed bag to be considered one of his best efforts. It features Charlton Heston at his most wooden and Janet Leigh playing a character so repellent that it's hard not to root for the ridiculous, black leather jacket clad delinquent refugees from *The Wild One* who menace her with dope-filled needles and worse. On the other hand, the picture can boast of an extraordinary performance by Welles as a border town cop so degenerate he makes Harry Lime look good, an all-too-brief appearance by Marlene Dietrich, lots of vintage Wellesian dialogue, and a bravura opening: a heart-stopping, three-minute-and-twenty-second tracking shot that follows a car as it meanders across the border from Mexico into Texas, where it explodes in a spectacular inferno of fire and smoke. If you can ignore Heston and Leigh, these gems alone are worth the price of admission, not to mention the entire careers of many directors. No exaggeration.

Despite his fitful success behind the camera, Welles directed eleven or so feature-length movies in the course of his career, including his outstanding Shakespeare trilogy—*Macbeth* (1948), *Othello* (1952), and *Chimes at Midnight* (1965), his tribute to Falstaff. The last feature-length picture he made, *F for Fake*, finished in 1973, and not released in the United States until four years later, was financed by Welles himself when he was unable to find backing elsewhere. Both fish and fowl, fiction and documentary, he called it an "essay film," which meant that it was a melange of everything he could lay his hands on in the vicinity of art forger extraordinaire Elmyr de Hory and faux Howard Hughes biographer Clifford Irving in sun-drenched Ibiza, as well as found footage of Picasso standing in a room behind a venetian blind, edited so that it appears that the artist is ogling Kodar as she parades up and down the street in a variety of chic outfits. Last but not least was Welles himself, dramatically draped in his signature black magician's cape skewering critics, while sharing his thoughts on illusion, art, and authenticity. *F for Fake* is an original, ingenious film, in which Welles bends the medium to his own ends and foreshadows pictures like Chris Marker's *Sans Soleil* (1983) and Banksy's *Exit Through the Gift Shop* (2010) that blur the lines between fact and fiction, but it was all too clever for its own good. However, the public never even got the opportunity to judge for itself since the distributor dumped the film.

These years, despite his more than respectable track record against daunting odds, tell a depressing tale of frustration, often featuring Welles as his own worst enemy. Like Kane, whose Xanadu was never finished, he accumulated a collection of incomplete pictures, earning him a reputation for walking away from his own movies before they were finished. True or false, the bad rap was impossible to shake, and made it difficult—not to say impossible—for Welles to raise money for his films.

Desperate for cash to complete old projects and/or launch new ones, he cobbled together an income by means of his performances in innumerable pictures, some very good and many very bad, ranging from B movies produced by fly-by-night producers in no-name countries to odds and ends like soaps, game shows, and TV commercials. It didn't seem to matter to him, so long as they put money in the bank, although hustling like this took its toll. He made Paul Masson a household name by intoning the slogan, "We will sell no wine before its time." (Outtakes of an inebriated Welles slurring his way through one of these commercials can be seen on YouTube.) But even Paul Masson turned him out when a slimmed down Welles reportedly explained on a talk show that he had given up snacks—and wine.

Henry Jaglom was born into a family of wealthy German and Russian émigrés. His father, Simon, was imprisoned after the 1917

Russian revolution for being a "capitalist," and left the Soviet Union with his brothers shortly thereafter, eventually making his way to London, where Henry was born in 1941, and then to New York City, where he grew up. He never knew exactly what his father did for a living, but when he applied to the University of Pennsylvania and was asked his father's occupation, Simon told him, "Write international commerce and finance."

Jaglom studied at the Actors Studio, and then joined the mid-1960s migration from New York to Los Angeles, where his friend Peter Bogdanovich had promised him the lead in his first feature, *Targets* (1968), a role Bogdanovich later decided to play himself. His acting career ended abruptly when he was washing his feet in the sink of his apartment and the phone rang, the caller notifying him that Dustin Hoffman had gotten the lead in *The Graduate* (1967), a role he was convinced he was born to play. He muttered an epithet and turned his attention to writing and directing.

In the wake of a worldwide explosion of film culture in the 1960s, movies became the medium of choice for aspiring artists. Under the sway of the French, Jaglom, like many of his contemporaries, wanted to do it all: not just act or write, but edit, direct, and produce as well. They didn't want to be directors for hire by some baboon in the front office with a big, fat cigar; they wanted to be filmmakers or, as the French would have it, *auteurs*, a term popularized in America by Andrew Sarris in the sixties. Simply put, an *auteur* was to a film what a poet was to poetry or a painter was to painting. Sarris argued, controversially, that even studio directors such as Howard Hawks, John Ford, and Alfred Hitchcock, or bottom-of-the-bill toilers like Sam Fuller, displayed personal styles, were the sole authors of their pictures, and were therefore authentic artists. Welles, of course, was the very avatar of an *auteur*. Jaglom and his friends venerated him as the godfather of the so-called New Hollywood. He recalls, "We used to talk about him as the patron saint of this new wave of filmmaking."

Partial to long, colorful scarves and floppy hats, Jaglom swiftly fell into bad company. He smoked dope at the Old World Restaurant on Sunset Boulevard with Jack Nicholson and was drawn into the orbit of Bert Schneider. Schneider, along with Bob Rafelson, had made a lot of money off the Monkees, and with the addition of Steve Blauner, ran a small production company called BBS. Schneider gave Jaglom a crack at editing the company's second picture, Dennis Hopper and Peter Fonda's *Easy Rider* (1969).

Easy Rider was a hit, and BBS was on its way. Jaglom discovered in himself the ability to talk people into things they didn't want to do. On the basis of his work on *Easy Rider*, he convinced Schneider to allow him to finance his first feature, *A Safe Place* (1971), with Nicholson and Tuesday Weld. Jaglom was desperate to add Welles to the cast. Bogdanovich was conducting a series of exhaustive interviews with Welles that would become a book and had become very friendly with him. Jaglom asked his friend to introduce the two of them. Bogdanovich warned him, "He won't do it."

"Well, tell me where he is, and I'll go meet him."

"He's in New York at the Plaza Hotel. But you musn't go to him without a script. He hates that. And you don't have a script."

Welles was an intimidating presence with an imperious manner, a slashing wit, and a reputation for not suffering fools. Jaglom was no fool, but he didn't have a clue how he was going to persuade the great man to join his cast. Undeterred, he flew to New York and went up to his hotel room. Welles opened the door wearing purple silk pajamas. Jaglom remembers, "He looked like this huge grape." Welles demanded, "What do you want?" in an unwelcoming way.

"I'm Henry Jaglom."

"Yes, but does that tell me what you want?"

"It should, if Peter Bogdanovich has spoken to you."

"Peter speaks to me often."

"The reason I'm here is because I'm making a film for Bert Schneider who Peter is making a film for. Which I arranged."

"I know who Bert Schneider is."

"Peter is making *The Last Picture Show*—"

"Yes, good for him."

"And I want to make my film, *A Safe Place.* With you in it."

"Where's the script?"

"I don't have a script."

"Why not?"

"Because if you're going to be in it, it's going to be completely different than if somebody else is going to be in it."

"No script? No interest."

"Your character is a magician."

"A magician? I'm a magician. An amateur magician, of course. But I don't do first scripts by first-time directors."

"What do you mean you don't do them? *Citizen Kane* was your first script."

"Did you really say 'A magician'?"

"Yeah. And I think I want him with a little Jewish accent. I know you go to lunch in London at that Jewish restaurant all the time. There are rumors that you think you're Jewish—"

"I am Jewish. Dr. Bernstein was probably my real father." He thought for a moment and then said, "Can I wear a cape?"

"Sure, wear a cape."

"OK, I'll do it."

Needless to say, the old-timers on the set, which meant most of the crew, looked askance at the young director, whose hair was gathered in a long pony tail and whose feet were squeezed into white Capezio dancing shoes. The second day of shooting, they all turned up wearing American flag lapel pins. (This was, after all, 1971, the middle of the Vietnam war.) During a lunch break, Jaglom was sitting with Schneider, Nicholson, and Weld. Welles joined them, saying, "You're the arrogant kid who pushed me into this. How's your arrogance doing?"

"Not very well. The crew hates me. They're totally negative. Everything I tell them to shoot, they say, 'It won't cut,' or 'it's not in the script.' I have to fight to get every single shot. I'm exhausted."

Jaglom talked a reluctant Welles into appearing in A Safe Place, *his first film. Here, he directs Welles and Tuesday Weld in Central Park, c. 1971.*

"Oh, my God, I should have prepared you. Tell 'em it's a dream sequence."

"What?"

"Just do as I tell you. Trust me. You trusted me enough to hire me. Do it." After lunch, they returned to the set. Jaglom had mapped out an intricate shot. The cameraman said, "Can't do it."

"Why?"

"It won't cut."

"It's a dream sequence."

"A dream sequence? Why didn't you say so? I'll get on my back and do it like this. It will be psychedelic." Jaglom went to Welles that night, and said, "What the fuck is this? Everything I want to do, I say, 'Dream sequence,' and they're pussycats."

"You have to understand, these are people who work hard for a living. They have tough lives. Structured lives. They work all day, then they have dinner, put their kids to bed, go to sleep, and get back to the set at five o'clock the next morning. Everything else in life except for dreams has rules. The only place they're truly free is when they fall asleep and dream. If you tell them it's a dream sequence, they will be freed of those rules to be creative, imaginative, and give you all kinds of stuff that they've got inside of them." That was the best advice Jaglom would ever get.

Welles taught Jaglom two other lessons: First, "Make movies for yourself. Never compromise, because those compromises are going to haunt you for the rest of your life." And second, "Never give Hollywood control over your tools because sooner or later, they will take them away from you."

When Jaglom screened *A Safe Place* for Schneider, the lights came up and Schneider was crying. Jaglom thought, "Oh, that's great, I moved him." Schneider said, "Yeah, I'm very moved. I'm also an asshole."

"Whaddya mean?"

"This movie can't possibly make a penny. Too abstract and poetic. The only person more self-indulgent than you in making this picture is me, for letting you. Why? Because it made me cry."

Jaglom was cutting his second film, *Tracks*, with Dennis Hopper when he ran into Welles in 1978 at Ma Maison, where the great man was having lunch with Warren Beatty. Now no more than a tarnished monument to an illustrious but checkered career, pursued by creditors, overweight and afflicted with depression—the "black dog" as he called it—Welles had pretty much given up. Schneider had been willing to finance a picture for him early in the decade, starring Jack Nicholson. As he put it, "Jack was ready to work for nothing, but when push came to shove, Orson just didn't have the courage to work anymore. It didn't matter what you put on his plate. He was frozen." Schneider was right. Welles's high hopes for *F for Fake* had been dashed on the rocks of public indifference.

As he himself explained, "I had begun to think I should stop and write my memoirs of twenty volumes so I could be paid for something and stop this misery." Or, as he put it to Jaglom, rather more succinctly, "I've lost my girlish enthusiasm."

Still, much as he might have wanted to, Welles couldn't or wouldn't give up. Welles's attitude toward the studios was ambivalent. He admitted to Jaglom that he had something to prove to a Hollywood that had turned its back on him. And vanity aside, he had an expensive imagination, and he was eager to take advantage of the resources only the studios could provide. On the other hand, he knew that he was temperamentally and aesthetically unsuited to the factory filmmaking practiced by the studios. He was forced to work as an independent filmmaker outside the system even in the late sixties and early seventies, when mavericks were courted, if only momentarily. But by the late seventies and eighties, when the studio system reasserted itself, his chances of finding a studio home vanished entirely.

Welles and Jaglom became fast friends. They were an odd couple, to say the least. Their backgrounds, personalities, ages (Jaglom was in his late thirties, Welles in his mid-sixties)—even their films were discrepant. What they did have in common was a fierce desire to go their own way. Moreover, the relationship was mutually advantageous. Jaglom was dazzled by the legend and seduced by the reality of Welles. Who wouldn't have been? He treasured his friend's advice, basked in his reflected glow, relished the role of Welles's gatekeeper. He also realized that he had something that Welles needed—energy, enthusiasm, and viability as a working filmmaker. He had bankrolled his own films by selling off the rights for foreign territories to a patchwork of overseas distributors and investors in much the same way American independents would do a decade later, and so he was perfectly positioned to navigate the maze of European financing to Welles's benefit. Although Jaglom had only a few films to his credit at the time he started to help Welles, he went on to make many more.

Welles blossomed in the warmth of Jaglom's admiration. As he put it, in the flush of a new optimism, "Henry has brought me back to life. Nothing can stop me now." With new movies in limbo and mired in unfinished projects, Welles had to know Jaglom was his best bet. More, Welles took a real interest in his friend's films, spending hours hunched over the flatbed editing machine with him, giving him the benefit of the narrative genius that lived inside him, and in fact, working vicariously through Jaglom.

Eventually, the younger man became Welles's sounding board, confessor, producer, agent, and biggest fan. He was the magician's magician who was going to turn the dross that Welles's career had become into gold, even if he had—figuratively speaking, more or less—to steal, cheat, and lie to do it.

Jaglom picked him up and dusted him off, set about buffing his image and laundering his legend. Using the playbook he had followed himself, Jaglom began lining up backers for Welles's various films. He got him good press, arranging interviews in which both men spoke enthusiastically about the projects on Welles's plate, many of which were so, so close to production, already cast, just waiting for the check to clear the bank. He energetically rebutted the conventional wisdom, that his friend suffered from cinematic ADD: "It's not that he didn't finish the movies. He ran out of money, somebody gave him more money to do something else, but he always planned to go back to everything." Admit it or not, however, Jaglom had set for himself a Sisyphean task. True, it's impossible to exaggerate the difficulties facing a filmmaker like Welles trying to get traction in a business dominated by a handful of powerful studios. There were more than enough extenuating circumstances to get Welles off the hook for the butchery of *Ambersons*, but even Barbara Leaming, his best and friendliest biographer, admits he had little excuse for disappearing to Europe before *Macbeth* was edited, replicating almost to the letter the *Amberson* fiasco. And doubly so, after he had made a point of coming in early and under budget to confound the doubters. It was the same old song. Victim of his own prodigious gifts, he was the man who did too much, and thus did, in the end, too little. Not even he—writer, actor, producer, and director—could execute all the films, plays, radio shows, and miscellaneous projects that popped into his head, especially while aiding the war effort and carrying on an energetic love life. His brain was like a boiling cauldron filled with bubbles that rose to the surface and burst—into thin air. He needed someone to yell, "Focus!" and this was the mantle Jaglom assumed.

Regardless of the reasons for Welles's spotty, post-*Kane* record, Jaglom discovered that indeed, none of the deep pockets that flapped about the Wellesian flame were willing to drop cash on the table. Welles found himself in the paradoxical position of being honored as America's greatest filmmaker yet unable to get backing for his projects. Buffeted by a blizzard of rejections, he struggled like any neophyte filmmaker just out of film school. "Orson couldn't get a movie done," says Jaglom. "He wanted to do this wonderful adaptation of these Isak Dinesen stories, *The Dreamers*. I went around to every studio, every producer, and I couldn't get him money. So I said, 'Orson, they don't want to do an adaptation. But I can sell you with a new movie, and new script. Tell me some stories.' He said, 'I can't write anymore, I'm no longer capable of writing.'

" 'That's bullshit. Just put it down on paper. Or just tell it to me; I'll put it down on paper.'

" 'I can't. I know what I can do, I know what I can't do.' Then "three weeks later, the phone rang at four in the morning," Jaglom continues. " 'I don't know what the fuck you're making me do this for. I can't sleep, but I've written three pages. They're terrible!'

" 'Read them to me.' Of course they were great. So for the next three or four months, I got him to write this whole script." It was called *The Big Brass Ring*, and it was about an old political advisor to Roosevelt, a homosexual named Kimball Menaker, who has mentored a young, Kennedy-esque senator from Texas with presidential ambitions named Blake Pellerin, who runs against Ronald Reagan and loses. Pellerin, according to Welles, as if describing himself, "is a man who has within him the devil of self-destruction that lives in every genius . . . Like all great men he is never sure that he has chosen the right path in life. Even being president, he feels, may somehow not be right: 'Should I be a monk? Should I jerk off in the park? Should I just fuck everybody and forget about everything else?' *That* is what *The Big Brass Ring* is all about."

Adds Jaglom, "*The Big Brass Ring* was about America at the end of the century, the way *Kane* was America at the beginning of the century. I couldn't fuckin' believe it—I've got the bookend to *Kane*." Now Jaglom was sure the wallets would open. "I told Orson, 'You know, all the people I came up with and struggled side by side with have become stars and production heads. I know them; they're my friends. They all worship you.' I went around to everybody, and I couldn't get anyone to do it. Every studio turned it down. The times had changed. Instead of talking about Orson Welles, they were talking about grosses. Orson understood this. He said, 'I expected the studios to turn me down. Why wouldn't they? I've never made any money for them.'"

After Jaglom failed to get the studios to show even a glimmer of interest in *The Big Brass Ring*, producer Arnon Milchan agreed to give Welles $8 million and final cut—for the first time since *Kane*—"if I got one of six or seven A-list actors to agree to play Blake Pellerin," Jaglom continues. "We celebrated, opened a big bottle of Cristal, because one thing Orson thought was that actors wouldn't betray him. He said, 'I know actors.'" But apparently not well enough. Clint Eastwood turned down the film because it was too left wing for him. Robert Redford said he already had another political thriller lined up. Burt Reynolds's person just said, "No." "Orson was really pissed about that," Jaglom continues. "He said, 'Burt Reynolds owes me so much, I wrote the foreword to a book about him, and he didn't have the guts to phone me himself and simply say, "It's not for me." His agent told me. Big money is the problem with these stars. When they get too rich, they behave badly.'

"One by one each of these actors came up with reasons, including my two friends Warren and Jack. Warren behaved better than anybody. He was very honorable, and Orson never blamed him. He had just come off of *Reds*, which Orson thought was the stupidest idea for a movie he'd ever heard. Warren said to me, 'Oh, God, tell Orson it's like coming out of a whorehouse after being there all night fucking, you're exhausted, and you walk out in the sunlight, and there's Marilyn Monroe with her arms out. I'd love to, but I just can't.'"

The best bet was Nicholson. Welles was ready to go in July 1982. He had a budget and a shooting schedule, as well as a crew and locations. Half a million dollars was slated to go to Nicholson. But the bigger the stars, the slower they are to respond, and by 1984, Welles still hadn't gotten an answer from him.

Welles was disappointed, but Jaglom refused to give up. In his words, unlike Hannibal, "he needed to bring the elephants over the mountains to Rome." Jaglom arranged a "coming out" press conference for Welles on the terrace of the Carlton Hotel at the Cannes Film Festival in 1983. Within ten minutes the great man had attracted a flock of journalists. To demonstrate that Welles was ambulatory, Jaglom hid his wheelchair.

Welles's unveiling was a success, generating a flurry of good press, but in some ways, the trip to Cannes was too much of a good thing. His diet had been drastically restricted by his doctor. Dining with his friend at L'Oasis, Welles ordered a salad, a light fish with lemon, and Perrier. "Then he made me order everything, three entrees, six desserts," Jaglom recalls. "'Just take a bite, and describe the taste to me,' he told me. What I didn't know was that he was going back to the hotel, waking up the chef, and ordering four steaks, seven baked potatoes, and a whole lot more in the middle of the night."

Beginning in 1978, Welles and Jaglom had lunch nearly every week—sometimes more often—at Welles's regular hangout, Ma Maison, where he ate almost every day. A celebrated French restaurant owned by Patrick Terrail, Ma Maison was located at 8360 Melrose Avenue, near Kings Road, in West Hollywood. It opened its doors in 1975 in a tiny, worn, and very unprepossessing bungalow formerly owned by a carpet company. It was set far back from the street, so that the area in between served as a "garden room," covered with leaky plastic that Terrail fondly referred to as a "shower curtain," and carpeted by Astroturf, colored a bilious green. The decor of the interior was nothing to speak of either; one critic mocked it as "the fanciest French restaurant in Kingman, Arizona."

But none of that mattered. Ma Maison quickly became the hottest restaurant in Hollywood. The kitchen served French cuisine with a nouvelle California accent and was the home of Wolfgang Puck for its first six years. It was so chic that it didn't even publish its phone number. It was a place where deals were made, where agents conned producers and producers conned agents.

Welles, who had ballooned to the size of a baby elephant, customarily ditched his wheelchair at the back door and entered the establishment through the kitchen. He used to sit in a mammoth chair to the right of the entrance at one of Ma Maison's few indoor tables. According to Gore Vidal, who also dined regularly with Welles, he draped himself in "bifurcated tents to which, rather idly, lapels, pocket flaps, buttons were attached in order to suggest a conventional suit."

Welles and Terrail were great friends, and Welles used to call upon Terrail to perform every sort of impossible, last-minute service. "The restaurant had become his office," he recalls. "We used to get all his mail and a lot of his phone calls." Terrail relayed messages from people who wanted to contact him, like George Stevens, Jr., who produced the telecast of the Kennedy Center Honors, and wanted to know if Welles would accept one of its distinguished awards, which usually meant the recipient was ready for the form-aldehyde. Terrail told Welles, "They'll fly you to Washington. Do you want to do it?" Welles replied, "No. I would have to sit next to Reagan in the box up there." On one occasion, the archbishop of the Greek Orthodox Church, dining at Ma Maison, asked to be introduced to Welles. As he reached over to shake his hand, Welles's constant companion, an ill-tempered toy poodle named Kiki that was no bigger than a box of Kleenex, leaped up from his master's ample "crotch," as Terrail puts it, and went for his arm. Neverthe-less, the orthodox pope invited the portly filmmaker to a high mass he was conducting at the Cathedral of Saint Sophia the following day, offering to dedicate the ceremony to him. Welles replied, "I am flattered by the invitation, but I must decline. I'm an atheist."

People of all sorts—friends, fans, and strangers—stopped by his table hoping for a golden word or two. Welles would roar at them, in his resonant, Orsonian voice, "HELLO, HOW ARE YOU?!" But he could also be rude. Recalls Jaglom, "People would say, 'So nice to see you.' He would say, 'So nice to see you too, but that's enough.' He would try to intimidate them." Jaglom asked him why. Pointing at his pug nose, he would answer, "You have to do something to let them know that you're not just a little creature. You have to be the ruler of the forest. People want me to be 'Orson Welles.' They want the dancing bear show."

"You don't need that. You're not so insecure that—"

"I'm much more insecure than even you know, Henry."

"I don't believe that. You're arrogant and sure of yourself."

"Yes, I'm sure of myself, but I'm not sure of anybody else."

According to Vidal, Welles's conversation "was often surreal and always cryptic. Either you picked up on it or you were left out." With Jaglom, he seemed to find a comfort zone that enabled him to show his vulnerabilities. His exchanges with his friend roamed over many subjects—movies, theater, literature, music, politics—of which Welles demonstrated an alarming mastery. There was no topic too insignificant or esoteric for Welles to weigh in on. The words he put in the mouth of Menaker in *The Big Brass Ring* suited him as well: "I am an authority on everything." Movies? "Ballet—that's the only thing less interesting." Eisenhower? "Underrated." Art Deco? "I deeply hate it." Kiwis? "Ruined by all the French chefs."

Although Welles was generous with his praise for people he respected, he invariably peppered his conversation with amusing if often unflattering anecdotes about those he didn't. He was particularly biting when his attention was directed toward former friends and enemies. Welles's outsized personality, as well as his early, dazzling success in the theater, radio, and movies, made him the envy of everyone in the arts, and a target of more than a few. Rightly or wrongly, and in the course of the lunches, he settled scores with those he thought had done him wrong. One of them was Pauline Kael, who became something of a celebrity in the sixties and seventies for her movie reviews in the *New Yorker*. Kael engaged in a decade-long feud with fellow critic Andrew Sarris. *Pace* Sarris, Kael argued that film is a collective art form, the fruit of a collaboration among many talents. A writer herself, she particularly lavished praise on the long-suffering screenwriter. Kael knew that if she could chip away at Welles's credit block, she could reduce the *auteur* theory—and Sarris—to a pile of rubble. In a notorious two-part essay published in the *New Yorker* in 1971 called "Raising Kane," she made the case that Herman J. Mankiewicz, not Welles, was largely responsible for the script of *Citizen Kane*. (On the film itself, both men are credited with the script.) To add insult to injury, the essay, since discredited, was republished that same year in *The Citizen Kane Book* as the introduction to the shooting script. Welles was deeply wounded. As Jaglom put it, "Everyone treated Orson badly, but the one thing that he had was that he made the greatest movie ever made, and she tried to undermine that by creating this mythology that he had nothing to do with the script, that he was taking false credit. He was furious."

Ironically, even Bogdanovich, who was a confirmed *auteurist*, was not proof against his ire. He had followed up *The Last Picture Show* with *What's Up Doc*, starring Barbra Streisand in 1972, and *Paper Moon*, featuring Ryan O'Neal and his daughter, Tatum, in 1973. With three hits in a row, he could have filmed the phone book and still found studio backing. His friendship with Welles endured throughout this period, but in the late seventies, it cooled. Welles complained that Bogdanovich never helped him when he was riding high and had the power to do so.

After his trifecta of hits, Bogdanovich went into a dramatic decline. Welles took a dim view of his late-seventies tabloid romance with Dorothy Stratten, a former *Playboy* centerfold, as well as the book he wrote about her, titled *The Killing of the Unicorn*, after she was shot to death by her estranged husband.

John Houseman, whom Bogdanovich called his "single most destructive enemy," was the target of Welles's most venomous barbs. He felt that his former partner had built his reputation with bits and pieces scavenged from the wreckage of his own. It was Houseman who had brought Welles into the Federal Theatre in 1934, where Welles quickly eclipsed his benefactor. "Houseman started out being in love with me, and then turned to hate," he once said. For the next decade or so, the two, like the proverbial scorpions in a bottle, were uneasily paired in a variety of projects, including the Mercury Theatre, until the ill will between them boiled over while Welles was at RKO. At a dinner at Chasen's, Houseman claimed Welles threw plates of food at him, including "two dishes of flaming methylated spirits," and accused him of stealing money.

In later years, when Welles's career went into free fall, Houseman's soared. After a lengthy career as a producer and director on both stage and screen, he won a Best Supporting Actor Oscar for *The Paper Chase* (1973) and segued into the long-running TV series of the same name. Houseman published several volumes of memoirs that to some degree framed the accounts of Welles's career thereafter, not to his benefit. The two remained enemies for the rest of their lives.

With Bogdanovich unable or unwilling to help him, Welles found himself only fitfully employed throughout much of the post-*Kane* period. He had decades to contemplate his mistakes and missed opportunities. He was never comfortable in Hollywood. Or perhaps it was the other way around: he was too comfortable, and despised himself for it. He loved to instruct Jaglom in the subtle ways the town distorted the values of the people who lived and worked there. A week or so after Welles delivered a tribute to Natalie Wood, Robert Wagner came up to the table. Welles asked, "Are you OK?"

"Yes, fine."

"Such a terrible thing."

"But you know, you were great."

"I was?"

"You were the best one."

"Thank you."

"The best one. It had so many elements. You were strong; you were poignant." After Wagner left, Welles turned to Jaglom and said, "You understand? You have just seen what Hollywood is really about. The man is in tears, he feels the tragedy, but he is so inured to reality, that for him it's a show. And I gave the best performance. He's giving me a review." Says Jaglom, "Even Orson was shocked."

In the spring of 1984, the movie version of *The Cradle Will Rock*, which Welles was slated to direct, and which was already cast, came crashing down when the main backer withdrew. Welles was desolate. He told Barbara Leaming, "It just shows me that I really shouldn't have stayed in this business . . . We live in a snake pit here. I've been keeping a secret from myself for forty years—from myself, not from the world—which is that I hate it."

Welles knew that Jaglom had recorded his own father's reminiscences for thirty years, and asked him to record their conversations as well. His only proviso was that the recorder be out of sight, concealed in Jaglom's bag, so he didn't have to look at it. Jaglom began taping the conversations in 1983 and continued until Welles was struck down by a fatal heart attack in the middle of the night of October 10, 1985. He died with a typewriter on his lap, working on a script. The conversations survived. Jaglom stashed the tapes—about forty of them—in a shoebox where they gathered dust for almost three decades.

I first met Jaglom in the early 1990s, when he shared his recollections and diaries with me while I was researching my history of the New Hollywood of the seventies, *Easy Riders, Raging Bulls*. He told me about these tapes, and I urged him to have them transcribed, but there was always another film to make, and of course that took precedence. The tapes sat and sat, even though he was eager for them to see the light of day. Eventually, they did. I read the transcripts with an eye to whether or not there was a book in them, and decided that there most definitely was.

Jaglom's tapes, a record of the last three years of Welles's life, may be the last undiscovered trove of Welles on Welles. Eavesdropping on Welles and Jaglom is the next best thing to sitting at the table. And what a table it was. Welles comes off as a fascinating bundle of contradictions, at once belligerent and almost childishly vulnerable, a schemer who often behaved impetuously at great cost to himself, a shy man who hid behind an endless array of masks but loved to display himself and liked nothing better than the thunderous roar of applause. He was forgiving and generous but tenaciously held grudges against those he felt had done him wrong. He could roar with anger one minute and laughter the next. Who knows to what darkness he was prey in moments of depression, but he rarely gave in to self-pity, at least not in these conversations with his friend.

The Welles who emerges here is a different Welles from either the fraud his detractors pilloried in their biographies or the genius his admirers enshrined in theirs. Because Jaglom was not interviewing Welles, but conversing with him, we have a Welles unguarded and relaxed, with his hair down, unplugged, if you will, willing to let fly with all manner of politically incorrect opinions—sexist, racist, homophobic, vulgar (let's be kind, call it "Rabelaisian")—driven, perhaps, by the impish pleasure he took in baiting his liberal friend, offending his progressive susceptibilities, or just by native, irrepressible ebullience. The more perverse Welles's views, the more fiercely he argued them. His antic wit, stringent irony, and enormous intelligence shine through these conversations and animate every word, making it difficult not to love the man.

"Orson is an enigmatic figure to most people," Jaglom wrote. "He presents a compelling challenge: how to reconcile the brilliant child prodigy, the precedent-shattering stage director, the iconoclastic radio figure, the celebrated Shakespearean artist, the groundbreaking filmmaker credited by almost everyone with having made the greatest movie of all time with the TV talk show buffoon, the corny wine commercial huckster, the willing participant in tasteless low-comedy "roasts," the bloated, seemingly self-destructive outcast whose unfinished works and aborted projects became legendary?"

These two may never be reconciled. And unplugged or not, this book makes no claim to discover the "real" Welles. There may never have been a real Welles. As Jaglom puts it, "The final scene of *The Lady from Shanghai* is perhaps the most autobiographically truthful metaphor in all of his work. It is ultimately impossible to find the real Orson Welles among all the fun-house mirrors he so energetically set in place." Welles appeared to prefer it that way. "Wait till I die," he once told Jaglom at lunch. "They'll write all kinds of things about me. They'll just pick my bones dry. You won't recognize me and if I came back to life and read them, I wouldn't recognize me myself. I've told so many stories, you know, just to get out of situations, or out of boredom or just to entertain! Who can remember them all, but I'm sure they'll come back to haunt me. Or rather, my ghost. Don't set them right, Henry. They don't want to know. Let them have their fantasies about me."

Welles's final turn in front of the camera occurred in Jaglom's *Someone to Love* (1987). Jaglom played the lead, a filmmaker, and Welles's character is known only as "the friend." "I gave him his farewell to the audience," Jaglom recalls. "He wouldn't let me ever show him laughing on screen, because he insisted, 'Fat men shouldn't laugh. It is very unattractive.' Once I caught him laughing, and he actually said, 'Cut,' to my cameraman. And my cameraman stopped the camera. 'What are you doing?'

"'Orson Welles told me to cut.'

"'Turn it right back on.' He turned it back on, and Orson, thinking that it was off, reached behind him, somehow producing a lit cigar. He puffed on it, and started to laugh, a roaring, embracing, wonderful laugh. I knew I wouldn't be able to get it in the film because he would have hated it. When he died, I felt the least I could do was give them his one last laugh."

Patrick Terrail closed Ma Maison in the autumn of 1985, a month or so after Welles's death. The decision had been made before Welles's heart attack, but regardless, the timing was appropriate. Generally, life goes on when one or another of us sheds this mortal coil, but in this case, the restaurant that was his second home, which sustained him in so many ways, died with him. It did survive, under new ownership in a different location, but in the absence of its most famous patron at his regular table, it was never the same.

A Note on the Text

My Lunches with Orson is divided into two parts, 1983, the year in which most of these conversations took place, and then 1984 and 1985. The organization is roughly, but not strictly, chronological. Welles's ruminations on like subjects, in fact separated by months or even years, have been grouped together. The quality of the tapes varies drastically. Many of them are clear, but some, with the recorder lying muffled in Jaglom's bag, are indistinct, and so I have taken occasional liberties with the text—adding or subtracting phrases, smoothing out syntax—for the purpose of making the conversations more concise and intelligible. Occasionally, I have attributed material to Welles that is quoted in Jaglom's diaries or was furnished by him in interviews with me. With his permission, I have sometimes altered his comments with an eye to furnishing context. Welles was, above all, a great entertainer, a fabulator who, like Scheherazade, learned early to sing for his supper. Some of the stories he tells in these conversations will have a familiar ring, and indeed, they have been told elsewhere, but they were too good to go unrepeated, and since he always provided fresh details or new twists in every telling, I have included them.

Part One

1983

Lunch companions at a star-studded reception c. 1983, thrown by the Hollywood Foreign Press Association, organized by Jaglom to show potential backers that Welles was still viable. Guests included Warren Beatty, Jack Nicholson, Jack Lemmon, and Michael Caine.

At lunch at Ma Maison, I encountered Orson standing with difficulty to embrace me after several months with great warmth (or what seems like great warmth, I have never been quite sure), and I am always moved, as I was today. And as always, amazingly for me, I was somewhat at a loss for what to say, and all I came up with was some general pleasantry/ banality on the order of, "How is everything?" Orson answered me with, "Oh, I don't know, do you?" And I, acknowledging that my question had been excessive in scope, reduced it to, "How is everything today?" To which he answered, happy that he had forced greater specificity: "Fine . . . as of this hour."

Then tonight, two hours ago as I twirled the television dial, I was astonished to find myself watching the opening newsreel segment of Citizen Kane. *I have just finished watching him grow old with makeup and acting skill on a body in its twenties, in a film designed by his mind in its twenties, and the film—and he in it—are so affecting and so near-perfect that the idea of watching anything else after seemed incomprehensible. I wonder, Was there nothing for him to do with the rest of his life after making it, is that his secret and does he know it? Is* Citizen Kane *his "rosebud"?*

—HENRY JAGLOM, Journal Entry, April 2, 1978

1. "Everybody should be bigoted."

In which Orson turns restaurant reviewer, confesses that he never understood why Katharine Hepburn disliked him, but knew why he disliked Spencer Tracy. He detested the Irish, despite his friendship with John Ford, and liked right-wingers better than left-wingers.

(Jaglom enters, Welles struggles out of his chair to greet him. They embrace, kissing each other on the cheek in the European way.)

HENRY JAGLOM: *(To Kiki)* How are you, Kiki?

ORSON WELLES: Look out—she'll bite you . . . All right, what are we gonna eat?

HJ: I'm going to try the chicken salad.

OW: No, you aren't! You don't like it with all those capers.

HJ: I'm going to ask them to scrape the capers away.

OW: Then let me tell you what they have on their hands in the kitchen.

HJ: It must be nuts in the kitchen. I've never seen it this packed.

OW: They're so busy, this would be a great day to send a dish back to the chef.

HJ: You know, Ma Maison is not my idea of the legendary restaurants of Hollywood. The romance for me was Romanoff's. And then I got here and there was no Romanoff's.

OW: Yeah! Romanoff's only stayed open until forty-three or forty-four. It had a short life. Romanoff's and Ciro's were the two restaurants that we did all the romancing in, and they both closed. Everybody was photographed with the wrong person coming out, you know? Romanoff's is a parking lot now, and when it was going broke, Sinatra came with sixteen violins and sang every night for three weeks for free, to try and help the business. We all went every night. It was sensational. Don the Beachcombers was another great place to take the wrong girl because it was dark. Nobody could see anybody.

HJ: What about Chasen's?

OW: Chasen's was a barbecue place, originally. I was one of the original backers of Chasen's—and Romanoff's.

HJ: You owned Romanoff's?

OW: Yes, and he never gave me anything. Nor did Chasen. I was a founder of both those restaurants. Me and a lot of suckers. We didn't expect anything from Romanoff because he was a crook. And Dave Chasen somehow forgot the original barbecue backers when his became a big restaurant.

Ma Maison was started in 1973, and continues. I wouldn't go for a long time because of the unlisted phone number. It irritated me so. It's a snobbish business not having a phone number. Somebody gave the number out on television, just to be bitchy. I don't envy these guys, though. It's a tough, tough business to run a restaurant.

WAITER: Going to have a little lunch today? We have scallops, if you want, Mr. Welles. Plain, or we have them prepared with a petite legume.

OW: No, it would have to be plain. Let's see what other choices I have.

W: Just in case, no more crab salad.

OW: No more crab salad. Wish you hadn't mentioned it. I wouldn't have known what I wasn't gonna get!

W: Would you wish the salad with grapefruit and orange?

OW: That's a terrible idea. A weird mixture. It's awful—typically German. We're having the chicken salad without . . . without capers.

HJ: They ruined the chicken salad when they started using that mustard. It's a whole different chicken salad.

OW: They have a new chef.

W: And roast pork?

OW: Oh, my God. On a hot day, roast pork? I can't eat pork. My diet. But I'll order it, just to smell pork. Bassanio says to Shylock: "If it please you to dine with us." And Shylock says: "Yes, to smell pork; to eat of the habitation which your prophet the Nazarite conjured the devil into. I will buy with you, sell with you, talk with you, walk with you, and so following, but I will not eat with you, drink with you, nor pray with you."

HJ: Isn't there something about the devil taking the shape of a pig in the Bible? Or did Shakespeare invent that?

OW: No, Jesus did put a whole group of devils into the Gadarene swine. Shakespeare was just trying to give Shylock a reason for not eating with them.

HJ: I would like the grilled chicken.

W: Okay.

OW: And a cup of capers.

W: Capers?

HJ: No, no—that's his joke.

OW: So I'll have a soft-shell crab. Alas, he breads it. I wish he didn't, but he does. I'll eat it anyway. *Est-que vous avez l'aspirine?* Have you any aspirin?

W: Of course. Here you are, Monsieur Welles.

HJ: Do you have some pain or something?

OW: I have all kinds of rheumatic pains today. The knees. I always say it's my back, because I get more sympathy. But I've got a bad right knee, which is what makes me limp and walk badly. The weather must be changing. I never believed that, until I became arthritic. I just started to ache the last half hour. I think it's gonna rain or something. Aspirin is great stuff. I have no stomach problems, and no allergy to it.

(Waiter exits.)

HJ: Isn't that terrible, the Tennessee Williams thing? Did you hear how he died?

OW: Only that he died last night. How did he die?

HJ: There was a special kind of pipe that he used to inhale something. And it stopped him from being able to swallow or breathe, or . . .

OW: Some dope? Or maybe a roast beef sandwich.

HJ: "Natural causes." Then they went to "unknown causes." So mysterious.

OW: I'd like to be somebody who died alone in a hotel room—just keel over, the way people used to.

Ken Tynan had the funniest story he never printed. He and Tennessee went to Cuba together as guests of [Fidel] Castro. And they were in the massimo leader's office, and there are several other people there, people close to El Jefe, including Che Guevara. Tynan spoke a little fractured Spanish, and Castro spoke quite good English, and they were deep in conversation. But Tennessee had gotten a little bored. He was sitting off, kind of by himself. And he motioned over to Guevara, and said (in a Southern accent), "Would you mind running out and getting me a couple of tamales?"

HJ: Do you think Tynan made it up?

OW: Tynan wasn't a fantasist. Tennessee certainly said it to somebody. But I've suspected that he improved it, maybe, by making it Guevara.

Did I ever tell you about the play of his I lost, like a fool, to [Elia] Kazan? Eddie Dowling, who used to be a producer on Broadway, sent me a play by a writer called Tennessee Williams. I didn't even read it. I said, "I can't do this; I just can't consider a play now." It was called *The Glass Menagerie*.

HJ: *The Glass Menagerie*—my God.

OW: If I had done *The Glass Menagerie*, I would have done all those others. A big dumb mistake.

HJ: A pity . . . By the way, I was just reading Garson Kanin's book on Tracy and Hepburn.

OW: I blurbed that book. I thought if I wrote something, I'd finally make it with Katie! But instead, I found out it was the worst thing I could have done!

HJ: I must say, reading it, I didn't understand why she was so upset about it.

OW: I think it was that he said she and Tracy lived together that—

HJ: A lot of people knew that.

OW: Particularly since she laid around the town like nobody's business.

HJ: Hepburn?

OW: Hoo boy! I sat in makeup during *Kane*, and she was next to me, being made up for *A Bill of Divorcement*. And she was describing how she was fucked by Howard Hughes, using all the four-letter words. Most people didn't talk like that then. Except Carole Lombard. It came naturally to her. She couldn't talk any other way. With Katie, though, who spoke in this high-class girl's finishing-school accent, you thought that she had made a decision to talk that way. Grace Kelly also slept around, in the dressing room when nobody was looking, but she never said anything. Katie was different. She was a free woman when she was young. Very much what the girls are now.

HJ: I wonder what she's got against you. Did you ever do anything to Tracy, or say anything about him?

OW: I was never a fan of his. When I was a young man, I got up and made a fuss at *Captain Outrageous*—uh, *Courageous.*

HJ: Well, you see, that probably got back to Hepburn at some point, and that's why she doesn't like you.

OW: Come on. Nobody knew who I was when I did that. I was nineteen years old. I stood up in the Paramount Theater and said, "You ought to be ashamed of yourself!" when he was doing the Portuguese accent. With the curled hair! The usher told me to get out because I was making such fun of his performance.

HJ: Did you bark?

OW: No, I was imitating his accent as he went along.

HJ: The single lapse in his career.

OW: That was not the only one. He had several. I'm having a hard time trying to think of a great Tracy performance. Well, he was gigantic in *Judgment at Nuremberg*, although it is not a great picture, but I couldn't stand him in those romantic things with Hepburn.

HJ: You didn't find him charming as hell?

OW: No, no charm. To me, he was just a hateful, hateful man. Tracy hated me, but he hated everybody. Once I picked him up in London, in a bar, to take him out to Nutley Abbey, which was Larry [Olivier] and Vivien [Leigh]'s place in the country. Everybody came up to me and asked for autographs and didn't notice him at all. I was the Third Man, for God's sake, and he had white hair. What did he expect? And then he sat there at the table saying, "Everybody looks at you, and nobody looks at me." All day long, he was just raging. Because he was the big movie star, you know. When he was on the set it was, "Why is that actor distracting everyone while I'm talking?"

But I don't think that's it, really. I think Katie just doesn't like me. She doesn't like the way I look. Don't you know there's such a thing as physical dislike? Europeans know that about other Europeans. If I don't like somebody's looks, I don't like them. See, I believe that it is not true that different races and nations are alike. I'm profoundly convinced that that's a total lie. I think people are different. Sardinians, for example, have stubby little fingers. Bosnians have short necks.

HJ: Orson, that's ridiculous.

OW: Measure them. Measure them! I never could stand looking at Bette Davis, so I don't want to see her act, you see. I hate Woody Allen physically, I dislike that kind of man.

HJ: I've never understood why. Have you met him?

OW: Oh, yes. I can hardly bear to talk to him. He has the Chaplin disease. That particular combination of arrogance and timidity sets my teeth on edge.

HJ: He's not arrogant; he's shy.

OW: He *is* arrogant. Like all people with timid personalities, his arrogance is unlimited. Anybody who speaks quietly and shrivels up in company is unbelievably arrogant. He acts shy, but he's not. He's scared. He hates himself, and he loves himself, a very tense situation. It's people like me who have to carry on and pretend to be modest.

HJ: Does he take himself very seriously?

OW: Very seriously. I think his movies show it. To me it's the most embarrassing thing in the world—a man who presents himself at his worst to get laughs, in order to free himself from his hang-ups. Everything he does on the screen is therapeutic.

HJ: That's why you don't like [Bob] Fosse either—*All That Jazz*.

OW: Yes, that's right. I don't like that kind of therapeutic movie. I'm pretty catholic in my taste, but there are some things I can't stand.

HJ: I love Woody's movies. That we disagree on. We disagree on actors too. I can never get over what you said about Brando.

OW: It's that neck. Which is like a huge sausage, a shoe made of flesh.

HJ: People say Brando isn't very bright.

OW: Well, most great actors aren't. Larry [Olivier] is very—I mean, seriously—stupid. I believe that intelligence is a handicap in an actor. Because it means that you're not naturally emotive, but rather cerebral. The cerebral fellow *can* be a great actor, but it's harder. Of performing artists, actors and musicians are about equally bright. I'm very fond of musicians. Not so much of singers. All singers think about is their throats, you know? You go through twenty years of that, what have you got to say? They're prisoners of their vocal cords. So singers are the bottom; actors are at the top. There are exceptions. Leo Slezak, the father of Walter Slezak the actor, made the best theater joke of all time, you know? He was the greatest Wagnerian tenor of his era. And the king—the uncrowned king—of Vienna. He was singing *Lohengrin*—if you're a Wagnerian, you know that he enters standing on a swan that floats on the river, onto the stage. He gets off, sings, and at the end of his last aria, is supposed to get back on the swan boat and float off. But one night the swan just went off by itself before he could get on it. Without missing a beat, he turned to the audience and ad libbed, "What time does the next swan leave?"

HJ: How can those people have such charm without any intelligence? I've never understood that.

OW: Well, it's like talent without intelligence. It happens.

HJ: If Tracy was hateful, none of that comes across in the work.

OW: To me it does. I *hate* him so. Because he's one of those bitchy Irishmen.

HJ: One of those what?

OW: One of those bitchy Irishmen.

HJ: I can't believe you said that.

OW: I'm a racist, you know. Here's the Hungarian recipe for making an omelet. First, steal two eggs. [Alexander] Korda told me that.

HJ: But you liked Korda.

OW: I love Hungarians to the point of sex! I almost get a hard-on when I hear a Hungarian accent, I'm so crazy about them.

HJ: I don't understand why you're saying that about the Irish.

OW: I know them; you don't. They hate themselves. I lived for years in Ireland. The majority of intelligent Irishmen dislike Irishmen, and they're right.

HJ: All these groups dislike themselves. Jews dislike themselves.

OW: Nothing like Irishmen.

HJ: That doesn't make them right, Orson, and you know that. And I don't accept this prejudice from you. I know that you don't really have it.

OW: I do have it. I do have it. Particularly against Irish-Americans. I much prefer Irishmen from Ireland. If I have to have an Irishman, I'll take one of those. And Irishmen in England are quite good. All the great Irish writers mostly left and went to England, except for [George William] Russell and [William Butler] Yeats. Yeats makes me shiver. I was in Dublin at the time when he was still—

HJ: I didn't realize he was still around in the thirties.

OW: Yeah. He was at every party, and you could see him walking in the park. And Lady Gregory. All those people were still around— the famous Gaelic nationalists. I got to know them all. And you know, some of my best friends are Irishmen.

HJ: Oh, God!

OW: But when I look at Tracy, I see that everything that's hateful about him is Irish. Everything that's mean. Every Irishman will tell you that. Seven hundred years of bitter oppression changed their character, gave them that passive meanness and cunning. All I can say is what Micheál Mac Liammóir said when we were making *Othello*, and I asked him, "Describe the Irish in one word." He said, "Malice." Look, I love Ireland, I love Irish literature, I love everything they do, you know. But the Irish-Americans have invented an imitation Ireland which is unspeakable. The wearin' o' the green. Oh, my God, to vomit!

HJ: That's boring and silly, and—

OW: No, it's to vomit. Not boring and silly. Don't argue with me. You're such a liberal! Of course there's no proof. It's the way I feel! You don't want me to feel that, but I do! I think everybody should be bigoted. I don't think you're human if you don't acknowledge some prejudice.

HJ: Yes. But acknowledging some prejudice and really having full-out hate, like you have against the Irish—

OW: Well, not so much that I'm rude to them or would bar them from my house. It doesn't *mean* anything, it's just a perception of their character. Or of the majority of them.

HJ: Okay. But if that's true, then all it means is that there's cultural conditioning.

OW: Well, of course there is!

HJ: So when they come to America, that changes them.

OW: Yes, they become a new and terrible race. Which is called "Irish-Americans." They're fine in Australia; they're fine in England; they do well in Latin America. It's in New York and Boston that they became so frightful. You know, the old Kennedy was a real Irish-American. That's what I mean.

HJ: But his kids weren't?

OW: No. They escaped it. You can see the Irish ancestry, but their character wasn't Irish. Their life wasn't based on malice. You know, if you're here in America long enough, you lose the faults and the virtues of your original culture. The Italians will lose the sense of family when they finally get to the next generation. They won't hang together, the way they still do now.

HJ: It's like in Israel, where there's no art now. All these Jews, they thought they were gonna have a renaissance, and suddenly, they're producing a great air force, but no artists. All those incredible virtues of the centuries—

OW: They left all that in Europe. Who needs it? They get to Israel, and they sort of go into retirement.

HJ: Their theater is boring; their film is boring. Painting and sculpture—

OW: Boring. You know, the only time they make good music is when Zubin Mehta, a Hindu, comes to conduct.

HJ: It's amazing. When the Jews were in Poland, every pianist in the world—

OW: Every fiddler who ever lived was Jewish. It was a total Russian-Jewish, Polish-Jewish monopoly. Now they're all Japanese and Orientals. [Arthur] Rubinstein is gone.

HJ: Last year.

OW: I knew Rubinstein for forty years, very well. I told you his greatest line. I was with him at a concert in Albert Hall, and I had no seat, so I listened to the concert sitting in the wings. He finished. Wild applause. And as he walked into the wings to mop his face off, he said to me, "You know, they applauded just as loudly last Thursday, when I played well."

HJ: Dying at ninety-five is not bad. He had a full life.

OW: Did he ever.

HJ: It's true, all that, then? That he fucked everybody?

OW: He was the greatest cocksman of the nineteenth century. Of the twentieth century. The greatest charmer, linguist, socialite, raconteur. Never practiced. He always used to say, "You know, I'm not nearly as good a pianist technically, as many of my rivals, because I am too lazy to practice. I just don't like to. [Vladimir] Horowitz can do more than I can. He sits there and works. I like to enjoy life. I play clinkers all the time." But, he says, "I play it better with the clinkers."

HJ: And Horowitz hates his life, and for fifteen years hasn't been able to play or even move.

OW: Rubinstein walked through life as though it was one big party.

HJ: And then ended it with this young girl. Didn't he leave his wife after forty-five years when he was ninety to run off with a thirty-one-year-old woman?

OW: Like Casals. Who suddenly, at the age of eighty-seven or something, came up with a Lolita.

HJ: Getting back to the Irish, some are liberals, like Robert Ryan. He was a brave man, politically and socially. Tell me Robert Ryan was not a decent man.

OW: He's a wonderful actor. I don't think of him as Irish; he just has an Irish name. He must be fourth-generation.

HJ: Now, Ford you liked. He was an Irishman.

OW: We were very good friends, and he always wanted to do a picture with me. He was a pretty mean son-of-a-bitch Irishman. But I loved him anyway.

HJ: When did you first meet him?

OW: When I was shooting *Kane*, he came to the set on the first day of shooting.

HJ: Just to wish you well?

OW: No, for a reason. He pointed to the assistant director, a fellow called Ed Donahue, who was in the pay of my enemies at RKO, and said, "I see you got snake-in-the-grass Donahue on the picture." And left. He came to warn me that my assistant was a fink.

HJ: I've always heard that Ford was a drunk.

OW: Never when he was working. Not a drop. Just the last day of a picture. And he'd be drunk for weeks. Serious, serious drunk. But for him, drinking was fun. In other words, he wasn't an alcoholic. Went out with all the boys. Irishmen, get drunk and fight. Everybody gets beat up in the pub, you know? I've lived through all that. Went to jail in Ireland for rowdyism. It was a culture where nobody got married until they were thirty-five, because they were always dreaming of emigrating, and they didn't want to be stuck with the kids, financially. So all these poor virgin ladies sat around waiting to get married, and the guys are all swinging at each other, reverting to the bestiality of the male.

HJ: There was not much fucking around, I would imagine, because it was a Catholic culture?

OW: Oh, my God, yes. By the girls. I could hardly draw a breath when I visited the Aran Islands. I was all of seventeen. And these great, marvelous girls in their white petticoats, they'd grab me. Off the petticoats would go. It was as close to male rape as you could imagine. And all with husbands out in their skin-covered canoes. All day, while I had nothing to do. Then the girls would go and confess it all to the priest, who finally said to me, "I had another confession this morning. When are you leaving?" He was protecting the virtue of his flock. When I told that story, there was tremendous excitement in America from the clergy, who said it could never have happened.

HJ: Wasn't Ford very reactionary, politically? Like his pals John Wayne and Ward Bond?

OW: Yes, but all those guys loved me, for some reason. And I loved them. I have a beer bottle that was put together on Ford's yacht, with different Mexican and American beer labels signed by that gang of people, all dedicated to me. Now this was at a time when I was a well-known Hollywood Red.

HJ: And their reactionary positions came from what?

OW: Irish, Irish, Irish. The Irish were taught, "Kill the kikes," you know. I really loved John Wayne. He had some of the best manners of almost any actor I've ever met in Hollywood.

HJ: Did you ever speak to him about politics at all?

OW: Why would I? I'm not like you. I'm not gonna set John Wayne straight. I never had any trouble with extreme right-wingers. I've always found them tremendously likeable in every respect, except their politics. They're usually nicer people than left-wingers.

HJ: Easy for you to say. You were in Europe in the fifties, during the blacklist, when all that shit happened.

OW: Yes, I was lucky. I wasn't in America during the McCarthy era. I was on every list in the world. Every time they asked for help for whatever cause, I said, "Sign me up." But in my *New York Post* column, all during the forties, I was in print attacking Stalinist Russia at a time when everybody thought God was smiling on Stalin. I wanted to explain to HUAC the difference between a Communist and a liberal, so I kept begging, "May I please go to Washington to testify?" But they didn't dare ask me.

HJ: But you're so forgiving about these kinds of very dangerous—

OW: Forgiving!? Supposing you go to the Amazon, and you live in a village of headhunters. Now, if you're an anthropologist, you can become very fond of those headhunters, but you're not gonna argue about head-hunting with them.

HJ: I don't understand how somebody with liberal feelings would not discuss politics with Wayne or Bond or Adolphe Menjou at a time when they had the power to hurt people, and in fact did a lot of damage.

OW: Well, Menjou was so fighting mad that you couldn't talk to him. But Noël Coward took care of him wonderfully. Menjou was heading a USO troupe. Noël Coward was heading the equivalent of the USO—whatever it was called in England—you know, entertaining the troops. And they met in Casablanca. And they were eating in the mess. Menjou was talking about how terrible it was in England, that those "nigger" soldiers were fucking all the English girls, and you didn't know what kind of race it was gonna be: "Isn't that true, Noël?" And Noël said, "Well, I think it's perfectly marvelous." Menjou said, "What?" Noël said, "At last there'll be a race of Englishmen with good teeth." No, with Menjou you couldn't talk. He was a raving maniac.

2. "Thalberg was Satan!"

In which Orson is rude to Richard Burton, was bored by Meyer Lansky, and argues that Irving "the Boy Wonder" Thalberg invented factory filmmaking with his producer system.

———————

HENRY JAGLOM: During these last two weeks, two studios have been taken over by their distribution chiefs.

ORSON WELLES: Well, if RKO hadn't been taken over by a distribution head, I would never have made *Citizen Kane*. That's why I got that contract with final cut. Because George Schaefer didn't know any better! None of the other guys would ever have given me a contract like that.

HJ: Were things really better in the old days?

OW: It's terrible for older people to say that, because they always say things were better, but they really were. What was so good about it was just the quantity of movies that were made. If you were Darryl Zanuck, and you were producing eighty moving pictures under your direct supervision, how much attention could you pay to any one picture? Somebody was gonna slip something in that's good.

I got along well with even the worst of the old moguls, like Harry Cohn. They were all easier to deal with than these college-educated, market-conscious people. I never really suffered from the "bad old boys." I've only suffered from lawyers and agents. Wasn't it Norman Mailer who said that the great new art form in Hollywood is the deal? Everybody's energy goes into the deal. Forty-five years I have been doing business with agents, as a performer and a director. As a producer, sitting on the other side of the desk, I have never once had an agent go out on a limb for his client and fight for him. I've never heard one say, "No, just a minute! This is the actor you should use." They will always say, "You don't like him? I've got somebody else." They're totally spineless.

HJ: In the old days, all those big deals were made on a handshake. With no contract. And they were all honored.

OW: In common with all Protestant or Jewish cultures, America was developed on the idea that your word is your bond. Otherwise, the frontier could never have been opened, 'cause it was lawless. A man's word had to mean something. My theory is that everything went to hell with Prohibition, because it was a law nobody could obey. So the whole concept of the rule of law was corrupted at that moment. Then came Vietnam, and marijuana, which clearly shouldn't be illegal, but is. If you go to jail for ten years in Texas when you light up a joint, who are you? You're a lawbreaker. It's just like Prohibition was. When people accept breaking the law as normal, something happens to the whole society. You see?

(Richard Burton comes to the table.)

RICHARD BURTON: Orson, how good to see you. It's been too long. You're looking fine. Elizabeth is with me. She so much wants to meet you. Can I bring her over to your table?

OW: No. As you can see, I'm in the middle of my lunch. I'll stop by on my way out.

(Burton exits.)

HJ: Orson, you're behaving like an asshole. That was so rude. He actually backed away, like a whipped puppy.

OW: Do not kick me under the table. I hate that. I don't need you as my conscience, my Jewish Jiminy Cricket. Especially do not kick my boots. You know they protect my ankles. Richard Burton had great talent. He's ruined his great gifts. He's become a joke with a celebrity wife. Now he just works for money, does the worst shit. And I wasn't rude. To quote Carl Laemmle, "I gave him an evasive answer. I told him, 'Go fuck yourself.'"

HJ: So you're saying he sold out, and you didn't.

OW: If I would have gone and done their scripts, I could've worked for any of the big studios. I was perfectly bankable even when the bad Welles legend was at its most virulent. I could still make pictures.

HJ: As long as it was somebody else's picture, and not an "Orson Welles picture." So would you have made a movie based on one of their scripts?

OW: No. I wouldn't. I was offered *Porgy and Bess* and—Sam Goldwyn offered me two or three pictures.

HJ: What was he like?

OW: In his time, he was considered a classy producer. Because he never deliberately did anything that wasn't his idea of the best quality goods. I respected him for that. He was an honest merchant. He may have made a bad picture, but he didn't know it was a bad picture. And he was funny. He made me laugh. He actually once said to me, in that high voice of his, "Orson, for you I'd write a blanket check." He said, "With Warner Brothers, a verbal commitment isn't worth the paper it's written on." He was there for me all the time. But Gregg Toland, who shot so many Goldwyn pictures, told me that in Russia, if you didn't see every actor's face brilliantly, they had to go back and reshoot it. Sam was the same way. Whenever there wasn't a bright light on a star's face for thirty seconds he went nuts: "I'm paying for that face! I want to see the actor!" Long shots, all right, but no shadows. It was all too much for me. I was just not constituted to deal with him.

HJ: You were never tempted?

OW: Never. To go through what Willie Wyler went through with him? Life is too short. Charlie MacArthur and Ben Hecht wrote *Wuthering Heights* in my house in Sneden's Landing, and Goldwyn was with 'em all the time. I was trying to sleep in the afternoon, before my radio show. And I heard the way Sam behaved with them. And I thought, "Never will I put myself through that."

He was really a monster. The last night I ever spent with him turned me against him forever. He was a guest at my house. I had come back to Hollywood, after years away, and I invited all these old dinosaurs, who were still around, and some other people. And he left right after dessert, because there were a number of guests who weren't on the A list. You know, he wouldn't have done that before. He got old.

HJ: Did anyone else offer you movies besides Goldwyn?

OW: [Louis B.] Mayer offered me his studio! He was madly in love with me, because I wouldn't have anything to do with him, you know? Twice he brought me over—spent all day wooing me. He called me "Orse." Whenever he sent for me, he burst into tears, and once he fainted. To get his way. It was fake, absolutely fake. The deal was, I'd have the studio but I'd have to stop acting, directing, and writing—making pictures.

HJ: Why wouldn't you have anything to do with him?

OW: Because he was the worst of them all. The rest of them were just what they were. The thing about Harry Cohn was: he looked like such a villainous Hollywood producer, there was nothing he could do that would surprise you. But L.B. was worse than Harry Cohn. He was self-righteous, smarmy, waving the American flag, doing deals with the Purple Gang in Detroit—

HJ: The Purple Gang in Detroit?

OW: Before the unions, it was all Mafia. But no one called it the Mafia. Just said "the mob." And, mainly, the Purple Gang. They controlled all the blue-collar guys who projected the movies, pushed the dollies, swept the floors. They controlled the Teamsters. They didn't control directors or anything—didn't need to. And when L.B. needed extra money, he got it from the Purple Gang. When he wanted strong-arm work, he'd call the Purple Gang, who'd send their tough guys into town.

HJ: Louis B. Mayer had people hit?

OW: Beat up. I wouldn't put it past him to have people killed. He liked to think of himself as a founding father and capo of the Mafia.

HJ: Did you know any of them? Meyer Lansky?

OW: Very well. He was probably the number-one gangster in America. I knew them all. You had to. If you lived, as I did, on Broadway during that period, if you lived in nightclubs, you could not not know them. I liked screwing the chorus girls and I liked meeting all the different people who would come in, and I liked staying up until five in the morning, and they used to love to go to nightclubs. They would come and sit at your table.

HJ: How did Lee Strasberg do with Hyman Roth, remember, in *Godfather II*?

OW: Much better than the real thing. Meyer Lansky was a boring man. Hyman Roth is who he should have been! They all should have been like that and none of them were. *The Godfather* was the glorification of a bunch of bums who never existed. The best of them were the kind of people you'd expect to drive a beer truck. They had no class. The classy gangster is a Hollywood invention. The classy gangster was the ideal of every real gangster, who then started to dress like George Raft, and tried to behave like George Raft, and so on.

HJ: They must have had something to get to the top.

OW: Energy, guts, luck, and the willingness to kill your friends in the interest of business. All this code of honor, and all that shit— pure invention. There was a famous cop on Broadway called Brannigan. I think I've got his name right, because his name was slightly changed by Damon Runyon and used as a character in *Guys and Dolls*. He used to go down Broadway every few weeks with a baseball bat, and I went with him a couple times, to watch it happen. Followed him, not went with him. He'd come into Lindy's—"Mindy's" to Runyon—and places like that, late at night. And if he'd see anybody, no matter who, he'd grab him, take him out in the street, and beat him up. Meaning: Get out of town. Don't sit around here—you make the town look bad. I saw him put Charlie Luciano, head first, into a garbage can outside of Reuben's, at five thirty in the morning.

HJ: "Lucky" Luciano?

OW: Yeah. He was never called "Lucky," except by the press.

HJ: In my mind, Luciano had forty people around him who would kill anyone who came near him.

OW: Not Brannigan—they all ran. They all had to go to the men's room when he came in with a baseball bat. He was just a tough Irishman. He said, "Fuck 'em."

HJ: But on the plus side, didn't Mayer create Thalberg, the greatest producer who ever lived?

OW: Thalberg was the biggest single villain in the history of Hollywood. Before him, a producer made the *least* contribution, by necessity. The producer didn't direct, he didn't act, he didn't write— so, therefore, all he could do was either (A) mess it up, which he didn't do very often, or (B) tenderly caress it. Support it. Producers would only go to the set to see that you were on budget, and that you didn't burn down the scenery. But Mayer made way for the producer system. He created the fellow who decides, who makes the directors' decisions, which had never existed before.

HJ: Didn't the other studio heads interfere with their directors?

OW: None of the old hustlers did that much harm. If they saw somebody good, they hired him. They tried to screw it up afterwards, but there was still a kind of dialogue between talent and the fellow up there in the front office. They had that old Russian-Jewish respect for the artist. All they did was say what they liked, and what they didn't like, and argue with you. That's easy to deal with. And sometimes the talent won. But once you got the educated producer, he has a desk, he's gotta have a function, he's gotta do something. He's not running the studio and counting the money—he's gotta be creative. That was Thalberg. The director became the fellow whose only job was to say, "Action" and "Cut." Suddenly, you were "just a director" on a "Thalberg production." Don't you see? A role had been created in the world. Just as there used to be no conductor of symphonies.

HJ: There was no conductor?

OW: No. The *konzertmeister*, first violinist, gave the beat. The conductor's job was invented. Like the theater director, a role that is only 150, 200 years old. Nobody directed plays before then. The stage manager said, "Walk left on that line." The German, what's his name, Saxe-Meiningen, invented directing in the theater. And Thalberg invented producing in movies. He persuaded all the writers that they couldn't write without him, because he was the great man.

HJ: F. Scott Fitzgerald must have been impressed by him, to make him the model for *The Last Tycoon*.

OW: Writers always fell for his shtick, knowing better. Writers are so insecure that when he said, "I don't write, but I'll tell you what's wrong with this," they just lapped it up. He could cut them off at the knees with all his "genius" stuff, and making them sit for three hours before he allowed them to come in to see him, and all that. By the way, there were better scripts written, on the whole—this is a generalization, but it's my opinion—even when writers considered that they were slumming by coming out here. Faulkner and everybody. "We're going out there to get some money." Still, they did an honest job for that money, because instead of going back to their little place up in the Hollywood hills to write their scripts, they had to eat with each other every day in the studio commissary, which made for a competitive situation. It was collegial—"What are you working on?"—and they shared funny stories about how dumb the producer was, how bad the director was, and all that. But they didn't want their peers to do better than they did, so they worked hard. Harder than these people now who want to be directors, who have done nothing but look at movies since they were eight years old, who have never had an experience in their lives. Or experienced any culture beyond movie culture.

HJ: But Thalberg was also creative. At least from Fitzgerald's point of view.

OW: Well, that's my definition of "villain." He obviously had this power. He convinced Mayer that without him, his movies wouldn't have any class. Remember that quote Mayer gave? All the other moguls were "dirty kikes making nickelodeon movies." He used to say that to me all the time.

HJ: When Mayer found you, you were very young, and very attractive, very magnetic.

OW: That's why he loved me; he thought I was another Thalberg.

HJ: Did you know Thalberg?

OW: I didn't know him. I was out here, playing in the theater, when he was alive, but I didn't meet him. Then he died.

HJ: Irene Mayer Selznick says in her book about L.B., her father, that everybody knew Thalberg had this sort of death sentence hanging over him from the beginning. He started at MGM knowing that at thirty he was gonna die. He had rheumatic fever. A bad heart.

OW: I know a lot of people who expect to die early. Thalberg turned it to his advantage.

HJ: He must have been incredibly skillful at manipulating Mayer.

OW: Thalberg used to manipulate everybody, brilliantly. Not only Mayer, but actors, directors, writers. He used his death sentence, his beauty, everything.

HJ: He was also beautiful, apparently, yeah?

OW: Yeah. Enormously charming and persuasive. Thalberg was Satan! You know, the classic Satan. And, of course, Norman worked around the clock.

HJ: Irving.

OW: Irving, yeah. I always think of him as Norman, and I don't know why. He would reduce people; and, having reduced them, flatter them. He was obviously a weaver of spells who was able to convince everyone that he was the artist. Thalberg was way up here, and the director was way down there. The result was that he negated the personal motion picture in favor of the manufactured movie. He was responsible for the bad product of Metro, and the style which continued afterwards: the Thalberg style.

HJ: That's true. Nobody knows who directed *Gone With the Wind*. Or, there were many directors on the same movie, like *The Wizard of Oz*. Metro's great, great movies somehow just happened.

OW: Yes. And they still look like any one of the Metro directors could have made them. At lunch in the commissary, you could play musical chairs with every movie—move every director to another movie—and you would not be able to tell the difference in the rushes the next day. Now, Warner's made the good pictures. It was rough there. Jack Warner tortured and murdered everybody, but he got great pictures out of them, obviously.

HJ: What directors managed to work under Thalberg that way?

OW: Vic Fleming, or Woody Van Dyke, whoever.

HJ: Were any of them gifted?

OW: George Cukor was.

HJ: Not as much as they say. His films were signature-less. Even the good ones.

OW: He was a very competent stage director. But it's true, you can't tell a Cukor picture.

HJ: *Holiday, Philadelphia Story.*

OW: Writers' pictures.

HJ: Or Tracy pictures, or Hepburn pictures; they're star pictures.

OW: Exactly—all of them. That's why, to me, Thalberg is the number-one villain. I think he was a real destroyer.

HJ: Okay. But, he didn't do anything to hurt people.

OW: Well, he destroyed [Erich] von Stroheim, as a man and as an artist. Literally destroyed him. And von Stroheim at that moment was, I think, demonstrably the most gifted director in Hollywood. Von Stroheim was the greatest argument against the producer. He was so clearly a genius, and so clearly should have been left alone—no matter what crazy thing he did—

HJ: But he was so extravagant that he reached the point where economically, it was impossible. If the stories about him are true. Or was he just so original he threatened everyone?

OW: They had to make him into a monster. I had a very interesting experience when I was making *Touch of Evil.* I had a scene in a police archive, and they let me shoot it in the real archive of Universal. And while they were setting the lights, I looked up von Stroheim, the budgets of his movies. They weren't that high. The idea that he was so extravagant was nonsense. Anita Loos wrote a brilliant book about Hollywood—*Kiss Hollywood Goodbye.* And she thinks [Josef] von Sternberg is a marvelous man. Sorry, not von Sternberg. Von Stroheim. Von Sternberg was a real louse. But nevertheless, the portrait of von Stroheim was a hatchet job. She said, "We all loved Von," and then she presents a picture of this terrible Prussian. Once she said to me, "The nicest Jewish actor you ever met in your life." You know?

HJ: Did you know von Stroheim?

OW: Yes, very well. But later, when he had become an actor and was living in France, Charlie Lederer and I wrote a movie for him in Paris, with Pierre Brasseur, and Arletty. It was called *Portrait of an Assassin*. It was about those guys that ride around on motorcycles inside a cage, going faster and faster. Kind of carny shit. They didn't use one word we wrote. But we wrote the story, which they did use. And we got paid by a black-market producer who came to the Lancaster Hotel with the money wrapped in newspapers— soaking wet; it was always raining in Paris. That's how we got to live it up in Paris, writing this story.

HJ: And you liked von Stroheim?

OW: Loved him. He was a terribly nice fellow. A French script girl who worked on *Grand Illusion* told me that he was the greatest prop actor she'd ever known. Because he'd have a newspaper, a swagger stick, a monocle, a cigarette—all of these things. And he would do a scene where he would put them down and pick them up on certain lines. You can't have that number of props and get it all right. But every time [Jean] Renoir would shoot a take, he'd do it right. On the syllable.

HJ: Did von Stroheim direct any movies in his later life?

OW: No, he didn't. He became purely an actor. He became a star in France in the thirties, but in bad pictures. A terrible loss. 'Cause there was a gigantic gift, really. No question.

HJ: Was he very frustrated? Was he very angry or sad?

OW: He didn't seem to be. By the time I knew him, he'd come to terms with it, so he didn't treat people badly out of his frustration. He was not a jolly fellow, but he was not brooding. He was very fond of being a star. And even after the war, he was still a star. That compensated a lot for him.

HJ: And he did that wonderful turn in *Sunset Boulevard*. That brought him back.

OW: Only in terms of Hollywood. In America it seemed as though he'd been reclaimed from obscurity, when the reality was he was coming from continuous stardom in France. But the success of *Sunset Boulevard* meant nothing to him, because it was Swanson's picture, and Billy Wilder's—compared to what he was getting in France. VON STROHEIM on top of every marquee.

HJ: So all the stories about von Stroheim were made up?

OW: He did some crazy things, but he didn't do anything as crazy as the young directors of the fifty-million-dollar pictures do today.

HJ: But his pictures were without precedent—eight hours long.

OW: Yes, they were, but Thalberg was the one without precedent. Without him, von Stroheim would never have been ruined. D. W. Griffith did much crazier things. But he was in charge, because he was the director, and "D. W. Griffith."

3. "FDR used to say, 'You and I are the two best actors in America.'"

In which Orson recalls sabotaging David O. Selznick's charades, claims that Carole Lombard's plane was shot down by Nazis, and says FDR's biggest regret was not having intervened in the Spanish Civil War.

HENRY JAGLOM: You were trashing Thalberg the other day. It's funny, because the myth gets handed down that Thalberg had great taste and culture.

ORSON WELLES: In his whole career he didn't make a picture that will last fifty years from now, and still he's revered. *Romeo and Juliet*, as produced by Thalberg, and directed by Cukor, was the cultural high point of his ten years of moviemaking. Now, you cannot sit through four minutes of it, it's so terrible. Norma Shearer with those tiny eyes, and Leslie Howard, a Hungarian Jew, as Veronese teenagers?

HJ: But he was so foppish, and so, so British. God, Hungarians made great Englishmen, didn't they? I wonder why.

OW: Well, there was a period during the Austro-Hungarian empire when the older aristocracy had all their clothes made in London. They spoke French with great chic, but their shoes were made in London; their hats were made in London; the nanny who raised their children was from London—and the greatest thing to be was an English gentleman. And I'm sure that's why Lord Leslie Howard, as Sir Winston [Churchill] used to call him, trilling his *r*'s, was such a good Englishman. And then to die in a plane crash, because of Churchill . . . Not killed by some angry Magyar peasant.

HJ: That was the incident where Churchill couldn't reveal that they'd broken the German code, so he let the Nazis shoot down the plane? Wasn't that the same plane that Norma Shearer was on? Thalberg's widow?

OW: No, no. Norma Shearer wasn't killed in a plane. That was another thing that is amazing. After Thalberg died, Norma Shearer— one of the most minimally talented ladies ever to appear on the silver screen, and who looked like nothing, with one eye crossed over the other—went right on being the queen of Hollywood, and getting one role after another.

HJ: Marie Antoinette.

OW: The biggest bust ever made, you know? And everybody used to say, "Miss Thalberg is coming," "Miss Shearer is arriving," and all that, as though they were talking about Sarah Bernhardt. You know, while there were Garbo and Dietrich and Lombard and all the good people. It was a continuation of the magic of this man.

HJ: But Thalberg was also responsible for careers of people like David O. Selznick, who came after him and who managed to make some extraordinary films.

OW: They would have been made by the directors, anyway—and better. The man was a simple pain in the ass! I knew him as well as I know you. He was a total monster, the worst of them all.

HJ: He has the image of somehow being elegant and classy.

OW: He wasn't elegant. He was gross. Tremendous energy and very intelligent. And very bad taste. He thought he was the greatest thing since Jesus. His job, like Thalberg's, was to efface the signature of the director. The man had a tremendous drive to be more than Thalberg. And he had no conscience. Selznick wanted to be the greatest producer in the world—and would have been happy to do anything to achieve it. It was unbelievable. Once I was on David's yacht, and we were all gathered together after dinner. He said, "We can either go back to Miami tonight, or we can go to Havana. I'd like to see a show of hands. Who wants to go to Havana?" Everybody's hands went up. We all went to bed, woke up in Miami.

HJ: That's what happens if you own the boat.

OW: I was close to David because friends of mine liked him. I used to go to his house on Sunday nights. Everybody in Hollywood would be there, and we'd play "The Game," which was just charades, you know. But Selznick played to *win*. Week after week after week. If our team lost, he would follow us in our cars down the driveway, screaming insults at us for having been such idiots, with his voice echoing through the canyons as we drove away. He would become so violent that it was worth it. It was funny just to watch him. And then he had us back the next week. "Now we're gonna win," you see?

Once Selznick wanted to have a fight with me. This was at Walter Wanger's house. After the ladies had left, the gentlemen sat around drinking port. He said how disappointed he was not to have Ronald Colman in *Rebecca*. Because he had this fellow Olivier. That irritated me. I said, "What's wrong with Olivier?" He said, "He's no gentleman." And I said, "David, what kind of shit is this? What are you talking about, 'no gentleman?'" "Well, he just isn't. You can tell that. But with Ronnie you know right away—he's a gentleman." And I said, "Why, you pious old fart." So David stood up, took off his glasses, and assumed the fighting position. We went out into the backyard, and everybody held us back.

HJ: You were really going to fight?

OW: Oh, yes. We used to do that all the time in Hollywood, always stepping out into the garden and fighting. While everybody held you, and nothing ever happened.

HJ: Bogart was always beating up guys, wasn't he?

OW: Now, Bogart, who was both a coward and a very bad fighter, was always picking fights in nightclubs, in sure knowledge that the waiters would stop him. Making fearless remarks to people in his cups, when he knew he was well covered by the busboys.

The great fistfight of the prewar days, though, was between John Huston and—who was the other fellow? It lasted a long time, and they kept running at each other, but neither one of them ever landed a blow. I only saw one great fighter in my life. I was sitting in Harry's Bar in Venice, in the afternoon, and there were four GIs, and their sergeant. Another soldier came in and made a remark, and the sergeant just turned to the soldier and knocked him out with the neatness of a John Ford movie, and they carried him away. Then another soldier made a remark, and he knocked him out. Now, you know, it is *impossible* to do that. But he did it, right in front of me, and each time the sergeant turned to me and said, "I'm very sorry, sir."

HJ: So if it wasn't Norma Shearer, who was killed in the plane crash?

OW: You're thinking of what's-her-name—the good one. I can't think of anybody's name, ever. Terrible.

HJ: Gable's girlfriend—Carole Lombard.

OW: His wife. I adored her. She was a very close friend of mine. And I don't mean to imply that we were ever lovers. I remember when Gable made a picture called *Parnell*, a costume picture. Nineteen thirty-seven, with Myrna Loy. Nobody came. They released it to *empty* theaters! Proving that there's no such thing as the star who can't empty a theater. I think it was the only MGM film that lost money. Not that it mattered to Mayer. Money was almost no object to Metro, 'cause they couldn't lose money.

HJ: You mean the way they had the distribution set up, owning the theaters, they were so locked in that—

OW: And when I learned to fly, I flew with Carole over Metro, at lunchtime. We buzzed the commissary, just as everyone was coming out, and she dropped leaflets that said, "Remember Parnell"! That's the kind of girl she was.

HJ: She looked to me like kind of a road-company Garbo.

OW: Not at all Garboesque! My God, she was earthy. She looked like a great beauty, but she behaved like a waitress in a hash house. That was her style of acting, too, and it had a great allure. She wasn't vulgar; she was just . . . I got to know her when I had to make peace between her and Charles Laughton. I was sort of an emissary for Laughton. They were making a picture called *They Knew What They Wanted*, about an Italian vintner who gets a mail-order wife, played by Lombard, you know? The movie was directed by Garson Kanin. Laughton was the simple Italian peasant. He would come to my office, and sit down across the desk from me, and put his head on the desk and cry.

HJ: Laughton?

OW: In the middle of the day. Said, "I can't go on the way they're making fun of me on the set." 'Cause they were sending him up so. And then I would go and talk to Gar, and talk to Carole, and say, "You know, he is a great actor. Take it easy with him. You're gonna ruin your own picture." Laughton was beside himself. Because he had been such a star in England with Korda. When he played Rembrandt for Korda, years before—a wonderful performance, one of the only times an actor has ever persuaded you he's a genius—he asked to be taken by Alex's brother, the art director, to Holland, to the museum in Amsterdam, to see *The Night Watch*, and other Rembrandt pictures. They arrived on Sunday, and the museum was opened just for Laughton. He walked up to *The Night Watch*, looked at it, and fell into a faint. From the beauty of it all. When he'd make an entrance, they had little sets built for him where he would be sitting, doing what he was doing just before he came on. You see?

HJ: A very Method actor for his time.

OW: Well, his own method.

HJ: Now, Lombard could not have been very bright.

OW: *Very* bright. Brighter than any director she ever worked with. She had all the ideas. Jack Barrymore told me the same thing. He said, "I've never played with an actress so intelligent in my life."

HJ: But Gable was certainly not bright.

OW: No, but terribly nice. Just a nice big hunk of man. If you're working hard that long—if you have to be in makeup at five fifteen, and you get home at seven o'clock—how much brightness do you want? The guys just wanted to stagger home—and, if they could, get laid. Otherwise, a happy smile and get ready for the next day's work.

HJ: So Lombard was also killed in a plane crash?

OW: Yes. You know why her plane went down?

HJ: Why?

OW: It was full of big-time American physicists, shot down by the Nazis. She was one of the only civilians on the plane. The plane was filled with bullet holes.

HJ: It was shot down by who?

OW: Nazi agents in America. It's a real thriller story.

HJ: That's preposterous. What was she doing on a plane full of physicists? Do people know this?

OW: The people who know it, know it. It was greatly hushed up. The official story was that it ran into the mountain.

HJ: The agents had antiaircraft guns?

OW: No. In those days, the planes couldn't get up that high. They'd just clear the mountains. The bad guys knew the exact route that the plane had to take. They were standing on a ridge, which was the toughest thing for the plane to get over. One person can shoot a plane down, and if they had five or six people there, they couldn't miss. Now, I cannot swear it's true. I've been told this by people who swear it's true, who I happen to believe. But that's the closest you can get, without having some kind of security clearance.

No one wanted to admit that we had people in the middle of America who could shoot down a plane for the Nazis. Because then everybody would start denouncing anybody with a German grandmother. Which Roosevelt was very worried about. The First World War had only happened some twenty-odd years before. He'd seen the riots against Germans. No one could play Wagner—or Beethoven, even. Germans weren't safe on the street. They were getting lynched. And he was very anxious for nothing like that to be repeated. He was really scared about what would happen to the Japanese if all the rednecks got started. Especially in California, with its coastline on the Pacific.

HJ: So his idea was to protect them? That's why he rounded them up and put them in camps?

OW: Yes. That was the motivation in his mind. But it was a ghastly mistake. Now, other people—the Pentagon types—thought we were riddled with spies. But his concern was the safety of the Japanese who lived here. Of course, they didn't know that. They're quite rightly indignant. They would never agree that it was a good thing.

HJ: You knew Roosevelt, right? Were you ever alone with him?

OW: Yes, several times. And then Missy [LeHand] would come in. And she hated it when I visited the White House.

HJ: Why?

OW: Because I kept him up too late. He liked to stay up and talk, you see. He was free with me. I didn't need to be manipulated. He didn't need my vote. It was a release for him, and he enjoyed my company. He used to say, "You and I are the two best actors in America."

HJ: Was he bright?

OW: Very bright.

HJ: What was that letter he wrote you about Spain?

OW: A four-page letter out of the blue, only a few months before he died, about the state of the world. It was lost in a fire. I never knew why he'd written it to me. He just sort of sat and dictated it one night.

HJ: He wrote he felt bad about Spain?

OW: Oh, no, he didn't write that. That's what he said to me. It was on the campaign train, not in the White House. We were talking about mistakes that other people had made—that [Woodrow] Wilson had made, that [Georges] Clemenceau had made. Yes, Spain. The neutrality with Spain was a big mistake. "That comes back to me all the time," he said.

HJ: It always struck me that the fact that some of our more progressive presidents—the Roosevelts and the Kennedys—came from wealthier backgrounds meant that they were less intimidated by other rich people, and therefore, less susceptible to special interests. The poor kids are the more dangerous ones—Reagan is so impressed with rich people—it is such an important part of his life.

OW: And they had Nixon in their pocket when he was still a congressman. From the beginning. But I still don't think your point is right. It's because of the old tradition of the Whig—of the liberal rich, the old tradition of public service and of liberalism—Roosevelt was a genuine, old-fashioned American Whig. The last and best example of it. And—

HJ: But I still say you can't be a poor person in the presidency and be surrounded by wealthy people.

OW: Well, a senator can be a poor person, but it's true, eventually he'll become a puppet of the rich. A senator used to be a tremendous office. Now it's really, more than it's ever been, what the money buys. The special-interest thing.

HJ: We always heard that Roosevelt really wanted [Henry] Wallace in '44 to run as his vice president again, and it was the reactionary Southern Democrats who forced Truman on him.

OW: He would have liked to have had a better Wallace.

HJ: William O. Douglas or someone.

OW: Yeah. He would have loved to have Douglas. But they did force Truman on him, and he didn't give Truman any kind of break. Roosevelt didn't think much of him. None of us did.

HJ: Were your sympathies with Wallace when he ran for president in '48 on the Progressive Party ticket?

OW: Oh, no. I thought it was just fatal. He was a prisoner of the Communist Party. He would never do anything to upset them. Not that I thought that in itself would make him a bad president. But it showed his weakness. I was very, very passionately against him. The left thought I was a real traitor. Had he won, I think we would have had a much bigger reaction after him.

HJ: Bigger McCarthyism?

OW: More dangerous, and more venomous, and more long-lived.

4. "I fucked around on everyone."

In which Orson and Rita Hayworth, who were separated, were reunited to make *The Lady from Shanghai*. He recalls that she stuck by him when he tried to leave Hollywood to do good works.

———————————

Henry Jaglom: Rita worked for Harry Cohn at Columbia, didn't she?

Orson Welles: Yes, he thought he was a great lover. He chased Rita around the desk all the years she was there. She was always going on suspension.

HJ: I just saw *Lady from Shanghai* again. She's so good in it.

OW: Are you kidding? She was magnificent! And she thought she wasn't. And nobody in the town would give her any credit for it.

HJ: It makes you realize what a waste her career was.

OW: She was a really talented actress who never got a chance.

HJ: They say that you ruined her in that film. Cut off her famous red locks, dyed what was left blond without telling Harry Cohn.

OW: Yes, that was supposed to be my vengeance on her for leaving me. I made her character a killer and cut off her hair, and all that. That's pretty profound psychological work, isn't it? Why would I want vengeance? I fucked around on everyone. And that's hard on a girl, very hard.

HJ: Did she believe that vengeance business?

OW: No, never. She always thought it was the best picture of her life. Defended me, and it. I was gonna make a nice little B picture with a girl I brought over from Paris—and get out, you know, in twenty days. I wasn't gonna get any money for it. So Rita came and cried, begged to do it. Of course, I said, "Yes." So suddenly, I'm stuck with the studio's bread-and-butter girl, from whom I've been separated for a year. I was dragged back into the marriage and the movie.

HJ: You were not divorced yet?

OW: No. So then we were reunited. Had to be, no other way to direct the picture. I moved back in with her. It wasn't really like working with an ex-wife, because we still loved each other. Then the hairdressers and people got after her. They worked her up with stories about who I was screwing. It's a regular Hollywood thing—all those people who live off of stars. She was deeply suspicious of everybody. She'd been so terribly hurt in her life, she wouldn't believe that I would not do that to her. So she threw me out. I was devastated.

HJ: Had you the intention of staying with her? Even though she was an alcoholic? And depressed?

OW: Forever? Yeah. 'Cause I knew she needed me desperately. I would have stayed with her till she died. There was nobody else who would have taken care of her like I would. I didn't know that she would be that sick.

HJ: And you didn't mind that?

OW: It doesn't matter whether you mind it or not—you do it.

HJ: Some people do it, and some don't.

OW: Yes. But I'm a terribly guilty-conscience person.

HJ: Yet you loved her, also.

OW: I loved her, yeah. Very much. But, by that time, not sexually.

I had to work myself up to fuck her. She had become so—such a figure of lust, and she just wanted to be a housewife. Marlene called her the perfect hausfrau. You know what Rita used to say: "They go to sleep with Rita Hayworth and wake up with Margarita Carmen Cansino." And she'd been so wonderful to me, absolutely wonderful. When I almost died of hepatitis, she spent five months with me while I recovered. And she never did anything except take care of me. When I said to her, "I want to give up the movies and theater. Will you do that with me?" She said, "Yes."

Later, when I was in Rome working on *Othello*, she sent for me. She said, "Come tonight." To Antibes. She didn't say why, and I thought something terrible had happened to her. There was no space on a commercial flight, so I flew in a cargo plane, standing up, with a lot of boxes. I arrived at the hotel, you know, *that* hotel, went up to the one great suite, you know, *that* suite. She opened the door, stood there in a negligee, hair flowing, gorgeous. The suite was full of flowers. The doors opened out onto the terrace, over-looking the Mediterranean. The smell, you know *that* smell. It was overpowering. Rita looked at me, tears in her eyes, said, "You were right; we belong together; I was wrong." But by then I was crazy for this ugly, little Italian girl who gave me so much shit, but I just had to have her.

HJ: The one with the face like a spoon.

OJ: I had to tell Rita, so I said, "I'm so sorry, but there's this girl. I'm in love; it's too late." She cried and said sadly, "OK. Then just be with me tonight, just hold me while I sleep." And I did. I held her. And nothing else. My arm was falling asleep. I was looking at my watch out of the corner of my eye to see when I could catch the morning flight back to Rome. I left the next day. Five days later Rita married Aly Khan. She was *dying* to stop being a movie actor. That's why she ran to him.

HJ: Relationships are so crazy. I'm devastated that Patrice [Town-send] has left me. I thought we had the perfect marriage.

OW: Women are another race. They're like the moon, always changing. You can only win by being the cool center of their being. You have to represent something solid and loving. The anchor. Even if you're not. You can't tell them the truth. You have to lie and play games. I've never in my entire life been with someone with whom I didn't have to play a game. I've never been with anyone with whom I could be exactly who I am.

HJ: Did you really want to give up the movies and the theater?

OW: Yes, at one point I decided that the best thing I could do, the most use I could get out of what I was born with, for my fellow man—unselfish use—would be in education. So I spent five months going to every big foundation, saying, "I'm going to give up my entire career." I was then very famous and very successful. I thought to myself, "I'll discuss with these people how to educate the younger generations, so that they know what's happening in the world, and the world will be a better place for it. We will use every method we can think of, and I will belong to you." Nobody wanted it. I got out of that by nobody taking me up on it. But I would have been very happy to do it. I had exhausted my real fire. I'm essentially an adventurer. I'd done all the things I wanted to do, and now I wanted to be of use. You know what I did instead? I made another movie.

HJ: Do you feel guilty for leading the good life in Hollywood while there are so many starving people in the world?

OW: I think most people here are bothered by the fact that in America we are incredibly fortunate. There are lots who have a bad conscience. A romantic conscience, depending on the person.

HJ: If they do, they don't talk about it.

OW: Because it sounds pompous. How can I sit at the table here with lunch and say, "I was talking to Henry in Ma Maison about these people who are starving in Africa, and thinking how I ought to be in Africa helping out." The answer is, "Go to Africa and shut up! Nobody is going to sympathize with you when you say that your problem is that you *aren't* going."

HJ: Has it occurred to you that if you went and did certain things, you'd be so caught up in it that you'd have to make dramatic changes in your life?

OW: It occurs to me every day. I am tormented by it. I live with it. The way I live with death, the way I live with old age, all those things.

HJ: What do you say to yourself about it?

OW: Well, you see, I'm not like you. I'm not judgmental. With me, it's, "Here I am, not going to Africa." I don't say to myself, "Why don't you go to Africa?" I don't discuss it with myself. Because if I did, I would go to Africa. So it is the self-indulgent devil in me that stops the dialogue.

HJ: I've been saying that to myself since I was seventeen, eighteen years old. That is the time you really feel it.

OW: That's the voice that should be leading you. It takes all the peer pressure and your self-indulgence and everything else to suppress that voice.

HJ: Isn't it shocking that we all do so little to alleviate all this incredible suffering?

OW: No. No, because it's only one aspect of our essential sinfulness. We are sinful in so many ways.

HJ: I never want to believe you have a religious bent, but, actually, you do.

OW: I know. I believe that we're much healthier if we think of our selfishness as sin. Which is what it is: a sin. Even if there is nothing out there except a random movement of untold gases and objects, sin still exists. You don't need a devil with horns. It's a social definition of sin. Everything we do that is self-indulgent, and that is selfish, and that turns us away from our dignity as human beings is a sin against what we were born with, the capacities we have, what we *could* make of this planet. Our whole age has taken the line that if you feel bad about yourself, it's something that you can be relieved of by your goddamn analyst. Psst!—it's gone! And then you'll be happy, you know? But that feeling is not something you should be relieved of. It's something you should *deal* with. And there's no remission for what I mean by "sin," except doing something useful. The confessional does the same thing as the shrink, rather more quickly and cheaper. Three "Hail Mary"s, and you're out. But I've never been the kind of religious person that thinks saying "Hail Mary" is gonna get me out of it.

HJ: The concept of sin is a difficult one for me, because it implies something other than our animal, material existence. I think we just have impulses, good ones and bad ones.

OW: Yes. But those impulses are *controlled* by us. I believe in free will. I believe that we are the masters of our fate.

HJ: But that means you do believe in some kind of a plan.

OW: That's right. You see, I'm religious, but you don't need God and his angels to feel that way. "The fault, dear Brutus, lies not in our stars, but in ourselves."

HJ: Well, we have the appearance of free will. But—

OW: It's real. With my history, why shouldn't I become a drunk, and a pathetic figure sitting around Hollywood, if there isn't such a thing as free will?

HJ: Because of, well, chemical balances, which are predetermined.

OW: If they are *truly* predetermined, you're more religious than I am. You're a fatalist. Every moment of life is a choice. I don't think it is possible to live a moral and civil life unless we accept the possibility of choice.

HJ: That I have never understood. Why do you need the belief in choice? Morality comes from your understanding of what is good.

I know it's good to help people. I know it's wrong to hurt other people. I don't need to believe that I have free will in order to be a decent human being.

OW: You think our lives are just ruled by chance? You think that if you want to make this movie and not that one, it's because of a series of chemical imbalances?

HJ: You're reducing it. I'm saying that I think that we are all the product of a long, long history of genetic construction that—

OW: But none of that eliminates free will.

HJ: Whether you get struck by lightning or not is—has nothing to do with your free will.

OW: Free will doesn't mean I can stop the lightning. Free will simply means that I can decide whether I'm going to go to Africa or not! It's demeaning if you think it's all a chemical accident.

There can be nothing more sterile than an extended conversation between two people who basically agree. If we basically disagreed we'd be getting somewhere.

(Waiter arrives.)

OW: I'd like a café espresso.

W: *Décaféiné?*

OW: *Oui, décaféiné—oui.*

HJ: And I would like a cup . . . uh . . .

W: Café au lait.

HJ: Café au lait. Please. With a little steamed milk on the side, as well. Thank you. *(To OW)* Um . . . do you want some berries?

OW: *(To Kiki)* Do you want a little sweet?

Oh, the irony of these kinds of conversations is that they end with: "Do you want some berries?"

HJ: I'm just not clear about why I am so good at doing nothing for those less fortunate than I. I guess it's because if I did anything, it would be a total commitment. And that would make my life something else.

OW: You see, I'm very clear. I have people whose lives depend on me. If I became some kind of fucking secular saint, I would strew misery among all the people who are close to me. Is the cry of the starving child in Africa louder than the people near me, who depend on me? That's an interesting moral question.

HJ: I've been involved in a lot of political things, and I tend to meet people who are fully involved. And I always find them very neurotic, disturbed . . .

OW: Politics is *always* corrupting. Even saints in politics. The political world, in itself, is corrupt. You're not going to satisfy that urge to spiritual perfection in *any* political movement without being betrayed and without betraying others. Only service, direct service, say, helping a lot of starving kids in a Third World country, is impeccable."

HJ: I should feel guiltier than I do.

OW: Guilt is an entirely masculine invention. No female has guilt. And that's why the Bible is so true!

HJ: How can you say that? The Bible was written by men!

OW: Yeah, I know. But the Garden of Eden story is such a perfect embodiment of the fact that—who feels guilty? Adam!

HJ: Yeah. But the men who wrote the Bible make Eve give him the apple.

OW: Sure. But she doesn't mind it!

HJ: Because it's a male's idea of a female.

OW: No, I think it's true. I think guilt is a vice, to a large extent, and I think it is a typically masculine vice. You may find it in women, but rarely. If you were religious, your absence of guilt would be a crippling thing.

5. "Such a good Catholic that I wanted to kick her."

In which Orson remembers entertaining the troops with Marlene Dietrich, explains why he detested Irene Dunne, and why movie-going in the thirties was like watching television today.

———————

HENRY JAGLOM: You toured for the USO during the war? With Marlene?

ORSON WELLES: Yeah. I said, "Why don't we have you do a song? And she said, "Oh, I'll play my musical saw." "Play what, Marlene?" "My musical saw." I said, "Well, all right."

HJ: She knew how to play the saw?

OW: Very well. It was the funniest thing. And she didn't do it to be funny. Toward the end of the war, I went to the South Pacific, and she went to Europe. She felt so lost being alone—"How can I go on without you?" and so on—so she began to sing, and that's how her cabaret act was born. Though she never sang with me.

HJ: And is it true that she's gained so much weight that she won't let anybody see her now?

OW: No, she won't. Not even her close friends. She makes dates to see people and breaks them. I made six trips to Paris to see her, and ended up talking to her from a phone booth. Every time she said she was ill. Once she said she had typhus!

HJ: Oh, so she probably plans and prepares—

OW: And then looks at herself and feels terrible. I'm sure Max Schell will never speak to me again. I'm going to have him as an enemy forever. He's doing a documentary about Marlene, and he has got all this audio of her on tape. But, then, when it came time to photograph her, she stalled and finally refused. So he built a set of her apartment in Paris. It's all about him—the director—in an empty apartment, with her voice piped in. And then I'm supposed to come as some kind of apparition—I think in double exposure. Well, when I heard that, I suddenly got awfully busy in another movie, you know? I sent word to him that I had a job that was too good to turn down, and I couldn't do this three-day appearance. He'll know that I was just pretending. But this movie can't be any good. It's a terrible idea for a picture. I admire him very much. But he's making a big mistake. It's not like him to be that nutty.

HJ: I like Schell as a filmmaker. Serious, you know? Very serious.

OW: Too serious. Too Swiss. He's a Swiss. He's not a Kraut. He and Yul Brynner are the two leading Swiss actors. Yul Brynner, however, seems to have—let's say—gone out to the Caucasus for a few years after leaving Zurich.

HJ: You mean all those biographies where he was supposed to have been born on—

OW: The steppes. Half gypsy, half Mongol! He had too much to drink on this long trip he took with me through the snow in Yugoslavia, and late one night he blurted out that his hometown was Brenner near Zurich, where everybody's name is Brenner. And he should never have said that, because there goes the whole story.

HJ: He only created one character, but he did it absolutely wonderfully. *The King and I.* I can't get over the fact you were offered the role in the earlier version, *Anna and the King of Siam*, instead of Rex Harrison.

OW: That's why he got it. Because I suggested him. Rex made pictures that only played in England, teacup comedies and things. The studio people had never heard of him. Sitting in the steam room at Twentieth? Rex Harrison, who's that?

HJ: Did you, by any chance, see *The Kingfisher* on cable, with him?

OW: Where he looks as though he's been on cortisone for eight years.

HJ: What was your reason for being so sure you didn't want to do *Anna and the King of Siam*?

OW: Because I couldn't stand Irene Dunne, who had already been cast. That's why I turned down *Gaslight*, too. She was going to do it. And then after I turned it down, they got Bergman and I was out. Irene Dunne. Dumb. Dumb, dumb.

HJ: Why did you have this terrible antipathy toward Dunne?

OW: You must stop trying to figure out why I have antipathies. Don't waste our time.

HJ: You mean just accept them?

OW: Yeah. That's right. Yeah. Irene Dunne was so dry-toothed and such a good fucking Catholic that I wanted to kick her in the crotch. Such a goody-goody. And she was always heading the censorship groups, and all that. Conservative, in a terrible Catholic-Christian way that I found peculiarly offensive. To me, she was the nonsinging Jeanette MacDonald, you know. And I hated her as an actress. She was so ladylike that I knew there wouldn't be any electricity between us.

HJ: Irene was in *A Guy Named Joe* with Spencer Tracy and Van Johnson. What do you think of Van Johnson?

OW: Well, I was responsible for his coming to Hollywood. I never told him that, so he doesn't know. He was a chorus boy in *Pal Joey*, and he was such a terrific personality I sent a wire to George Schaefer at RKO and said, "Get this guy Van Johnson," and they sent for him. They didn't like him, and didn't use him. And then he went to MGM and—

HJ: He wasn't a great actor or anything.

OW: Pitiable now. Most men get better looking when they get old. He's a kind of queen that doesn't. He had to be young to be attractive.

HJ: His movies are terrible.

OW: Oja [Kodar] won't go to the movies with me; she says that if I stay, I'm making groans, these awful noises.

HJ: Sitting in front of the television you don't have that experience?

OW: No. Total idiot. Other people want to switch channels. I don't. I'd much rather see junk on the TV than bad movies because bad movies stay with me for too long. And if they get a little good, then they're gonna haunt me. And who needs to be haunted?

HJ: Warren Beatty was just saying that TV has changed movies, because for most of us, once you're in a movie theater, you commit, whether you like it or not. You want to see what they've done, while at home . . .

OW: I'm the opposite. It's a question of age. In my real movie-going days, which were the thirties, you didn't stand in line. You strolled down the street and sallied into the theater at any hour of the day or night. Like you'd go in to have a drink at a bar. Every movie theater was partially empty. We never asked what time the movie began. We used to go after we went to the theater. We'd go down to the Paramount where they had a double bill, and see the B picture, and go to laugh at bad acting in the Bs. You know, childish, stupid things. There was an actor called J. Carrol Naish. Anything he did, we'd laugh at. I didn't like the screwball comedies, at all, with the exception of Carole Lombard. Anything with her—that was fine.

HJ: You didn't feel you had to see a movie from the start?

OW: No. We'd leave when we'd realize, "This is where we came in." Everybody said that. I loved movies for that reason. They didn't cost that much, so if you didn't like one, it was, "Let's do something else.

Go to another movie." And that's what made it habitual to such an extent that walking out of a movie was what for people now is like turning off the television set. Oja and I do it still. Last time we were in Paris, we saw five movies, one or two reels of each one.

HJ: There was entertainment between the features in those days?

OW: Sure. There was Kate Smith and travelogues and the newsreel and an *Our Gang* comedy, you know.

HJ: So, for people like you, it's very important that filmmakers grab you in the first reel. The first ten to twenty minutes.

OW: If not, I'm up the aisle.

HJ: Up and out. No slow and leisurely getting into it, no misdirections?

OW: No. If you stand in line, of course, you want to see what you were standing in line for. But in those days, we only ever committed like that for Sinatra when he was singing at the Paramount. No movie ever had that kind of business. The truth is, I was not very fond of the movies of the late thirties, the few years just before I went to Hollywood. The so-called "Golden Age."

HJ: I'm reading Budd Schulberg's autobiography, called *Moving Pictures*. It introduced me to the world of silent movies that I didn't know anything about.

OW: I'd rather not read it. I don't read books on film at all, or theater. I'm not very interested in movies. I keep telling people that, and they don't believe me. I *genuinely* am not very interested! For me, it's only interesting to do. You know, I'm not interested in other filmmakers—and that's a terribly arrogant thing to say—or in the medium. It's the least interesting art medium for me to watch that there is. Except ballet—that's the only thing less interesting. I just like to *make* movies, you know? And that's the truth!

But I do know quite a bit about early movies, because I was interested in movies before I made them. And I was interested in the theater before I went into it. There is something in me that turns off once I start to do it myself. It's some weakness. In other words, I read *everything* about the theater before I became a theater director. After that, I never went to plays or read anything. Same thing with movies. I believe that I was threatened, personally threatened, by every other movie, and by every criticism—that it would affect the purity of my vision. And I think the younger generation of filmmakers has seen too many movies.

6. "Nobody even glanced at Marilyn."

In which Orson greets Swifty Lazar, remembers dating Marilyn Monroe when she was just another pretty face and failing to interest Zanuck in her career, even though the mogul's weakness for starlets nearly wrecked his.

(Swifty Lazar enters.)

Swifty Lazar: Just wanted to say, "Hello."

Orson Welles: You look wonderful.

SL: I feel good. I'm good. Orson, see you Wednesday. You take care of yourself.

OW: What, do you think I look badly?

SL: No, you look great.

(Lazar exits.)

OW: I don't like people to say, "Take care of yourself." He hasn't changed in thirty years. Lives in a hotel. Orders a whole lot of towels, and when he goes from the bathroom to his bed, he lays down a path of towels.

Henry Jaglom: So he doesn't have to walk on the carpets? He's that nuts about germs?

OW: Yes.

HJ: And what if he wants to go to the closet?

OW: Then he'll make another path. I've seen it. With my own eyes.

HJ: What does he think he'll get through his feet?

OW: Hookworm. From the Ritz, you know? Mania.

HJ: I was going to ask you about Zanuck when Swifty interrupted us. What did you think of his movies when he headed Fox?

OW: He was the greatest editor who ever lived. But only for his kind of pictures. In other words, he was at a loss if a picture got too good. But he could save any standard picture. He would automatically make it better. He was awfully good making the corniest pictures—which I didn't like, for the most part. I think the musicals were awful. But if he knew he had an art film on his hands, he left it alone. Including pictures we don't think are art films, like what is that hanging picture? The western that was considered very high art at the time.

HJ: Henry Fonda?

OW: Yeah. And a lot of other good actors, standing around kind of projecting gloom. The lynching. *The Ox-Bow Incident*!

HJ: Did Fox make any good pictures during that period?

OW: Yes. A few. A very few. They made *How Green Was My Valley*.

HJ: What was he like?

OW: Zanuck was a great polo player. When I first came out here, he was using the old polo grounds by the Palisades. It was funny, the head of the studio playing polo. I had the usual New York sneer. You know that for years, on the drive to work and back, he had a French teacher with him? Imagine a movie head wanting to learn something!

HJ: Why, if Zanuck had that quality as a human being, was that not reflected in the films?

OW: Because he wanted to be a successful head of a studio, and he was. Until he fell in love with that terrible Juliette Gréco. I made two pictures with her.

HJ: That *Crack in the Mirror* picture.

OW: And another one, that I've forgotten. He lost everything over her, his power, left his wife—everything.

HJ: For Juliette Gréco?

OW: To serve her. He'd take her little dog and walk it around the lot while we were shooting. So help me, it was awful. I don't believe a director should ever fall in love with his leading lady. Or at least show it.

HJ: He had Marilyn Monroe under contract, didn't he?

OW: She was a girlfriend of mine. I used to take her to parties before she was a star.

HJ: I didn't know that!

OW: I wanted to try and promote her career. Nobody even glanced at Marilyn. You'd see these beautiful girls, the most chic girls in town, who spent a fortune at the beauty parlor and on their clothes, and everybody said, "Darling, you're looking wonderful!" And then they'd ignore them. The men, not the women. The men would gather in the corner and start telling jokes or talking deals. The only time they talked about the girls was to say whether they scored with them the night before. I would point Marilyn out to Darryl, and say, "What a sensational girl." He would answer, "She's just another stock player. We've got a hundred of them. Stop trying to push these cunts on me. We've got her on for $125 a week." And then, about six months later, Darryl was paying Marilyn $400,000, and the men were looking at her—because some stamp had been put on her.

HJ: God, that's amazing.

OW: Then Darryl disappeared to Europe with Juliette Gréco. We thought we'd never hear from him again.

HJ: When I arrived, in the mid-sixties, in the later part of his career, he was trying to put together a big war movie in Paris, *The Longest Day.*

OW: Twentieth was in terrible trouble.

HJ: With *Cleopatra.*

OW: He heard about it, so he rolled up his sleeves and made *The Longest Day*, which got them out from under—like that, you see. It made a fortune, and brought him back as president of Fox, because he had become a figure of fun, you see. Then his son and another group maneuvered him out.

HJ: Richard Zanuck maneuvered him out? Richard, who's partnered with David Brown?

OW: Yeah. He was the front man for those who were trying to get rid of him.

HJ: His own son? Not Jewish, in other words. It's not like Jews to—

OW: Zanuck? Everybody thought Darryl was Jewish, because Zanuck is sort of a foreign name. He was Christian. The only Christian head of a studio.

HJ: Except for his boss, [Spyros] Skouras.

OW: If you could call him Christian. He's Greek Orthodox. Twentieth was the only Christian studio. It was the worst studio in town. Yes. Zanuck is Czech, from Nebraska. He had begun his career by publishing, at his own cost, a novel. And putting it on the desks of the various producers. At nineteen he became the white-haired boy by writing the Rin Tin Tin movies, which, of course, made a fortune.

HJ: Isn't *Jane Eyre* a Zanuck movie? I watched it last night. You put on a nose for *Jane Eyre.*

OW: Yes.

HJ: Why?

OW: Because I was so baby-faced. I looked sixteen years old. How was I gonna be Mr. Rochester with this baby face? I had a nose in *Kane.* Then we made it longer as I got older. Noses do get longer.

HJ: I didn't like the acting at all.

OW: What acting?

HJ: In *Jane Eyre*.

OW: My acting?

HJ: No, I like your acting immensely.

OW: Oh, her. Joan Fontaine. No, she's no good in it. She's just a plain old bad actor. She's got four readings, and two expressions, and that's it. And she was busy being the humble governess—so fucking humble. Which is a great mistake. Because she's supposed to be a proud little woman who, in spite of her position, stands up for herself. That's why she interests this bastard of a man.

HJ: I guess that's the thing that I always have trouble with in the film, that she looks so mousy and unappealing. And I can't understand why she appeals to him.

OW: You should get the feeling that this mouse roars, but you don't. The trick of the story is that she is, by virtue of the nature of society as it was then, doomed to a position of total servility. But because of her tremendous independence of spirit, she causes the man to become interested in her. Even though she's not a beauty. It's her *character* that makes the impression on him. And that's why he loves her, finally.

HJ: What you see is an actress trying to play not a beauty.

OW: Yeah, that's all you see. The whole point of the story is ruined by that. Because you're supposed to see that the visiting lady— what's her name?—is the great beauty. And that's the sort of pearl that he ought to have, and all that. And here is this girl who not only is in a position of being a mere hired servant, but she's not even a beauty. But she finally commands this man's whole life. Because of her character. Standing up for herself. Being a fierce little girl. And that isn't the movie at all! It isn't even indicated. Nobody told her that, you know.

HJ: Neither she nor her sister Olivia de Havilland could act. I never understood their careers.

OW: Yes, you do. There are always jobs for pretty girls who speak semi-educated English. I don't think either one of 'em is worth much—

HJ: I understand their careers, but I don't understand how some people hold them in such high regard.

OW: There are a lot of bad actors.

HJ: It's like Merle Oberon is another one for me.

OW: Yeah. But very beautiful. She was mainly wonderful in one movie, but wonderful because she was not asked to do any acting. It was a very strange French movie. She played a Japanese—before she ever came to Hollywood. I've forgotten what it was called. *Sayonara 1*, or something. Now there's a bad picture for you—*Sayonara 2*.

HJ: Poor Marlon.

OW: Anybody who was trapped in that movie would have been at a loss. Yet, he got an Academy Award for it. That shows you where we were then. The picture was, on every level, an abomination. It looked like a musical that didn't have any numbers in it. The Orient is the graveyard of American directors. The only really bad [Frank] Capra picture I've ever seen is this *Shangri-La*. It's terrible—terrible. Absurd! I screamed with laughter! Shangri-La, where they were kept, was this sort of Oriental country club. Still, I was a great Capra fan.

HJ: *It's a Wonderful Life.* You want to hate it, but—

OW: Well, yes—hokey. It is sheer Norman Rockwell, from the beginning to the end. But you cannot resist it! There's no way of hating that movie.

7. "*The Blue Angel* is a big piece of shlock."

In which Orson mocks the excesses of *auteurism*, and Peter Bogdanovich in particular for falling at the feet of studio directors such as Howard Hawks. He recounts his adventures with the kings and queens of the Bs, who churned out bottom-of-the-bill fillers.

ORSON WELLES: I'm going on ABC-TV this afternoon. Just before the Oscars. That's why I'm made up. Myself and Peter Bogdanovich. And Hal Roach. I suggested Hal Roach. Because I saw him on TV the other night. He's eighty-six, but he still makes great sense! He's cute as hell. They wanted Capra, and I said, "Capra may be the best living director, but he's the worst living guest. He'll talk about how beautiful America is, and so on. Forget him—get Hal Roach!" They'd already gotten Bogdanovich, and they were angling for Francis Ford [Coppola]. I said, "You have too many people—I don't really want to go. You won't have any time for any of us to say anything. All you'll get is Bogdanovich."

HENRY JAGLOM: So Bogdanovich is gonna be on this show today.

OW: He's good on TV.

HJ: Yeah, but he antagonizes a lot of people. Cynical.

OW: That makes me look better. Always nice to have a heavy man.

HJ: When I first met Bogdanovich—

OW: You thought he was nuts.

HJ: He was always finding great virtues in all of those studio directors.

OW: Unwatchable.

HJ: What's the name of that stupid director?

OW: Sam Fuller. Peter gets furious with me for not expressing enthusiasm for Fuller. Fritz Lang, you know? He thinks is great. Lang, whose mother was Jewish, told me that Goebbels, who was trying to get him to head up the Nazi movie industry, offered to make him an honorary Aryan, of which there were only a handful. Lang said, "But I'm Jewish," and Goebbels replied, "*I* decide who is Jewish!" *That* was when Lang knew it was time to leave Germany.

What were we talking about? Peter also thinks von Sternberg is great. Von Sternberg never made a good picture.

HJ: What about *The Blue Angel*?

OW: It's a big piece of shlock. Painted on velvet. Like you buy in Honolulu. Peter stopped talking to me for several days when I said von Sternberg was no good. Then Hawks, Howard Hawks. The so-called greatest ever. Hawks is number one, and all the rest ate the scraps from his table.

HJ: Yeah. Yeah, *Bringing Up Baby*.

OW: Yes, the greatest picture ever made. I recently saw what I've always been told was Jack [Ford's] greatest movie, and it's terrible. *The Searchers.* He made many very bad pictures.

HJ: You're talking about *The Horse Soldiers* and stupid *Sergeant Rutledge*.

OW: I was in Peter's house one night, and he ran some John Ford picture. During the first reel I said, "Isn't it funny how incapable even Ford—and all American directors are—of making women look in period? You can always tell which decade a costume picture was made in—the twenties, the thirties, the forties, or the fifties—even if it's supposed to be in the seventeenth century." I said, "Look at those two girls who are supposed to be out in the covered wagon."

Their hairdos and their costumes are really what the actresses in the fifties thought was good taste. Otherwise, they're gonna say, "I can't come out in this." Peter flew into a rage, turned off the projector, and wouldn't let us see the rest of the movie because I didn't have enough respect for Ford. But Jack made some of the best ever.

HJ: When I first met Bogdanovich, I was very snide about John Ford movies. I made fun of them. When I grew up, I realized that they were perfectly good. Say hello to Peter if you see him. Is that book on Dorothy Stratten ever gonna come out?

OW: I have a terrible fear that it'll be a runaway best seller. Really, I have a dread! He'll behave so badly. He'll become such a pompous ass again. Right after *The Last Picture Show* he came out to Arizona to play his part in *The Other Side of the Wind*—and sat for five hours at the table talking to me, with his back turned to [my cinematographer] Gary Graver, whom he knew very well. He never said hello or goodbye to him. You want to know about your friend Peter?"

HJ: He was your friend, too.

OW: You know when vaudeville died, and all the great vaudeville performers—the comics, the singers—were thrown out of work. They couldn't make the move to radio or film. They used to huddle around these barrels in Times Square, where they made fires, and ate roasted potatoes off sticks. Then television arrived, and the TV producers came looking for these guys to use them in their variety shows. One of them was the biggest star of vaudeville. While he was on top, he treated everybody like shit. So when the bad times came, they wouldn't share their fires with him, or their food. But gradually they started to feel sorry for him. Years passed. They all forgave him. Now, the *Ed Sullivan Show* is going to do the best of vaudeville, at the Palace Theater. This guy gets a plum part. He tells all his friends, who didn't get chosen, "Guys, I just got lucky. I'll never forget you. You can't imagine what you mean to me; you've saved my life; here are some tickets, front row; come backstage afterwards; we'll go out for drinks, celebrate. I've learned my lesson." The show goes on, this guy is sensational, he's going to be a big TV star now. All his friends come backstage, knock on the door. He comes out in a velvet robe, says, "Fellas, I've got that old shitty feeling coming over me again." And he slams the door in their faces. That's Peter.

HJ: Nonetheless, say hello for me.

OW: Yeah—if I get a chance to say anything.

HJ: You'll have a few moments before, in the dressing room.

OW: Oh, but by then he'll be telling me about himself, you know. He knows that I'll listen to it all.

HJ: By the way, before I forget, I got your contract for *Two of a Kind*. John Travolta and Olivia Newton-John are set, along with your favorite, Oliver Reed, playing the devil. They want you for the voice of God, for two consecutive days. I love playing your agent. They said to me originally, "What kind of price do you think would be right?" I said, "If he does it at all, it's because he's interested in the work. The money is not what he would do it for. But, of course, you can't make it an insulting offer." And they said, "Well, we were thinking ten, fifteen . . ." I said, "Really. For the voice of *God*? Maybe you should get somebody else. I don't even want to submit that to him. I don't think it's fair. Why don't you round it out at $25,000." And they did. Now I have this agent's fantasy, which is: Could I have gone to thirty-five?

OW: Well, I once had a radio director get mad at me. Sent me a wire saying, "When I want God, I'll call heaven!"

HJ: What is it with Oliver Reed, that you like him so much? Weren't you stuck in Greece with him on some B movies?

OW: A movie, for which the money never arrived. It was a Harry Alan Towers production. 1974. Harry Alan Towers is a famous crook.

HJ: He's the guy who was charged with running a vice ring out of a New York hotel in the sixties, and also of being a Soviet agent!

OW: I worked for him for years. He always took the money and ran. He once fled Tehran, leaving a mountain of unpaid bills. When we made *Ten Little Indians*, Towers stuck Oliver Reed with the hotel bill. Oliver went down to the nightclub at the Hilton, which was in the basement, and broke it up. All the mirrors, chandeliers; wrecked the whole place. Destroyed the whole nightclub. Everyone was in such awe of the violence that they all just stood back in horror, including the police. And he just walked out—and went to the airport. Nobody ever laid a hand on him! I admire him greatly!

Then there were the Salkinds, who produced *The Trial*, that I directed. I ended up paying the actors out of my own pocket to stop them from walking off the set all the time. About seventy thousand bucks.

HJ: The Salkinds? I assume this was way before they made *Superman*?

OW: Yeah. Oh, they were broke, they had nothing. To this day, I can never go to the Meurice, in Paris. I can't go to Zagreb because the Salkinds never paid my hotel bill for *The Trial*. I was in Belgrade, making a terrible version of *Marco the Magnificent* with Tony Webb—a whole lot of tatterdemalion actors of that sort. There was a big snowstorm. And word came that the manager of the Esplanade Hotel in Zagreb was on his way to Belgrade to get me for my hotel bill on *The Trial*. But he was stuck in the snow. And I managed to finish the picture and fly out before he arrived!

HJ: You'd think, after *Superman*, they could retroactively take care of these things.

OW: Not for a minute. Not for a minute. And when they did those all-star *Three Musketeers*, I was the only star from *The Trial* not in those. They could've given me a job, at least, for all the money I'd put into *The Trial*.

This kind of thing happened to me all the time. My Spanish producer never paid my hotel bill for the three months that he kept me waiting in Madrid for the money for *The Other Side of the Wind*. So I'm scared to death to be in Madrid. I know they're going to come after me with that bill.

HJ: Why do they go after actors? You'd think it would be good for business to have them stay at their hotels.

OW: Actually, actors are rather well thought of in Spain. Particularly in the theater. Although, how theater actors manage to get along in Spain I don't know, because they do two shows a night. Same thing in a lot of Latin American countries, still—two shows a night. I had a friend who was the last really great illusionist, whose stage name was Fu Manchu. His real name was Bamberg, and he came from seven generations of great magicians. Born in Brooklyn, played a Chinese magician, with a Chinese accent in Spanish, you know? He had to finish a movie he was making. And he said, "I've got this show. And if I close it, I'll never get it open again with any business. Will you do it? What'll you take?" And I said, "I'll do it for free." So for a week I did his show, while he finished his movie, but there were two performances a night. And at the end of that week, I didn't know how I—or he—lived through it. He died at seventy-five last year. His father, who worked silently, was a famous magician called Okito, and played as a Japanese.

HJ: All these Jews from Brooklyn playing Japanese and Chinese!

OW: Dutchmen—Dutch Jews. The father was born in Holland, and a great variety-hall star. And he had the most ter—

HJ: *(Calls out)* Excuse me! Waiter! Can I talk to you?

WAITER: Talk to me, monsieur.

HJ: Uh, you gave me cold chicken. And I wanted warm chicken salad, like it's advertised—and it's cold chicken. The plate is very good and hot—the plate is excellent. If I were eating the plate, I would have been happy. But the chicken—

OW: Terrible thing happened to him. Whenever I have any trouble professionally, I remember Okito, 'cause I know that I will never be in the trouble he was in. He and his father and his grandfather had all been magicians to the court of Holland. And he was playing a show for the King and Queen of Holland, as well as the visiting King and Queen of Denmark. And his opening trick was producing a large bowl of water from a cloth—no, a large duck from a cloth. To complicate the story, even though he worked under the name of Okito, he wore Chinese clothes.

And he had that Chinese robe that's open here, and the duck was between his legs, in a sack. And on this occasion, the duck got its head out of the sack and grabbed him by his jewels. A death grip. Just as he made his entrance. Now that is what I call being in trouble. He said, "I did a lot of jumping around. I acted like a sort of crazy Chinaman."

(To waiter) He's looking for capers in his chicken salad.

HJ: To make sure that they gave me the right—

OW: He looks like a customs inspector. Is there a caper in it?

HJ: It's the exact same as when they had the capers in and took them out. After all this discussion, there is the same taste of caper. Here are capers. They lied to me.

OW: Don't get tiresome about the chicken salad.

HJ: Why am I being tiresome, Orson? I want to get it the way it always is, without the capers. The waiter doesn't understand.

OW: This is the way this chef makes it now.

HJ: They keep writing in the papers that, ever since Wolfgang left, this place has gone downhill. And his restaurant, in turn, has become the number-one one. He's begging me to get you to come to it.

OW: I'll never go.

HJ: Why?

OW: I don't like Wolfgang. He's a little shit. I think he's a terrible little man.

HJ: Why?

OW: I don't know. God made him that way. What do you mean, "Why"?

HJ: Well, I mean, what makes him terrible?

OW: I don't need to explain that. It's a free country. Anybody who sits down at my table without being invited is a shit.

HJ: Wolf did that?

OW: Yes.

HJ: You wouldn't want to call him just "informal," rather than "a shit"?

OW: What?

HJ: You wouldn't want to refer to that as informality, rather than being a shit?

OW: No. Shitty, shitty. A self-promoting little shit. And I'm very sorry he has all this success, because I'm very fond of Patrick. And I wouldn't do that to him.

HJ: What is wrong with your *moules*?

OW: It's not what I had yesterday.

HJ: You want to try to explain this to the waiter?

OW: No, no, no. One complaint per table is all, unless you want them to spit in the food. Let me tell you a story about George Jean Nathan, America's great drama critic. George Jean Nathan was the tightest man who ever lived, even tighter than Charles Chaplin. And he lived for forty years in the Hotel Royalton, which is across from the Algonquin. He fancied himself a great bon vivant— ladies' man and everything. I heard him say to a girl—as he was dancing by me in the old Cub Room at the Stork Club a thousand years ago—after she laughed at something he said, "I can be just as funny in German and French." And away he went, you know? He never tipped anybody in the Royalton, not even when they brought the breakfast, and not at Christmastime. After about ten years of never getting tipped, the room-service waiter peed slightly in his tea. *Everybody* in New York knew it but him. The waiters hurried across the street and told the waiters at Algonquin, who were waiting to see when it would finally dawn on him what he was drinking! And as the years went by, there got to be more and more urine and less and less tea. And it was a great pleasure for us in the theater to look at a leading critic and *know* that he was full of piss. And I, with my own ears, heard him at the 21 complaining to a waiter, saying, "Why can't I get tea here as good as it is at The Royalton?" That's when I fell on the floor, you know.

It'd be a wonderful thing to tell somebody you hated, when it isn't true. To say, "Don't you know that the waiters are doing that to your tea?" Then you don't have to even do it! You could drive a man mad! A real Iago thing to do. Better than the handkerchief, you know. I've remembered it, probably, because he was no admirer of mine. He was very anxious for you to know that he'd seen everything ever done in Europe. So whatever I did was done better in Prague in 1929. Those kinds of notices. It probably was better, but he was showing off, too.

8. "*Kane* is a comedy."

In which Orson speculates on why Jean-Paul Sartre disliked *Kane* and snubbed him, remarks on the great number of novelists who wrote film reviews, and recalls that he got his best notice from John O'Hara.

HENRY JAGLOM: I just saw a Renoir film I had never seen. I don't understand why there is such unevenness to the work of—

ORSON WELLES: He actually made bad movies.

HJ: It was a sweet little film, but terribly acted, called *The River*.

OW: Very bad picture. It's considered one of the great monuments of film. Greatly overpraised. When he isn't on pitch, Renoir comes off as an amateur. It's always mystified me. I have nothing to explain it. I don't talk about it, because it just irritates people.

HJ: What do you feel about *Grand Illusion*?

OW: Probably one of the three or four best ever. I burst into tears at *Grand Illusion* every time. When they stand up and sing "The Marseillaise." And [Pierre] Fresnay is so wonderful—all the performances are divine.

HJ: What about *Rules of the Game*?

OW: I love it, too—but, to me, it's a lesser work, by just a tiny bit. I think *Rules of the Game* is a better picture. It's like listening to Mozart. Nothing can be better than that. But I don't like the love story. And *Grand Illusion* just simply grabs me.

HJ: Did the French know about *Kane*?

OW: I thought it had been a big success in Paris. When I arrived there, I found that it had not been. They didn't know who I was. They didn't know about the Mercury Theatre, my troupe, which I thought they would, because I knew about their theater. And I was snubbed terribly by them. *Kane* only got to be a famous picture later. And then a lot of people really hated it. Americans got it, but not Europe. The first thing they heard about it was the violent attack by Jean-Paul Sartre. Wrote a long piece, forty thousand words on it or something.

HJ: Well, maybe it politically offended him in some way.

OW: No. I think it was because, basically, *Kane* is a comedy.

HJ: It is?

OW: Sure. In the classic sense of the word. Not a fall-in-the-aisles laughing comedy, but because the tragic trappings are parodied.

HJ: I never thought of *Kane* as a comedy. It's profoundly moving.

OW: It's moving, but so can comedies be moving. There is a slight camp to all the great Xanadu business. And Sartre, who has no sense of humor, couldn't react to it at all.

HJ: Was that really why?

OW: When he wasn't being a German philosopher, which he was good at—late Heidegger—most of what he wrote as a critic of the modern scene, political or otherwise, was full of shit.

HJ: And as a playwright he wasn't very hot, either.

OW: Very overrated. But he was such a god at that time. My friends forbade me to go into the Café Philippe, where he used to hang out. They said it would be unpleasant. "Go across the street to Le Dôme, where your people are, the Americans."

Years later, I was visiting Dubrovnik with one of my dearest friends in the world, Vladimir Dedijer, who was the number-three man to Tito during World War II. At that moment in the Vietnam

War, a group in Europe headed by Sartre, Bertrand Russell, and Vladimir Dedijer had formed a committee to bring the Americans to trial for war crimes. The three of them were there for a high-level meeting before going to Paris. As we approached, Dedijer and I saw Sartre and Russell sitting in a café. Dedijer said to me, "Don't go any closer." He was one of those fuck-you kind of fellows, who could have just as easily have said, "Come on, Sartre, don't be an asshole, you're gonna like Orson." But no, he says, "Don't go any closer." It was strange. I never understood it. As though Sartre was going to take off his kid glove and slap me, invite me to a duel. This wasn't 1890, you know. You can't imagine Sartre challenging anybody to a duel.

HJ: Sartre was profoundly anti-American. I wonder what the roots of that were.

OW: Well, most Frenchmen are, especially the brighter ones, so his was more carefully worked out. He thought up a lot of reasons.

HJ: Did you ever know Simone de Beauvoir?

OW: No, I never met her. How could I? We would have had to meet in secrecy.

HJ: Maybe that's the reason. That would have been the way to get even. Maybe she saw the movie, loved it, loved you, and said something like, "I think he's very attractive."

OW: Like Peter Sellers. That was the reason I could never act on the same set together with what's-her-name, that pinup he was married to, Britt Ekland, during *Casino Royale*. Because she apparently said, "Look at that Orson. That's the sexiest man I've ever seen." And someone told him.

HJ: What did they think of *Kane* in England?

OW: It was not gigantically big in England. Auden didn't like it. Nor *Ambersons*.

Some people called it warmed-over Borges, and attacked it. I always knew that Borges himself hadn't liked it. He said that it was pedantic, which is a very strange thing to say about it, and that it was a labyrinth. And that the worst thing about a labyrinth is when there's no way out. And this is a labyrinth of a movie with no way out. Borges is half-blind. Never forget that. But you know, I could take it that he and Sartre simply hated *Kane*. In their minds, they were seeing—and attacking—something else. It's them, not my work. I'm more upset by the regular, average, just-plain critics.

HJ: How did you feel about James Agee?

OW: He didn't like me. He and Dwight Macdonald, who just died.

HJ: Didn't Agee write a negative review of *Citizen Kane*?

OW: Yeah.

HJ: Why did he dislike it?

OW: I don't know. Who cares? I don't want to go into it, you know. He didn't attack it. He just didn't like it. Do you know who Indio Fernández was?

HJ: He was the guy who posed naked for the Oscar statuette?

OW: Yes. He was the only Mexican director worth anything. While cutting a movie, he once sent an invitation to the critics to see a rough cut. Told them, "Why should I only hear what you people have to say after it's too late to do anything about it? Come to the rough cut and tell me what you think, while there's still time for me to do something about it, to improve the film." So Indio Fernández ran his rough cut for the critics. Asked them afterwards to tell him what they thought. They all liked it except one critic. This guy stood up, said, "It's no good." So Indio Fernández pulled out a gun and shot the critic.

HJ: I can understand that.

OW: For a couple of years after *Kane*, every time I walked in the streets in New York they shouted at me, "Hey! What the hell is that movie of yours about? What does it mean?" Not, "What is Rosebud?" but always "what does it mean?" The Archie Bunkers. It was

[Michelangelo] Antonioni to them. All those mixtures of things—
"What kind of thing is that?" Nobody says that now. Everybody
understands.

I told you about John O'Hara's review of *Kane*? In *Newsweek*.
He was the movie critic. You'd be amazed how many novelists
wanted to be movie critics. Graham Greene was a movie critic for
about six years. His reviews were not very good. They were neither
witty, amusing, nor original. They were just intelligent, plain, ordinary reviews. If you're going to be an interesting critic, you've got
to have a little zing. It's all right to be wrong, but you've got to be
interesting. We're all in the same business. We're entertaining the
public.

HJ: What about O'Hara?

OW: He wrote the greatest review that anybody ever had. He said,
"This is not only the best picture that has ever been made, it is the
best picture that will ever be made."

HJ: What do you do after that?

OW: Nothing. I should've retired.

9. "There's no such thing as a friendly biographer."

In which Orson says he doesn't want to know about the lives of his favorite writers. He mourns *F for Fake*, denies he tried to steal sole writing credit for *Kane* from Herman J. Mankiewicz, as Pauline Kael said he did, and speculates about his parentage and progeny.

HENRY JAGLOM: Orson, there's a wonderful writer, Barbara Leaming, who has written a book about Roman Polanski, among other people, who wants to write a book about you. She says it's going to be a critical biography—your life in relationship to your works, not gossipy.

ORSON WELLES: God help us. I have turned so against biographies in the last few weeks, because I read the great biography of [Isak] Dinesen and the great biography of Robert Graves—both brilliantly written and very sympathetic. Two of my gods, you see, and Graves's is written by an *adoring* biographer, who was close to him for twenty-five years. But I learned a lot of things about him I didn't want to know. If you do the warts, the warts are gonna look bigger than they were in life. If these people were my friends, the warts wouldn't be as important to me as they seem in the book. We all have people that we know are drunks, or dopeheads or have bad tempers or whatever, and they're still our friends, you know? But in a book you focus on it. And these biographies have diminished those two people so much in my mind, I wish I had never read them. They deny me somebody who I've loved always. I like Dinesen a lot less, now. In other words, Dinesen was brilliantly careful to present herself as the person I wanted to love. And if she was somebody else, really, I'm sorry to know it. And I suddenly think to myself, "You know, there's no such thing as a friendly biographer."

If it were a military leader or a politician, or somebody who didn't write—if it were a director—it wouldn't matter so much. But with writers, they become my friends from the testimony of the pages that they have written. And anything else diminishes what I feel. If I'm enraptured by any writer's work, I don't want to know about him. Somebody's come out with a snide biography of [Joseph] Conrad now. Just reading the review of it made me sick.

HJ: But doesn't it add another dimension that—

OW: Nothing. I know everybody thinks that way, but I don't believe it. I don't want to keep hearing that [Charles] Dickens was a lousy son of a bitch. The hateful Dickens, you know. I'm very glad I don't know anything about Shakespeare as a man. I think it's all there in what he wrote. All that counts, anyway.

HJ: I'm constantly trying to understand: why has there been nobody since Shakespeare who has approached his genius? And how is it possible that one individual, three hundred years ago—

OW: Definitively, he wrote all the plays that we need. And he knew it. He knew it. He wrote a short verse in which he said that nobody would match him. He was apparently an enormously charming man. Nobody ever spoke against him. Everybody loved him. And what's interesting are the new discoveries about his acting career, that he probably played much bigger parts than we had heretofore thought. It's now almost certain that he played Iago. It was [Richard] Burbage who played Othello. Burbage must have been wonderful, because you don't get those plays written for somebody who can't do it. We know he was chubby, of course, to the point of fatness, because of the line in *Hamlet*, when the queen says, "Our Hamlet is fat and short of breath."

The mystery surrounding Shakespeare is greatly exaggerated. We know a lot about his financial dealings, for example. He was brilliant in arranging his finances, you see. He died very rich from real-estate investments. The son of a bitch did everything! And finally he got what his father had always wanted—a coat of arms. His father was a butcher. And a mayor of Stratford.

HJ: Wouldn't that make an incredible film, a biography of him? Or is it impossible? 'Cause there's just too much—

OW: They hate movies about geniuses. *Rembrandt*, the only one I ever liked, emptied the theaters, a total failure.

HJ: Do you read the books about yourself?

OW: No. They make me wince. Either because they're too nice, or not nice enough. I'm terribly thin-skinned. I believe everything bad that I read about myself. And even if I reject it, it remains in my mind as probably true. So I protect myself by reading as little about myself as I can, out of cowardice.

I had to go to court in France this year to stop a book in which that old fellow—Maurice Bessy—who's always been a kind of professional friend of mine, wrote that I was an impotent latent homosexual.

HJ: How would he know that?

OW: Turns out he's my intimate friend, you know? I never laid a hand on him! He's a mean, little, crooked fairy. And he's one of those people who declares himself your friend, follows you everywhere, saying, "I'm a devoted friend." So he's *made* himself your friend, and you can't say, "No, you're not a friend."

HJ: Is Bessy a homosexual?

OW: No. Well, it never occurred to me. Maybe he is. What probably happened is that when I was making *Othello*, I was based in Paris for about six weeks, rehearsing with Micheál Mac Liammóir. And Bessy used to join us for meals. Well, when I am with a homosexual, I get a little homosexual. To make them feel at home, you see? Just to keep Michael comfortable, I kind of camped a little. To bring him out. So he wouldn't feel he was with a terrible straight. Bessy may have seen that.

HJ: Homosexuals and Jews both have one thing in common. They want everybody else to be Jewish, or everybody else to be homosexual. I was eavesdropping in a restaurant once and the people at the next table were insisting you were Jewish because—"He has a Jewish father, Bernstein."

OW: My biggest success was with *Jew Süss*, the first play I ever did. In Dublin. And somebody overheard a couple of Dubliners— women—saying, "Orson Welles. Oh, he's a Jewman, too." And they all thought Hilton Edwards was, 'cause he had a splendid hook nose. He wasn't. He was Anglo to the marrow of his bones, but to them he was a "Jewman." They liked that. A Jewman is a clever fella, you know.

HJ: So if you went to court to stop Bessy, why didn't you try to prevent Pauline Kael from using *Raising Kane* as the introduction to the script in *The Citizen Kane Book*?

OW: How could I? You see, I had held out and refused to have the script published for years. But then I was so poor that I couldn't turn it down—I just had to have some money. And it never occurred to me to think about who would write an introduction. I should have said, "I must have approval of the introduction." Or, "Let me write it." But I just took the money and ran, you see?

I love Pauline, because she writes at length about actors. Which nobody writing about movies does. I think she's wrong a lot of the time, but she's always interesting. I wish she hadn't attacked me, because I've studied her, and I'd like to attack her, but now it will be seen as payback. She has a couple of extraordinary bad habits. First of all, she's spoiled by [William] Shawn, the editor of the *New Yorker*, and given more space to talk about movies than anybody gets for the theater, or for art, or for music. She's allowed to go on and on, and she abuses the privilege. Secondly, she misuses "we" and "us": "We" feel that, and so on, for entirely subjective criticisms, which are nothing more than her own personal opinions. And she has a third thing, which is a schoolgirl use of language. Everything is "glitzy" and all kinds of things that you'd hear in a girls' boarding school. That's the voice she's developed for herself. It doesn't work. But I've never understood the *New Yorker*, anyway. The *things* that they give length to have always amazed me. Like somebody's memories of a middle-class childhood in Bombay gets a full book-length article.

You know, four pieces on me were written and not printed before they finally ran the fifth, written by Wolcott Gibbs. And you know why they wouldn't print the first four? Because they were too sympathetic to me. Harold Ross told me that. One guy wrote a rave review about me. So Ross said, "That's no good." And he gave it to another fellow. Finally Ross just gave up and ran Gibbs's very nice piece. When I was writing a column in the *New York Post*, Ross used to write me criticisms of the column all the time, as though I were sending it to the *New Yorker*. In a sort of friendly but hostile way. His basic feeling was, "He's an actor. What's he doing writing?"

HJ: You may not read all this stuff about you, but other people do. When Diane Sawyer interviewed you on TV she asked—

OW: She was very scared of me for a long time.

HJ: Yes, because of the mythology around you. That's what scares the money people away, too. You have to debunk it.

OW: She said, "In the world, there are only four or five with your kind of legendary—" While I'm trying to think, "Who are they?" This at the beginning. And finally she got to her prepared dirty question, which she held for the end. She looked at me in a hurt way and said, "Why did you try to take Mankiewicz's name off the credits?" She'd just read Kael.

HJ: Of course that's ridiculous. You should have set the record straight. But you can't if you're not even interested in your own biography!

OW: There are a lot of things I don't remember, you know. I got a letter three days ago from a woman who says that her mother and I had a great love affair. Absolutely no recollection. According to this woman, she is the issue of this affair, and she claims that I offered to support her when she was born, but the mother said, "No." Nevertheless, she says, I bought a perambulator for her. She has enclosed photographs of what she claims is my grandson. I know it's a fantasy.

HJ: You don't know anything about this?

OW: Clearly a disturbed woman. Did I ever tell you, once after a matinee performance, I was visited in my dressing room by a beautiful, exquisitely dressed, extremely elegant young woman. She said: "I just wanted to see you . . . because we are brother and sister." And then she left. I've always wondered about that—about who she was, what she meant. I've told you about my doubts about my parentage, who my father really was. I really think it was Feodor Chaliapin, I really do.

HJ: You mean the Russian opera singer?

OW: He had an affair with my mother, at just the right time.

HJ: In England, you know, you have a man named Michael Lindsay-Hogg, of quite considerable stature and prominence, going around insisting that he's your son. Says that on television.

OW: It's extremely unlikely, which I've never told anyone, because I never slept with his mother, Geraldine [Fitzgerald], all the time she was staying with me. She lived in my house when I was divorced from my first wife, for the first six months I was in Hollywood. She was not my type.

HJ: It's true, you like the dark, Mediterranean types. People say, "I didn't know that he was such an extraordinary Don Juan."

OW: I used to love everybody thinking I was having sex with everyone. But in this case it would have had to be an immaculate conception. That's the reason I've always said no, and she's always said no.

HJ: Maybe you just forgot.

OW: Well, the dates are right. So there's just a chance that he is. He believes it. I have no idea. He's a talented fellow. He acted in a play that I did in Dublin when he was a young boy. I also saw a television movie he made. Awfully well done. He's a very good director. And he smokes cigars well.

HJ: He made the first few of those *Brideshead Revisited* episodes that I like very much. The pilot, and about six others—the best ones.

OW: Really? I didn't know that. *Brideshead* is the only [Evelyn] Waugh novel I don't like. Waugh was my idea of the greatest writer of the century. I read Waugh through, all the works, except *Brideshead*, once a year. That's how much I like him. It's the greatest therapy. *Black Mischief* and *A Handful of Dust* and *Vile Bodies*.

HJ: Back to artists showing themselves in their work, isn't *F for Fake* at least partially biographical or autobiographical? Don't you reveal yourself there? At least it poses as a confessional film. Within which Elmyr de Hory, the art forger, is the fake. And then, on the second level, Clifford Irving is the fake, for having fabricated that biography of Howard Hughes, and then written a biography of de Hory called *Fake*. And, finally, the filmmaker—you—is the fake.

OW: Not at all. It's a fake confessional. I'm not really confessing. The fact that I confess to be a fraud is a fraud. It is just as deliberate and manipulative as that. No, I think I'm absolutely genuine— that's a lie. I *never* tell the truth.

HJ: So, you're not really beating your breast in *F for Fake*?

OW: I don't get anything off my chest. That's a kind of romanticism that I don't like. The personal aspect of romanticism. I don't want to know about the hang-ups of the writers or movie people, either. I'm not interested in the artist; I'm interested in his work. And the more he reveals, the less I like it. Proust holds me by his enormous skill. But the subject matter is not that interesting. He wants us— It's not—he's being— I don't know how to explain it. Here's a way to put it: I do not mind seeing the artist naked, but I hate to see him undressing. Show me your cock. That's all right with me. But don't striptease.

HJ: So in real life, how can we trust you when you say favorable things? Or unfavorable things, for that matter.

OW: You can't. You have to ask me to repeat it. I never lie twice about the same thing. What I hate is when filmmakers ask my opinion, saying to me, "We know that you wouldn't say anything but the truth. That's why we're asking." At that moment, I'm preparing the biggest lie in the world, you know. They're going to ask about some piece of *merde*—always. I've come up with one good answer, at least, which is this: "There are no words . . ."

HJ: And your other one, that I've heard you say, is, "You've done it again."

OW: I never lie with a laugh. It's much easier to lie about an intense tragedy than about a comedy. It's very hard to sit and go, "Ha ha ha ha." It's easier to say, "It's too touching, isn't it?"

HJ: I'll never understand why *F for Fake* didn't do better here.

OW: The tragedy of my life is that I can't get the Americans to like it. Outside of New York, the critics hated it. In Chicago, Cleveland, St. Louis—they were *furious* with it. They seemed to think I was attacking critics. Which I wasn't, but why not? It did make fools of them. In France, for instance, all the art critics denounced it. That's what happens when you show a [Kees] Van Dongen that Van Dongen didn't paint, and the critics say that he did. The great Andre Malraux, with tears coursing down his face in the Museum of Tokyo where there were five Modiglianis, came up to one of them and said, "At last the true essence of Modigliani has been revealed to me." All five of them were fakes, painted by de Hory. Who should go down in art history as a serious forger. But you can't *say* that to critics, you know. Anyway, I think, *F for Fake* is the only really original movie I've made since *Kane*. You see, everything else is only carrying movies a little further along the same path. I believe that the movies—I'll say a terrible thing—have never gone beyond *Kane*. That doesn't mean that there haven't been good movies, or great movies. But everything has been done now in movies, to the point of fatigue. You can do it better, but it's always gonna be the same grammar, you know? Every artistic form—the blank-verse drama, the Greek plays, the novel—has only so many possibilities and only so long a life. And I have a feeling that in movies, until we break completely, we are only increasing the library of good works. I know that as a director of movie actors in front of the camera, I have nowhere to move forward. I can only make another good work.

HJ: *F for Fake* is a new form, film in the form of an essay, which is one of the things that appeals to me. You created a new language.

OW: I hoped *F for Fake* would be the beginning of a new language that other people would take up.

HJ: I wish you had done more films in that format.

OW: I wish so, too.

HJ: Maybe the critics' scorn for Clifford Irving damaged the film itself.

OW: He's the unsympathetic fellow in this film. But he's kind of fascinating, sitting there and talking about what makes a poseur.

HJ: And what makes something art.

OW: And, really, what is art? It's a very interesting question, you know? One that has never been sufficiently answered. I'm deeply suspicious of the unanimity that people have about the whole range of art and music. Because I don't think it's humanly possible for everybody to have the right opinion about something. Therefore, some of it must be wrong. I wish some critics would say, "You know, this is all trash!" But nobody has.

HJ: Do you mean that the reputations of Beethoven or Picasso should be challenged?

OW: Yes. Why are we admiring some painters now, like [Bartolome] Morillo, who are going to disappear? Conversely, nobody took El Greco seriously until seventy-five years ago. Why is there this absolute unanimity and certainty that everybody has not only about painting, but about everything—movies; anything you want to name. Everyone agrees on what is classic and what is not.

HJ: But don't you think there are some works that transcend—

OW: That's the question. Are there? I'd like to think so, but I'm not—

HJ: You've made one, arguably two. The fact is that everyone agrees about *Kane*. It's on everybody's list.

OW: Who knows how it will fare in thirty years?

HJ: It's already withstood the test of time. I don't know why, because I don't think *Kane* is better than *F for Fake*.

OW: I think we can't pursue this conversation if we do it around my work. Because I get coy.

HJ: I don't think we can question a Beethoven symphony as being anything less than—

OW: One would think not. And I would personally die for Bach and Mozart, Bartók, Beethoven. I'm sure I'm right about them—and about Velázquez, too—but what troubles me is when people accept the whole edifice—the movies, the books, the paintings, what's in, what's out—just because it's already been accepted. That arouses my suspicion. Even if it's right. I also don't believe, in literature, that anybody can have taste so catholic that he genuinely likes Joyce and Eliot—and Céline. And yet, many people accept *all* of them. I say there's a point where somebody can't really dig that other fellow if they dig this one. Our eyes, our sensibilities, are only so wide.

HJ: But I wonder if you and I are defining art in the same way. Because, for instance, Beckett, for me, who I consider a great—

OW: I agree that he probably is. But I don't understand it—the greatness. I believe that people are right when they say he's great. But I cannot find it, and I—

HJ: Why do you believe it, then?

OW: Because I suspect that I'm tone-deaf to it. Just like I think there is music that I don't understand. I know when I sense something is wrong. I know when I think something is a fake. I know when the emperor has no clothes. But I don't see a naked emperor with Beckett. He's just opaque to me. I think [Francis] Bacon is a great painter, but I hate his paintings. I don't really question his reputation; I just keep walking, rather than stopping and staring, you know. I believe that there is no law, and should be no law under the heavens that tells an artist what he ought to be. But my point of view, my idea of art—which I do not propose to be universal—is that it must be affirmative.

HJ: Really?

OW: Life-affirming. I reject everything that is negative. You know, I just don't like Dostoevsky. Tolstoy is my writer. Gogol is my writer. I'm not a Joyce guy, though I see that he's one of the great writers of this century.

HJ: God knows, he's not affirmative.

OW: No, and that's why I don't like him.

HJ: But, wait a minute, Orson, what are you talking about? This is a stupid conversation. *Touch of Evil* is not affirmative.

OW: Listen, none of my reactions about art have anything to do with what *I* do. I'm the exception!

HJ: Oh, my God.

OW: It doesn't bother me, because it comes out of me. I'm dark as hell. My films are as black as the black hole. *Ambersons*. Oh, boy, was that dark. I break all my rules.

HJ: What about film versus theater?

OW: Films are either superior to or inferior to the theater. The battle between the two will always exist. The lack of live actors will always be to the advantage of movies and to its disadvantage. There are things you can do in movies that *require* the absence of live actors. Therefore, it's a more versatile medium. But theater, which requires live actors, can achieve things that films can never reach, because what's up on the screen is dead. It's only an image—there are no people there. Nobody who didn't see him in the theater will ever know how great W. C. Fields was. He was a *shadow* of himself in films. A shadow! A *tenth* as funny as he was on the stage. [Al] Jolson, too.

HJ: But that's performance you're talking about. Not filmmaking.

OW: Yes. Well, that's all that's important. The making of a film is secondary to the performance.

HJ: Oh, how can you say that? You, the man who made *F for Fake*! Your own work belies that.

OW: Basically, when you speak about the performing arts, the most important thing is the performer, even if he is the *result* of the director. What you are looking at is a performance. That's my point.

HJ: Wait a minute. In *F for Fake*, it's not the performance—it's the *form* you create.

OW: The hell it's not the performance.

HJ: You center it on the performance, but it's the form! The best indication of it is that whole section where you use a still photograph of Picasso's eyes behind the images, where Oja is walking in the streets while his eyes flick up. It's you, the filmmaker, who created that!

OW: I don't argue with this at all. I don't say that the filmmaker can't be the most important thing. But, *basically*, in the great mass of films, it is the performance in the film as photographed that we see. That performance may be the result of the director or may not! And when it's at its best, it's both.

HJ: But I think film is more analogous to music than to theater.

OW: I do, too. But I wasn't talking about analogous. I was talking about the battle, the curious tension between the two performing media. I agree that film is more musical than theater—and more literary. It's more narrative than drama. A real movie is a narrative—it's a story. For [Sergei] Eisenstein, on the other hand, montage is the essence of cinema. But he is the most overrated great, great director of them all.

HJ: He doesn't value actors or performance. He's the exact opposite of you. I'm not surprised that you gave *Ivan the Terrible* an unflattering review in your *New York Post* column.

OW: Yeah. It didn't bring the hands together. And he then wrote me letters month after month. Hundreds and hundreds of words each time. Until he went into hiding.

HJ: What happened to those letters?

OW: They burnt up. I felt badly about that review. It was a stupid thing to do. I published it when I was in San Francisco where the charter of the United Nations was being written. But I was spending so much time with Yugoslav partisans who were there, in San Francisco, that I felt—and with Harry Bridges, and other known card-carrying members of the Communist Party—that I thought I could attack Soviet art with a good conscience, you see?

HJ: Stalin didn't dare touch Eisenstein, did he?

OW: He apparently was touched. He was hiding in phone booths at the end, and he was very badly off. He was not allowed to release the third part of *Ivan the Terrible*. Because it suddenly occurred to Stalin, who thought he was going to be glorified, that in *Ivan the Terrible* you couldn't help but see that he was terrible. So, of course, Stalin's displeasure then moved to Eisenstein. Who should have anticipated that at the beginning. If he was so good at dialectical materialism, he should have looked around him and said, "I think I'm going to do a pastoral story of a happy collective farm," you know?

HJ: He died in forty-eight. The time of the Doctors' Trials. All the Jews were being purged.

OW: The theater suffered much more than film. All the good theater people got it. You know, Meyerhold—

HJ: Meyerhold was shot in an earlier purge in 1940 . . .

OW: I don't know why they were persecuted more severely. Maybe because all these terrible functionaries had the habit of going to the theater as a sort of official event. So they saw all the plays. The Russians have terrible taste. I saw it at its worst when they came here to buy films while the war was still on in the Pacific. I was talking to them about Eisenstein and all that. So certain was I that my work would be taken back to Russia that I took the commissar, who'd been given the job, to all the Hollywood parties, and to Romanoff's, and poured champagne down his throat. And he went home with a list that began with *Sun Valley Serenade*, a bunch of pictures like that, mostly with Don Ameche. Crummy musicals. Not even the good ones. Just dumb. Peasant dumb. Idiots that I wasted my time on. You know, not one movie of mine has ever been shown in any theater in the Soviet Union.

HJ: You would think they would love *Kane*, because they could interpret it as a big attack on capitalism.

OW: But they don't have enough sense to understand it. The critics frothed at the mouth, because it shows the good side of the oppressor.

HJ: They thought you admired Kane? And his opulence?

OW: The truth is, if any of them got to be the premier of Russia, they would be living in Xanadu themselves. The one they really couldn't stand was *Touch of Evil*, because that showed the final decadence of the capitalist world.

HJ: That's why they should love it!

OW: But they thought it was *my* decadence. The Russians are a people of genius, you know, in every department. But instead of it flowering under this great revolution, it all withered. And they're very literal. What we used to think the German mind was like. People who don't really understand German culture always think Germans are very literal. But they're not literal at all. They're mystics—you know, hysterics. The Russians are "machine-made," "tractor-made." Poor people.

None of this is true of the satellite countries. In Yugoslavia, for example, *F for Fake* has run three times on prime-time television with Yugoslav subtitles. Here, the film is almost unknown. It just broke my heart that it never caught on. Because that would have solved my old age. I could have made an essay movie—two of 'em a year, you see? On different subjects. Various variations of that form.

HJ: Weren't you thinking of making *Don Quixote* as an essay film?

OW: That was the way I wanted to finally get it done, with the title *When Are You Going to Finish Don Quixote?* That would be the name of the movie. And it would be all about Spain, a country I've known since I was a boy. What's happened to it, and why *Quixote* is still important. That film would be much more expensive than *F for Fake*, because I'd need to shoot footage in modern Spain. You know, de-Francoed Spain. But how to sell *Quixote* without having sold *F for Fake*? It's hard if you haven't got in the door with your first Fuller brush.

10. "The Cannes people are my slaves."

In which Orson perks up when he hears there is interest in Lear *and* The Dreamers. *He plans to "come out" at Cannes, where he always traveled under a foreign flag because the French hated to give Americans the Palme d'Or.*

Henry Jaglom: Speaking of unfinished and new films, did you read that article about you that Mary Blume wrote in the *International Herald Tribune* I gave you?

Orson Welles: Yeah, sort of. You know, I don't read those things very carefully. I read the end to see how they sum it up. I'm always afraid of reading something bad along the way. It's not arrogance on my part, but cowardice, sheer funk that keeps me from reading the articles. I should, but I don't. I will.

HJ: That one's significant, because I've gotten a great many calls from Europe. They all want to be your hero. As if Hollywood didn't understand, or appreciate you, and they want to show them up. Germany, now, is back in the picture. They were mad, because they hadn't heard directly from me since *The Dreamers*, which I had offered them, and they had proposed, remember, good partial financing.

OW: Yes.

HJ: And we ended up thinking it wasn't enough. I don't recall what it was. Now they're saying, "*The Dreamers*, is that still available?" And they said, "Why didn't you come to us about *Lear*? Welles and *Lear*."

OW: Yes, I do remember.

HJ: I have reason to believe that, for the German-speaking countries, I could get a million dollars. And now they're not demanding stars.

OW: In other words, the game has changed since what's-his-name told us, "Without stars, nothing doing"? We don't need A-list actors? That's progress. *Lear* must be done. I work on it all the time. I would feel very unfulfilled if I couldn't bring this one off. And I think it is a dream tax-shelter thing.

HJ: So let's talk about *Lear*.

OW: If God gives me basic health, I can go on to make several pictures over the upcoming few years. But because I'm increasingly arthritic, I must play *Lear* in the next year. I'm worried about doing it after that. Just sheer getting around.

HJ: The energy of that part.

OW: Not so much the energy of the part, but the physical moving around. Which is fine for me to do and use as the old man. But I must be *able* to. And who knows, with arthritis, when the moment comes when I really can't get around? You see? I have to be realistic about that.

HJ: So if you can't do *Lear*—

OW: I can do *The Dreamers*, for which I almost have a new script. Which I don't want to show you, because you'll love it, and then you won't want to do anything else, it's so good. I've rewritten it and completely sharpened it and made it—

HJ: You can't do this! You're not allowed to do this to me! You say that I'll love it, I won't want to do anything else, so you won't show it to me?

OW: No, I will, I will. I'll send it to you today. And when you get it, be sure you have time to read it. Try to read it as though you never read it before. Oja thinks that it should be the second picture, because even if the knee should get worse and I can't move around in that part, I don't have to. I can do *The Dreamers* even if I can't move.

HJ: I want to talk about your knees, also, though, because I have an idea.

OW: My knees?

HJ: Knees.

OW: Knees.

HJ: Knees. Do you rub anything into your knees?

OW: Never mind. Let's talk about the medical part of it later.

HJ: I just found something very interesting.

OW: Give it to me. I'll rub anything in. But let's not talk about my knees; let's talk about *Lear*. If there is real interest in it, I really must do it.

HJ: The hardest thing for me has been to pin you down about the budget. How much money do you really require to do it?

OW: Well, I'll tell you. Because of the constant changes in rentals— When I first talked to you, the rentals of studios in Hollywood were 40 percent less than they are now for independent productions. And Italy has a new production agreement that has raised the rates 30 percent. In other words, nothing is fixed. We have to decide at what moment we're really going to go after it, and make the budget then.

HJ: Well, which budget do we work from?

OW: The budget I sent you. That is the budget that allows me shorter working hours, and addresses the problem of the five- as opposed to six-day shooting week that is routine throughout Europe.

HJ: That's a doable budget. We could get that money.

OW: I also need to have some money for myself, as an actor. I want to play the part that I was born to play. And I cannot bear to lose it. And I've done the script for it already. Big job, making a movie of Shakespeare. Because you have to take terrible risks, do things that people don't like you to do. And always criticize you for it. But I think it's what he . . . would do.

HJ: Sure, if film had existed then.

OW: For one thing, his stage at the Globe Theatre was very big— people forget that. The distance from the inner theater out to that platform was a long way. And he had to march these armies on and write these boring speeches to give them the time to get off again. He turns into a different kind of writer when he's moving armies. You could almost write the stuff yourself, the level is so mundane. Now, in a movie you don't have to do that.

I'm gonna do it in 16 millimeter black-and-white. The camera is so small that you can carry it like a typewriter. If only the people who put up money didn't turn white with terror when you say "16 millimeter." It's the only way to go. Even though it still has to be turned into 35 millimeter.

HJ: Which makes no sense.

OW: Especially in an age when most of your public is gonna see it on a television screen anyway, and the other people are gonna see it on a small screen in these smaller theaters.

HJ: Regular 16? Not Super 16? It'll have to be mostly close-ups.

OW: It will be mostly close-ups. With my little machine, I can cut in my bedroom. You know, just get out of bed and—

HJ: I don't even think it's necessary to tell people you're going to shoot in 16.

OW: But how do you do that? Unless we made a 35 millimeter blimp and hide the 16 millimeter camera inside it. And never say a word about it.

HJ: And use the money we save for . . .

OW: Just leave the word *35* out of the contract. When I think that in the last decade of my career I have to make pictures which are essentially much cheaper—require more ingenuity and faking around than when I started—and yet, they will be judged by the standards of the time when I had more money, I don't like that at all, you know.

HJ: Do you want to finance *Lear* through any of these cable people who have been interested?

OW: I don't think so. It should be a small movie that plays in small theaters everyplace in the world. And then there's the casting. I'll have to do it with people who are eager to work with me, you know. They'll share a piece of it—or nothing, or whatever.

HJ: I think you should make the rounds in Europe again, to take advantage of the interest that article has stirred up.

OW: I think that I should consider, very seriously, going to Cannes this year. The cultural importance of the festival vanished years ago. It's now ceased to be anything except a market. But if you get one of the top prizes, it helps your business.

HJ: We should make arrangements.

OW: Oh, there's nothing to arrange. You know, the Cannes people are my slaves, pretty much. But I don't want to go as a guest of the festival, if I can help it. I'll let 'em pay for the hotel, as long as I'm not obligated to do anything. They'll probably want me to do some things that I don't want to do. And if there are too many of them, I'll pay my own hotel bill.

HJ: I bet they want to give you some award or something.

OW: It's a disadvantage to be an American there. They don't *like* to give the Palme d'Or to Americans. I experienced that several times. The most notable time was with *Othello* in 1952. I didn't know whether I was getting the prize or not. Because they never tell you, you see, that you've won it, until the very last minute. And the way I learned it was when they came to my room in the Carlton, desperate, and said, "We can't find anybody who knows the national anthem of Morocco." Because I had entered the picture as a Moroccan picture! The Moor of Venice, you know? All the things I've entered in Cannes for prizes have always been as Italian or Spanish—or Moroccan.

HJ: Didn't you get some kind of consolation prize for *Chimes at Midnight*?

OW: That one was nominated for the Palme d'Or in 1966, and it was "the" picture that year because the competition was so weak. All my old French friends were on the jury: Marcel Achard, Marcel Pagnol, somebody else, I've forgotten. And it was that thing of [Claude] Lelouche, his first movie, *Un Homme et Une Femme*, that got it.

When I got word that I was being given a special prize, I said, "I don't want to come to the ceremony." Because it's very undignified. But then I thought, "If I don't show up, it'll look like I'm a sorehead." So I went. And it was the greatest triumph of my life. Because when they announced that *Un Homme et Une Femme* had won the Palme d'Or, the audience stood up, booed and yelled for ten minutes. Then they said, "We're giving a special prize to Orson Welles," and there was a fifteen-minute ovation. So it was clear what everybody thought—except the jury, you know.

HJ: And did you ever get an explanation from people like Pagnol?

OW: No. It was a French thing. To promote their industry. I hadn't figured on that. I should have insisted that *Chimes at Midnight* be shown out of competition. Instead of enduring the humiliation. The year you make your masterpiece, the Rumanians will get it, you know. I was in Cannes the year of the revolution. In '68. When all the leading directors withdrew from the festival. And I joined them. It was "to the barricades!" They all said to me, "We don't even think of you as an American." But I'm very American! My pictures are very American! All they mean is that they like them.

HJ: And you're content to let them think your pictures are un-American because it helps you there?

OW: I'm a hypocrite. A sellout. You know, Louise de Vilmorin told me a story about Malraux.

HJ: De Vilmorin. You mean the writer? *Madame de . . .* , from which [Max] Ophuls made *The Earrings of Madame de . . .* ? She was Malraux's mistress, called herself Marilyn Malraux, was she not?

OW: The very same. You know, de Gaulle made Malraux Minister of Cultural Affairs. She told me, "The limousine meets him in the morning and takes him to the ministry."

HJ: My God! A hero of the Spanish Civil War, of the French Resistance, in a limo? With a driver?

OW: And then he ended up a stooge. There was a picture in *Paris Match* at the height of the '68—the "troubles," as we called them in Dublin—in which there was a great right-wing demonstration in Paris where they all filled the Champs-Élysées right up to the Arc de Triomphe. And there was de Gaulle, standing by the Unknown Soldier, with a flame coming out. And there was Malraux, with his head leaning over onto de Gaulle, with tears running down his cheeks. That's what can happen to intellectuals, you know? They are the biggest pushovers. They love power. They cluster around whatever golden boy, or man, is in power and begin to justify it.

HJ: I wonder if it's because they feel that sense of being an outsider so early in life . . .

OW: Yes. And suddenly they have access to power. We saw that with Kennedy. It was such a beehive. I got a letter from Arthur Schlesinger, who wrote an article in a magazine called *Show* in which he talked about me as a person who inexplicably had a certain cult following. Now he's forgotten all that, and wants me to be a member of the Academy of Arts and Letters. They can't do better than make me an honorary one, because there is no category for films. And I am rather tempted to say, "Create one or do without me." They're all feebly trying to imitate the Académie française, which is a useless institution, anyway.

HJ: I wonder why they don't have a category for film.

OW: They're the last holdouts. Because when I was young, the movies were considered to be not quite serious. The theater critic is what mattered. The movie critic was a little fellow who covered hockey or the dog show.

HJ: Does the Académie française have a category for film?

OW: They do. René Clair. Pagnol. Cocteau. By the way, when is Cannes this year?

HJ: May something—tenth? To the seventeenth. In that week or so. When are you going to Paris?

OW: I go to Paris for the show at the Louvre. I'm committed to that.

11. "De Mille invented the fascist salute."

In which Orson displays his grasp of ancient history, art history, and French history, venturing several dubious theories while scheming to hijack an ambitious French television series on the Louvre.

HENRY JAGLOM: What are you going to do at the Louvre?

ORSON WELLES: Between the Socialists and TV, the French have put up an enormous sum of money for thirty hours of programming on the Louvre.

HJ: What do they want you to do?

OW: To rewrite the thing. Not wanting to do it much, what I did was to make conditions that I thought rendered it impossible for them to say yes. It was a little bit like my contract for *Kane*. They asked me, "What are you interested in, what subjects?" So I said, "Well, considering it's the Louvre, I would like to do the Egyptian collection, because I have a particular thing I'd like to say about it in France." To my great astonishment, they said yes. The scripts only arrived the day before yesterday. You've never read anything so terrible in your life.

HJ: Why am I not surprised?

OW: The director of the whole show is also the writer, thus making it impossible to argue, because he's the one who calls the shots. A voice from heaven, never explained, delivers the commentary, and two people—Elle et Lui—go trotting around the Louvre. Saying banal things like, "Oh . . . the Egyptians, I believe? They're the people who invented a writing called hieroglyphs," and, "Then the mummy is placed in a coffin, which is called a sarcophagus." Any intelligent fifth-grader knows what a sarcophagus is. Every once in a while there's a little spirited remark, such as—they've been looking at the zodiac things and Elle says to Lui, "What's your sign?" So much for the great patrimony of Egyptian art. There's no story; there's no theme, no revelation, no point of view, just a number of stupid statements that aren't true, beginning with, "Like all ancient religions, the Egyptians were obsessed with death." So I immediately said, "I will name you several ancient religions in which death is incidental: Judaism, to begin with. Confucianism. Taoism. Shintoism."

So I thought to myself, legally I can say, "I don't like the script," and everybody goes home. The French will be deeply embarrassed by this, and it'll look like I'm being capricious. So I decided, I won't attack the director and his script. I'll say what I want to do, and ask to write it, not just rewrite it.

WAITER: Gentlemen, bon appetit. How is everything?

HJ: Thank you.

OW: We're talking, thank you. *(Waiter leaves.)* I wish they wouldn't do that. If I ever own a restaurant, I will never allow the waiters to ask if the diners like their dishes. Particularly when they're talking.

HJ: You were saying?

OW: The great story is that Egypt was an incredibly closed society, which lasted longer than any other society in the Mediterranean world, in a state of total rigidity. Egypt is like the Japan of the Mediterranean, elegant, cruel, inexplicable, and then suddenly opened up. Who by? Napoleon. That's why the story of the Egyptian collection is fascinating. That never occurred to these French people. It's also very nice, because it's the one moment in Napoleon's career when it's possible to speak well of him without reservations. So the half of the population that adores him is not gonna hiss me off the screen. Napoleon in Egypt is beyond criticism.

And I pointed out that not only did Napoleon give us all these savants and the Rosetta Stone and [Jean-François] Champollion, who broke the code and therefore opened up Egyptian art and culture to the world, but Egyptian art and culture dominated the aesthetics of the First Empire.

HJ: I didn't know that.

OW: Study the interior decoration. It's full of Egyptian elements, just as the Deuxième Empire of Louis Napoleon drew on Arabic and Algerian sources for exoticism. Just as the English used India for exoticism. Paris is full of imitation Arabic places left over from the Second Empire. To which was then added Caesarism—Roman elements—foreshadowing Mussolini. Because every dictatorship has always adapted the gestures and costumes of an ancient nation. That's the kind of thing I would like to do on TV, to take people through all these kinds of connections. Including when you go into the Caesarism of Mussolini, there is the fascist salute. [Cecil B.] DeMille invented it. He had to come up with something for the crowd, all those extras, to do, and Mussolini picked it up from there. Then it went to Hitler. And everybody else has been doing it ever since.

HJ: So Mussolini sees DeMille's version of ancient Rome, and . . .

OW: Oh, you'll get historians who'll scream about it and say it isn't true, but I've never been able to find one who could *dis*prove it. And I've had some arguments in Rome with historians. I said, "Come back to me when you can show me that everybody always saluted like that." They weren't doing this at the beginning of the fascist era; it only started after the movie came out. They took up Caesarism, because it was the era, in both Italy and America, of big Roman spectacles.

HJ: And why did Napoleon stand like that?

OW: A great actor of the time instructed him, "You're an Italian, and you're very short. You look ridiculous. And when you talk you wave your arms about. Keep your hand tucked under your tunic." This was still in the days of the Directory, when it was possible to talk to him like that. And Napoleon added, "Never wear a uniform higher than a corporal."

HJ: You're making this up. Why did he say that?

OW: You know his saying. "Every French soldier carries a marshal's baton in his knapsack." In other words, they could all rise to this, you see. But what he gave the marshals was everything except final power. And since they had all the gold braid that has ever been put on a uniform, what could this little dago dress up like that would make him stand out? Leave the marshals to have their gold braid. Of course, the French hate that story, because they don't even like to hear that he's Italian. Corsican. Straight from Genoa, on both sides of the family. And the behavior—the loyalty to the family, you know? It's just like the Mafia. With the old woman running the whole thing in the back room, you know?

HJ: Which old woman?

OW: The mother.

HJ: And he puts the brother—

OW: Sure. Take care of Giuseppe, you know? Makes him King of Naples. It's a real, real Mafia story.

Anyway, I told the French, "You have two choices: either accept my proposal, or pay me $5,000 and give me the rights to what I wrote. Because I cannot do your script. I am somebody who is supposed to know something—whether it's true or not, it's a certain image—and that is greatly reduced when I become a fool, and in that case, I am done an injury. And furthermore, if I don't do your show, you won't be able to sell it in the English-speaking market." They might, but I tell 'em that to scare the shit out of 'em. Then I throw in the blackmail: "I will show my tape to the press in Paris, and explain to them what I wanted to do. On the other hand, if you do like it, I'll give it to you for free, but your director is working for me. And it has to be "Orson Welles Goes to the Louvre." Half an hour ago they got back to me. I won the point. I said, "You were gonna use Charlotte Rampling with Dirk Bogarde, but it's going to be me and Oja."

HJ: You know, in Jewish history Napoleon is quite a hero.

OW: Yes. My Dadda Bernstein taught me, as a child, that he was a great man. He had rows of books on Napoleon.

HJ: He freed the Jews in France. And in all of the French Empire. Took 'em out of the ghettoes. He was the first person to consider the Jews citizens of the country, and treated them accordingly.

OW: He did all kinds of admirable things. I'm not a mad Napoleon fan, but there's no denying his genius. A very complicated man. But had he never been born, there are millions of people who wouldn't have died. There were unnecessary wars that he fought for his own glorification, which makes him a villain in the last analysis.

HJ: That's terrible, of course. But, at least, he was good for the Jews.

OW: It's like older Hungarian Jews still worshipping Franz Joseph because he was the only king who didn't make pogroms. He wasn't a liberal, but at least he didn't go out and beat the Jews over the head! Did I tell you the story of his visit to the provinces? It's a great movie story. You can use it on a set almost any day with an assistant director.

HJ: What is it?

OW: Franz Joseph is riding in his carriage through this tiny provincial town, plumes and all. The trembling mayor is sitting next to him. He says, "Your Imperial Highness, I have to apologize to you in the profoundest terms for the fact that the bells are not ringing in the steeple. There are three reasons. First, there are no bells in the steeple—" And Franz Joseph interrupts him and says, "Please don't tell me the other two reasons." Now, that's a good answer for every assistant director, everyone in the world that you've had working for you in any capacity.

HJ: Where you just want to get a straight answer. But clearly, it's apocryphal. I mean, it can't . . . Who could have been there?

OW: He told it to his mistress, said, "I got off a pretty good one the other day, with a moronic mayor," and she told it—

HJ: To her lover, who was a writer.

OW: And somebody improved it, some Jewish writer . . . I tell that story when I make a movie, always. When somebody starts with the excuses, I say, "Bells in the steeple." It stops them every time. That's one of those you can die with, you know. Like Alex Korda's "any bloody duke," you know?

HJ: No, you never told me that one.

OW: Well, I've ruined it, 'cause that's the tag line. It won't be as funny, but it's still funny. I heard it only a few months ago, in Paris. Well, Douglas Fairbanks, Jr., was asking to see Korda.

HJ: Which Korda?

OW: Alex.

HJ: The director, or producer, or whatever he was.

OW: And Korda said, "My God, he's such a snob and a bore." But his secretary says, "Please see Douglas. You know, you've been refusing to see him and giving him evasive answers. And it's rude." So Douglas Fairbanks, Jr., comes in and sits down. There's a long silence, and then Douglas says, "Well, I think it's going to clear up." Or, "Even for England it's been raining an awful lot. But, still, when you see that green . . ." Another moment of silence. Suddenly Korda says, "Tell me, how's the duke?" And Fairbanks replies, "Which duke?" Korda says, "Any bloody duke," to this famous snob.

12. "Comics are frightening people."

In which Orson suggests that John Huston was little more than a hack, and recalls Olivier and John Barrymore. When Jack Lemmon pulls up a chair, he describes his encounters with Johnny Carson and Joan Rivers.

HENRY JAGLOM: You know, Miloš [Forman] is making *Amadeus* into a movie. I don't know why he wants to do that. It's the stupidest play in the world.

ORSON WELLES: Well, you know, it's been a worldwide hit. Paris, London, New York.

HJ: People are describing Roman [Polanski]'s performance in Paris as Mozart as—

OW: It's terrible. Embarrassing. He's a bad actor.

HJ: I liked him when he cut Jack's nose in that movie that I didn't care for, *Chinatown*.

OW: He was all right in that. Because he did nothing but stand still, you know. I hated the movie. That's John [Huston] at his worst. I have to make the big speech for him at his tribute. He's been campaigning for four years now for the AFI Life Achievement Award, and he's got it.

HJ: Did he ask for you specifically?

OW: Probably. I'm almost sure. After all, I've acted in four or five movies of his, and he's acted in some of mine. So—

HJ: And he's stolen from you so liberally.

OW: His first picture, *The Maltese Falcon*, was totally borrowed from *Kane*. It was made the next year, you know.

HJ: It's hard to look at it now without thinking of your shots. I mean, the lighting; the angles; the setups; the ceilings . . .

OW: For three or four years, everybody was doing that.

HJ: I just saw *Annie* yesterday, with Huston directing.

OW: It's really bad. On every level, I think. Don't you?

HJ: No—I was entertained, in some way.

OW: I wasn't. I thought it missed all over the place.

HJ: But the real point is, how can he bring himself to work with the studios?

OW: What you don't understand is that he doesn't. He just knows how to make a picture without directing it. He just sits and lets the choreographer or somebody else do it. He stays up and plays poker all night, and when he's shooting, *that's* when he's resting.

HJ: You mean he's able to step back, because he doesn't have a need to really be the creative artist. The fact that you've not been able to do that is testimony, in many people's minds, to a kind of—you're gonna hate the word—*purity*. It comes from a kind of insistence on making your own films . . . I'm disgusting you with my effusiveness . . . All right, so what are you reading?

OW: I was reading Montaigne last night again. I was reading the great passage where he says something like, "If you walk on stilts, you're still walking on your feet. If you sit on the highest throne in the world, you're still sitting on your ass." He was a beautiful, beautiful man.

HJ: You have an actor's memory.

OW: Not really. I can read any detective story a year later with perfect pleasure, because I totally forget the plot. So I never have to buy another book. I don't even remember the names of the characters in my own scripts, you know? I say "the girl," or whoever is playing the part. I have a terrible time with fictitious names.

HJ: You have a bad time with the names of real people, too.

OW: No. I just have a selective— It's usually the one I know best whose name I can't remember. That's what really drove me out of the theater, because of the way you're trapped in the dressing room. People come backstage—and they come from every period of your life and they're all gathered together. There's dear old Pete—or whatever his name is—and his wife, standing there, waiting to be introduced to the celebrity who's next to them. And waiting to be shown that you're a snob and won't introduce them. I've perfected the mumbling now. "You all know each other"—all that.

What I do like is when they come up to me and don't know who *I* am. I was in the airport in Las Vegas last year, and a man on crutches, an older man, looked at me with that finally-found-his-favorite-movie-star expression, and started limping toward me. Of course, I met him halfway, and he said, "Milton Berle! I'd know you anywhere." So I signed *Milton Berle* for him. True story. I swear. I finally figured out that he meant Burl Ives, who is a big fat bearded fellow. And out came "Milton Berle."

(Jack Lemmon enters.)

OW: THERE HE IS!

JACK LEMMON: May I invade for a moment?

OW: Please.

JL: You know, if I had to pick a single moment of any performance—let alone just a reading—of anything that Shakespeare ever wrote, that was you one night on the *Johnny Carson Show*, a number of years ago. Now, you take an average, goddamn audience of the *Johnny Carson Show*, and you have a knowledge of Shakespeare that is that of a newt. But you were reading, and, bang! The fucking place gave you an ovation! And I was sitting at home applauding. It was brilliant—it was fucking brilliant! And I don't remember what you were reading.

OW: I remember what it was—it was the speech to the players from *Hamlet*.

JL: Fucking wonderful.

OW: I screwed it up in the middle.

JL: Nobody realized it. And there was a great lesson in it. Because, you know, most actors create characters they want you to identify with, and all of that shit. But you just did it like you were talking to Johnny. I think it was Johnny.

OW: Yes, it was Johnny. That was just before Ken Tynan wrote a profile of Johnny in the *New Yorker*, in which he quoted somebody on Johnny's show—one of the assistants—as saying there was only one guest that Johnny was visibly in awe of, and that was Orson Welles. Since then, I haven't been on the show. For five years. There goes two million copies of my autobiography when I publish it, because I can't even get on to plug it!

HJ: Well, you can if somebody else hosts. Joan Rivers.

OW: I did go on once with "John Rivers," as she ought to be called, when she was replacing Carson. After four and a half years. Obviously, just so that I couldn't go around Beverly Hills saying I was blackballed by Carson. And I knew she was all set for me; I knew. Before I even sat down I began telling her how my wife thought she was the best-dressed woman in show business. And so on. Cut her right off at the knees. She couldn't do a fat joke to save her life.

HJ: So she was on good behavior.

OW: She had to be, after that! How could she sail into me?

JL: She runs on impulse. God knows, she's got balls. And talent. Very, very bright and talented.

OW: Yes, I'm sorry to say. In her terrible way, she's very talented.

HJ: I just heard her do this incredible line. I couldn't believe I was hearing it on television: "Brooke Shields is so dumb, she flunked her Pap test."

OW: To me it sounds like you're bugging the girls' bathroom in a particularly low-class establishment.

HJ: She really makes incredible reaches, and has no sense of limits, of stopping before—

OW: Well, she has a sense—she senses it's gold! That's the trick.

HJ: You know, the talk shows have really gone down tremendously.

OW: In the days when there were four talk shows, and I was on *Carson* every other week, and I was approached for magazine interviews, who needed an interview? I used to say, "I don't give interviews. You want to know about me, tune in to Carson." Now I'm getting in a tough spot with this line. Today, tune into what? I better start getting nice to these cocksuckers with typewriters.

I saw a very long interview with your friend Richard Pryor. Interviewed by a not stupid, but rather square and dull, black man. Pryor had decided to open up and talk. He is very moving. I've always been very fond of him as a person, without knowing him.

HJ: I used to sit with Richard Pryor every night at the Improv in New York when we were starting out, and we had a game, which was that one of us had to make the other laugh. And you couldn't go to the bathroom, you couldn't go home, you couldn't do anything until the other person laughed. So I did something, and then it was his turn to do something. It was very funny, but I didn't laugh. An hour went by, and a second hour. By then we had a crowd around us, a third hour, and he was doing everything he could think of. Richie is brilliant, but fuck it, I was refusing even to smile. There was a relish tray on each one of the tables. He took the mustard. Poured it on his head. He took the ketchup and splashed it on his face. It was a horrible mess. He had every possible color of condiment dripping down his face. Hysterically funny, but I was able to control myself until he took a napkin and with infinite delicacy, dabbed the corner of his mouth. Just like Charlie Chaplin. That got me. Five hours. He ran to the bathroom—he'd been waiting all that time to go—and I realized I would never be a standup comic.

JL: I've always been fascinated by the phrases that we all used, that are so destructive, like "I killed them!"

OW: "I murdered 'em."

HJ: "Destroyed them."

OW: It shows the hostility of the comic. Comics are frightening people. Do you know the story about the comedians sitting around the table at Lindy's? They're all telling jokes. A fellow comes in very sad. He just sits there. He says, "Well, I just finished three weeks at the Paramount—held over another week—and they booked me down in Philadelphia. I guess I shouldn't complain, but, you know, everything I earn goes to my poor kid, who's been in a wheelchair all of his life. He has polio." There's a long silence. Then somebody said, "That's good. Have you heard this one?"

HJ: I remember in childhood, when I was really lonely and scared, I fell off chairs in school to get laughs. The harder I fell, and the more I hurt myself, the bigger the laugh. There's such a clear relationship between getting attention, getting that laughter, and hurting yourself. I used to be compelled by Jerry Lewis for that reason.

OW: He plays a spastic. And he will die to make you laugh. He will do anything! Cut his head off if he needs to, you know. The speech to the players, where Shakespeare has Hamlet say, "Let not those that play your clowns speak no more than is set down for them"—he must have had a big problem with some of his successful clowns. With his Jerry Lewises. Got on there in *Macbeth* as the porter and wouldn't get off. Right in the middle of the murder.

HJ: I remember seeing Milton Berle take bow after bow after bow. He had the world at his feet. Then he came on for his last bow, and he blew his nose on the curtain. He just couldn't not do it, that's all. And he didn't even get a laugh!

JL: Yeah, that's the thing of it: the tremendous need to get the attention of the audience.

OW: But, also, you know, with a comic it's different than any other form of show business, because you are instantly rewarded by laughter. You are on the greatest high in the world. And if you are not rewarded, you're dying. Even playing in a comedy, getting a good laugh on Thursday, is not the same thing as being a comic.

HJ: *(To Lemmon)* You did the TV version of *The Entertainer*?

JL: Yes, I did.

OW: I loved it. But it's an overrated play. You would be astonished at what a rattletrap piece of crap it is. It does not hold up at all! It's all vehicle.

HJ: It was Americanized, right?

OW: No—yeah. But that wasn't important—it was essentially the same play. Fakey and off-pitch. Like Larry. The thing that was better about Jack's performance, and the great mistake that Larry made— You see, Larry can't bear to fail, even if he's supposed to fail. So when he played the comic onstage, he played for real laughs from the paying audience, instead of giving the feeling that he was in a half-empty theater where nobody was laughing. He did not play a failed comedian. Success to Larry demanded being an effective comedian, even though it made no sense! Because if he was that good, what was he doing out in a Brighton theater? What was his problem? But Jack played it like the theater was empty and nobody was laughing. A couple of guys with raincoats on, and that was it, you know?

HJ: Did you see Olivier's *Lear* on the BBC?

OW: The first two scenes are the worst things I ever saw in my life, bar none. Remember, this is the man who, when he played *Hamlet*, began the movie saying, "This is the story of a man who could not make up his mind."

HJ: I understand that Olivier plays Lear as senile in the first scene.

OW: And he mustn't be senile in the first scene! He has to *fall* from grace, you see. Such a vulgar conception. You know, Larry is in competition even with the people who were doing Shakespeare *before* he was doing it.

HJ: Dead actors! Your Jack Barrymore did Hamlet.

OW: When Larry talks about Jack Barrymore, he says, "That ham." But Jack is wonderful! There's nothing *remotely* hammy about him. He was the greatest Hamlet of the century, and the greatest Richard the Third, without any doubt. I can still hear it. And I've heard his records, too. *(As Barrymore)*:

> "Ay, Edward will use Women honourably:
> Would he were wasted, Marrow, Bones, and all,
> That from his Loynes no hopefull Branch may spring,
> To crosse me from the Golden time I looke for . . ."

Jack never intended to be an actor. He began as a newspaper cartoonist, you know, and he was just a guy around town. And Arthur Hopkins said, "You're it."

HJ: Arthur Hopkins the director?

OW: Yes. And they did *The Jest*, the Sam Benelli play. He and Lionel did *Richard III* and *Hamlet*, and they did *Justice* by [John] Galsworthy. Those were the great years of acting in the American theater. In order for Jack to play *Richard III*, Hopkins sent him to Margaret Carrington, who had been the first singer of [Claude] Debussy's songs and was a great authority on voice production. She was a millionaire and the aunt of John Huston. Jack spent four months, summer months, with her, every day, saying, "Mee, mee, mam, mum," and, suddenly, this great organ was born, you see.

HJ: How did you first meet Olivier?

OW: We met when he was playing in the *The Green Bay Tree*, in

New York, and I had just finished playing Mercutio in *Romeo and Juliet*. It was a very nice gathering of people, and we were sitting talking together. The hostess was Margaret Carrington, who had been my voice teacher as well as Jack's. That's why I can imitate Barrymore, because I took lessons from her. She charged neither Barrymore nor me, and ruined me and made Barrymore. It took me years to recover. But anyway, she came up to us and, according to me, said, "Mr. Olivier, you must stop boring Mr. Welles." And, according to Larry, she said, "Mr. Welles, you must stop boring Mr. Olivier." And both of us believe that our version is right! To this day, I honestly don't know who is right.

HJ: How is Larry? Has anybody heard anything more about his health?

OW: I hear all kinds of stories, none of them very cheerful. He has three kinds of cancer. It's particularly a shame, because Larry wanted to be so beautiful. I caught him once, when I came backstage to his dressing room after a performance, he was staring at himself with such love, such ardor, in the mirror. He saw me over his shoulder, embarrassed at my catching him in such an intimate moment. Without losing a beat, though, and without taking his eyes off himself, he told me that when he looked at himself in the mirror, he was so in love with his own image it was terribly hard for him to resist going down on himself. That was his great regret, he said. Not to be able to go down on himself!

He was supposed to be in this last movie I was in, and he couldn't make it. And he's supposed to be in another movie they want me in, and they guess he won't be able to do that, either. And that's rough on him, because he has to act. He doesn't care if it's a bad movie or a bad play. He has to work. Which is admirable. That's why he went so far beyond me as an actor. I envied him that so much, but that was the great difference between us. He was—and is—a professional, whereas I don't see acting as a profession, as a job, never have. I am an amateur. An amateur is a lover—*amateur*,

the word, comes from "love"—with all the caprices and the difficulties of love. I don't feel compelled to work. And Larry does. A
professional turns up on Wednesday afternoons.

HJ: I never asked you—how did you get into acting in the first place?

OW: I finished high school in two years and had a scholarship to
Harvard. I *hated* school! *Hated* school! The trouble with school is
that it's very good for some minds, and very bad for others. It's giving you opinions. All the time, opinions about history, opinions
about people, opinions about everything. Schools are opinion fac-
tories. So I went into the theater so as not to go to Harvard!

HJ: Candice Bergen has just finished her book on growing up as
the daughter of a ventriloquist. I don't know what reminded me.

OW: Edgar Bergen was an ice-cold fellow.

HJ: He never told her, "I love you."

OW: I believe that. I knew him very well, because we were fellow
magicians. We went every Thursday night to the same magic club!
Here's a story about him. We were in a show—I was doing a run-
through with him—he was up there with a dummy. And his two
leading writers were sitting in front of me in the CBS Theater,
which was empty. They didn't know that anybody was behind
them. One of 'em turned to the other and said, "You know, to look
at him, you'd swear that Bergen was real."

HJ: You know, for the first three years of her life, Candice had
breakfast with Edgar and Charlie McCarthy, and thought Charlie
was her brother? Charlie would sit there and talk to her: "Drink
your milk." Her father never spoke directly to her. Till one day she
opened a closet she wasn't supposed to open and found five of her
brothers hanging there.

JL: Have to leave. It's been fun.

OW: Bye, Jack.

13. "Avez-vous scurf?"

In which Orson claims Chaplin "stole" *Monsieur Verdoux* from him, or at least the writing credit, and explains how the Tramp wore out his welcome with the Hollywood set, compares him invidiously to Keaton, and recalls Garbo snubbing Dietrich.

HENRY JAGLOM: Orson, speaking of comics, I'm dying to hear about Charlie Chaplin. He was the hero of my youth, and I still adore his movies. Do you know whether he planned his jokes in advance, or mainly improvised?

ORSON WELLES: No. He didn't improvise much, but he wasn't the one who planned the jokes, either. He had six gagmen.

HJ: Chaplin had *six* gagmen?

OW: Yes. Oh, yes, of course. I'll tell you a story. There was a fellow who later became a director, called Mal St. Clair, and he was one of the gagmen. This was a day when Rebecca West, Aldous Huxley, and H. G. Wells were coming to watch the shooting of *City Lights*.

HJ: My God.

OW: And Chaplin has the chairs out, ready for them, and they sit down. He starts his scene, something they had been shooting the night before and hadn't finished. He has a brick. And he's going to throw it through the window of a shop to take something—because he's hungry or whatever it is—and then realizes a policeman is standing behind him. They start to roll. And Mal comes into the studio and says, "Charlie, I've got it! None of us could figure out what to do in that scene you were shooting last night, but I've got—" Chaplin says, "Go away." Mal says, "Charlie, I'm telling you, I've got it. What you do with the brick—" Chaplin says, "Get out, please. I told you not to come in." Mal says, "But we were all trying to find a kicker for this scene last night, and I've got it!" Chaplin's really angry now, says, "Listen, will you get out?" And Mal says, "As you start to raise the brick—" Charlie yells, "Get out of my studio!! I never want to see you again!!" So Mal says, "Yes, I'm going." Just as he reaches the exit, he turns around, and adds, "You are nothing but a no-good quidnunc."

HJ: Quidnuck?

OW: Quidnunc. Don't interrupt. Listen to the story. "No good quidnunc." Now, Charlie, every day after lunch, went to the can, his private can. And there he had the short Oxford dictionary, and he read a page of it to improve his mind. On this day he turns to Q. He sees that it's circled, and Mal has written, "I knew you'd look it up."

HJ: So it doesn't matter what it means.

OW: Exactly. That has nothing to do with it.

HJ: He did it in advance, was sort of saving it up, to humiliate Chaplin?

OW: Charlie was uneducated, you see, and embarrassed about his vocabulary.

HJ: Right. And he didn't want anybody to know that he had gag-men.

OW: That's why he fired Mal St. Clair. Never allowed him on the set again! Because he was blowing it in front of these highbrow, grand people, who thought he was the genius of comedy—

HJ: I'm completely stunned. It makes him Johnny Carson to me.

OW: Of course. He was Johnny Carson! He did think up gags, but he also had gagmen. The only one who didn't was Harold Lloyd, who was the greatest gagman in the history of movies. If you look at his movies, the gags are the most inventive—the most original, the most visual—of any of the silent comics.

HJ: But they weren't touching like Chaplin's were.

OW: C'mon, who's talking about touching? We're talking about gags! A gag isn't supposed to be touching.

HJ: I'm trying to talk about Chaplin's special genius . . .

OW: We're not talking about Chaplin's genius, we're not talking about his art, or whether Lloyd is better than Chaplin. We're talking about gags. The joke. You've got to separate jokes from beauty and all that. Chaplin had too much beauty. He drenched his pictures with it. That's why [Buster] Keaton is finally giving him the bath, and will, historically, forever. Oh, yes, he's so much greater.

HJ: Because he was not as schmaltzy.

OW: Because he was better—more versatile, more, finally, original. Some of the things that Keaton thought up to do are incredible.

HJ: I feel like a little child told there's no Santa Claus.

OW: But think what gags are. They're essential in a slapstick comedy. A picture has to be full of them. Chaplin had a guy who wrote better gags than he did, you see? But still, he made the pictures you admire. With his sensibility, plus all the things he did around the gags.

HJ: To me, nobody else is diminished by having writers, but it's different with Chaplin.

OW: He understood that. That's why he wanted people to think that he composed, directed, designed—everything. The day he ran *Monsieur Verdoux* for me—you know I wrote it—the credits said, "Charles Chaplin presents *Monsieur Verdoux*, produced by Charles Chaplin, directed by Charles Chaplin, music created by Charles Chaplin, executive producer Charles Chaplin." And then it said, "Screenplay—Orson Welles." Story and screenplay. And he said, "Don't you find it monotonous, my name all those times?" Not thinking he's being funny.

HJ: I don't understand. Was that his way of saying he didn't want Orson Welles?

OW: No. My name had to stay. It was in the contract. He was already being sued for plagiarism by Konrad Bercovici over *The Great Dictator*—and he did steal. So he came to me, and he said, "I have to, for my defense, say that I've written everything I ever did. And if I put it in the credits that you wrote the story and the screenplay, there goes my case. I'll put you back the minute the case is over.

HJ: But he never did.

OW: Never meant to. But I said, "Okay," and it opened in New York without my name at all. And all the papers said, as their chief criticism of *Monsieur Verdoux*, "Whoever put it into Chaplin's head to do such a thing?"

HJ: You mean to make such a dark movie about a bluebeard?

OW: Of course. So one day later the credits say, "Based on a suggestion by Orson Welles." Or "a story suggested," something like that. "Suggest" is in it. In other words, something I said to him one night over dinner. And it has said that ever since! But I wrote the whole script, which he then—

HJ: You wrote the whole script of *Verdoux*?

OW: I had a script, and I was gonna direct him in it. For two years. And he kept stalling, and finally he said, "I can't. I have to do it myself." He didn't want to be directed. He said, "I want to buy it from you." I said, "Of course, Charlie. I just want it to happen." I practically gave it to him. I said, "I'll leave the price to you." So a check came for $1,500—something like that. Cheapest man who ever lived. You love him, and I don't. And you wouldn't have loved him if you'd been through what I went through with him. It was really rough, and I have real contempt for him, because I worked very hard. Offered him something out of my love for him. It was not a suggestion, it was a *screenplay*. Do you know why I thought of Chaplin? There used to be an ad in the subways for something called Eau de Pinot. Which was the sort of thing that barbers put on, that smelled a little, and was supposed to stop dandruff. French. And they had a fellow with a little mustache saying, "Avez-vous scurf?"

HJ: Scurf?

OW: Flaky skin. And I looked at that, and I said, "Chaplin! Got to play [Henri-Désiré] Landru," you know, the real Bluebeard, eleven killings, all women except one, during World War I. Of course, Chaplin changed the script. Mine was called "The Lady-killer." Based on Landru, and I called the character Landru. He called him Verdoux. And he had to make it socially conscious, have Hitler, and so he changed the period.

HJ: So you had set it twenty years earlier, World War I?

OW: Yes. I've told you about the great sequence in the Alps that he cut out. Landru finally finds a woman whose profession is killing her husbands. His equal. And they go on a honeymoon together, a walking trip in the Alps. And each one wants to kill the other. And he cut it out, 'cause it was too good a part for the woman.

HJ: Oh, my God. Really? Who was gonna play it?

OW: It didn't matter. Because even those who loved him, and were close to him, have said, "You know Charlie will never let another actor be good on the screen with him, not for one minute." So he changed the script and came up with what was a very funny scene, but nothing like mine. His was the scene in the rowboat, in the Bois de Boulogne. If you listen carefully, you will hear yodeling in the distance. Because, in my script, I accompanied this scene in the mountains with yodeling, and he never stopped to wonder why the yodeling. That's how dumb he was!

Actually, Chaplin was deeply dumb in many ways. That's what's so strange, great hunks of sentimental dumbness with these shafts of genius. And he blew it, too. He performed *Verdoux* for two years in everybody's drawing room, so that there was nothing left when it came time to shoot it. He did the same thing with *The Great Dictator*. But he didn't get invited out that often. Because, after a point, people didn't want their whole party taken over by one entertainer. They knew he'd come, and he'd totally dominate—if you had Chaplin, you had Chaplin performing. That limited his social life terribly.

HJ: He was that insecure, that he had the need to prove himself?

OW: Or had that much pleasure in performing, whatever. He may just have enjoyed showing off. Chaplin showed me the rushes of the original *Limelight* scene with Keaton, before it was cut.

HJ: Keaton had more to do, I presume.

OW: Not only more to do, but he gave the bath to Chaplin! Washed him right off the screen. You saw who was the best. Just no argument.

HJ: And you think the reason Chaplin cut it was 'cause he was jealous of Keaton?

OW: There's no "thinking." I can't blame him, because it was almost embarrassing.

HJ: You would think that the brilliance of Chaplin would give him the generosity of spirit to recognize—

OW: I don't think *brilliance* is the word, *genius* is.

HJ: His creative brilliance, I mean. I never have understood the word *genius*.

OW: Well, you can't—any more than you'd understand *soul, love.* They're all the big words that no one understands.

HJ: I mean, he was some kind of genius. Right?

OW: No, not some kind of genius—he was absolutely a genius. But so was Keaton. There's nothing Chaplin ever made that's as good as *The General*. I think *The General* is almost the greatest movie ever made. The most poetic movie I've ever seen. To my great sorrow, I've got to the age now where all my old minority opinions are ceasing to be minority. I spent all my life saying, "You're all crazy—it's Keaton!" And now I've got nothing to argue about! Now Keaton is coming in. I used to say, "What are they doing all that Wagner for? Why don't they do *Don Giovanni*? Now everybody's doing it.

HJ: I don't know why Keaton to me is more farcical, broader, not as real as Chaplin.

OW: But Chaplin isn't real. He's—

HJ: Oh, how can you say Chaplin isn't real?

OW: Chaplin is sheer poetry, if you want, but it's not real.

HJ: But it's poetry based upon reality, a heightened form of reality.

OW: Not for me, no. What Chaplin did is—there are two basic kinds of clown. In the classic circus, there's the clown who is white-faced, with a white cap, short trousers, and silk stockings. He has beautiful legs, and is very elegant. Every move he makes is perfect. The other clown, who works with him, is called an *auguste*, and he has baggy pants and big feet. What Chaplin did was to marry them, these two classic clowns, and create a new clown. That was his secret—that's my theory.

HJ: You look at some of Chaplin's shorts, and they don't feel dated.

OW: They don't date because they were dated then. They were period pieces when they were made. The silent pictures always look as though they happened in a world earlier than they did when they were shot. They all derive from the nineteenth century.

HJ: That must be why, when he tried to tackle anything contemporary it was so bad. That's why there was such a gulf between his silents and his talking pictures. *Limelight* is a fake, sentimental film, but I happen to like it very much.

OW: Yeah. Well, as I said, you love him, and I don't. The visual difference between *City Lights* and the movie he made with Paulette Goddard is extraordinary.

HJ: *City Lights* is still the greatest Chaplin film.

OW: No question. But that other film is bad. From that time on, he went down so fast that he's almost unrecognizable . . . *Limelight*!

HJ: *Limelight* didn't have Paulette Goddard.

OW: No, no, the picture I'm talking about was made before, when I was still a boy.

HJ: *Gold Rush*?

OW: No, no.

HJ: No. Which one was it with her? I forget. *(Pause)* Not *Modern Times*.

OW: *Modern Times*! That's the bad picture. I saw it again just six weeks ago. It doesn't have a good moment in it. It is so coarse, it is so vulgar. It doesn't touch—I knew Paulette well.

HJ: So you knew her when she was going down on people at Ciro's, or was it Anatole Litvak going down on her under the table? Or something like that.

OW: She's a wonderful girl, but she's a living cash register, you know.

HJ: You should see Chaplin's female impersonation movie, *The Woman*, it was called. A short, about twenty minutes. He was wearing a fur muff and a fur hat.

OW: He looked terrific as a woman.

HJ: He looked gorgeous and he was so incredible and touching and flirtatious and charming and romantic and teasing. And sexual . . .

OW: He wasn't effeminate, just totally female as a performer. There was no masculine element there. And he was like that as a man, too, terribly female as a man. It's that smile, that little female smile. He was so beautiful when he was young. And he didn't want any of us not to notice it. He beaded his eyelashes. You know how long that takes? He made himself up to be the most beautiful fellow in the world, and then put that little mustache on. Vanity is very much part of that character. He didn't think he made himself look prissy. He thought he looked beautiful, and delicate and sensitive, and so did all the world. They took it on his terms. I never thought he was funny. I thought he was wonderful—wonderful—but not funny. I thought he was sinister. That's why I thought of him for *Verdoux*. I had another idea for Chaplin—with Garbo—but neither one of them would touch it. A farce. They're in the maze in Hampton Court, and he deliberately loses her.

HJ: Could she have played farce, do you think?

OW: Yes. Well, she played comedy wonderfully. I wouldn't have made her ridiculous, but I would have made her herself. I would have made her the distinguished actress that she was. I told it first to her, and then to him, and they were just—nothing. So that went nowhere.

HJ: Why did she stop acting? Was it just because of the bad reviews?

OW: Of *Two-Faced Woman*. No business.

HJ: You mean she was that unprepared for a flop? She must have, somewhere along the line, figured that, eventually, one of her pictures wouldn't work.

OW: No, I think she was getting older, and I think she hated to act. And I think she was waiting for the flop.

HJ: To go out with.

OW: I think so. I was always a wild Garbo fan. But when I saw her in *Grand Hotel*, at first I thought it was somebody else making fun of her, like somebody taking off on Garbo. She was totally miscast as a ballerina. She's a big-boned cow. She did everything that you would do if you were a drag queen doing an imitation of Garbo, you know.

Did I ever tell you about the time I introduced Marlene to

Garbo? Marlene was my house guest, and for some unaccountable reason had never met Garbo, and she was her hero. I arranged for Clifton Webb to give a party for Garbo so I could bring Marlene. I was living with Rita at the time, and she didn't want to go. That was very much like her. She never wanted to go anywhere, just stay home. So Marlene and I went without her. Garbo was sitting on a raised platform in the middle of the living room, so that everybody had to stand and look up at her. I introduced them. I said, "Greta, it's unbelievable that you two have never met—Greta, Marlene. Marlene, Greta." Marlene started to gush, which was not like her at all. Looking up at Garbo, she said, "You're the most beautiful woman I've ever seen, it's such a pleasure to meet you, I'm humble in your presence," and on and on. Garbo said, "Thank you very much. Next?" And turned away to somebody else. Marlene was crushed.

14. "Art Buchwald drove it up Ronnie's ass and broke it off."

In which Orson ridicules Ronald Reagan, explains why he lost his respect for Elia "Gadge" Kazan, and argues that old people, especially macho men like Norman Mailer, come to look like their Jewish mothers.

ORSON WELLES: Did you see the tribute to the five distinguished people at the Kennedy Center the other night?

HENRY JAGLOM: No. I missed it.

OW: I saw it. It was a riot. Art Buchwald came on, and for seven minutes drove it up Ronnie's ass and broke it off. He didn't have one joke that Ronnie could even laugh at. He said, "And Mr. Reagan . . ." you know, with that voice of his, "We have to be careful. We ought not to treat the arts the way you treat Central America." And he said, "Because, if the Kennedy Center goes Communist, the next thing is the Hollywood Bowl!" You could see the audience wondering whether they'd be photographed by the FBI on their way out if they laughed too hard.

HJ: Did they cut to Reagan at all?

OW: At the very beginning, doing a kind of wince, and then never again. The whole dressed-up audience had these frozen smiles. Art was the licensed jester. They couldn't cut. I wanted to see how Old Blue Eyes was taking it. But we didn't even get to see that.

HJ: Who else was there?

OW: It was a great group. Besides Sinatra—Kazan, Katherine Dunham, Jimmy Stewart, and Virgil Thompson. First we had a speech by Reagan, from the White House, instead of his speaking from his box or coming on the stage. They'd written a very short, gracious speech, which he read with that Reagan skill, which can be very good. Followed by Warren Beatty, who introduced Kazan, calling him "our greatest living film director." A very bad speech. And badly delivered. He looked terrible. Any thought that he's gonna be president was written off last night. Katherine Dunham is a fake dancer if ever there was one. And Virgil Thomson, introduced by John Houseman. I didn't stay for that. They roomed together— they were lovers. Why shouldn't he introduce him?

HJ: Yeah, yeah. They were lovers, really?

OW: Oh, yes.

HJ: Is he that old?

OW: Houseman is eighty-one. Something that gives me comfort every night. Every night when I get a twinge of rheumatism. He's holding up awfully well, though.

HJ: More extraordinary, that Warren would choose to introduce Kazan!

OW: Kazan gave Warren his first job, *Splendor in the Grass*. Why couldn't he have pretended that he wasn't in town, or something? When I saw Gadge it made me sick. I still can't forgive him. The people I got most mad at were people from my side who gave names. And he was one of the biggest sellers of people up the river in the whole bunch. I am not a vengeful person, but Kazan is one of the people that I feel really badly about. I was—in fact, in a terrible way, I'm still fond of him—I like Gadge. But I think he behaved so badly that it's just inexcusable. I cannot honor him. Or sit with him.

HJ: You won't give anything to *On the Waterfront*?

OW: Nothing. Because it's so immoral.

HJ: Forgetting the politics for a moment . . .

OW: I wish I could. But that was made at a time when I was very sensitive on those subjects, and it was an excuse for all those people who gave names. All those collabos with McCarthy, of which Kazan was one. And this film was to show that the hero is the man who tells.

HJ: And Budd Schulberg, who wrote it, was another.

OW: That's right—all that. So I'm bigoted. Then we had Zorba the Greek. Straight from Broadway. Tony Quinn came out and neither danced nor sang. But kind of stood there, as though we're all supposed to think that this is the biggest set of balls that's ever been seen in New York. And then he told us that he loved Kazan more than any man alive. Zorba the Testicle, to Gadge.

HJ: I'm trying to think when they even worked together.

OW: In *Viva Zapata!* He played Zapata's brother. He was quite good.

HJ: I love that movie.

OW: Above all, not a good movie. Zapata is so important to me, and I have such a clear picture of what the story is, that I was profoundly offended by the movie. On the grounds of its—

HJ: I just took it as a progressive fairy tale.

OW: I was not free to appreciate it on those terms. And it wasn't progressive. Zapata—here's a true story. Did I ever tell you what happened when he heard about the trouble Lenin was in? Because at one point Lenin had said, "If we can hold out another sixty days, the revolution is won. If we don't, it's lost." And word of this got to Mexico, where Zapata was fighting. So Zapata says, "Where is he? We will ride over and help him." He thought Moscow was somewhere over the hill.

HJ: I guess *Viva Zapata!* was another anti-left film, if you think about it. Because the revolution is betrayed by the arch revolutionary, the Lenin figure. And better to have had no revolution at all. Do you think *Streetcar Named Desire* is a good film?

OW: No. I think Gadge did it better in the theater. I don't think he's a very good filmmaker compared to his work in the theater.

HJ: You don't make allowances for people with talent, like Kazan?

OW: Let me tell you the story of Emil Jannings.

HJ: I know who he is. He played opposite Marlene in *The Blue Angel*. He won a Best Actor Oscar for something or other, I think the first one ever awarded. Not only did he collaborate with the Nazis, Joseph Goebbels named him "Artist of the State."

OW: When the allies got to Berlin in the last days of the war, he fled to his hometown. As the American troops entered the town with their tanks looking for collaborators, he stood in front of his little house waving his Oscar over his head, yelling, "Artiste, artiste!"

You know, Gadge has begun to look like a minor figure in a Dostoevsky novel. His face has become long, like a junior inquisitor. And he was standing on that stage like some terrible bird. The face he deserves, with a beak, a beak—it's a beak. A face that turns into a beak.

HJ: My mother once said, "All old people look Jewish."

OW: True. You either look Jewish or you look Irish—you have your choice. It has nothing to do with the nose. It's an expression that happens to people when they get past sixty—they usually look like their Jewish or Irish mother. Like Mailer, who looks exactly like his Jewish mother. He never looked Jewish before at all! He looked like an Irishman, if anything. If you met him and his name had been Reilly, you would have said, "Sure—that's Reilly." And Lenny Bernstein is getting to look like his mother, too, you know.

HJ: I just saw him in New York. He conducted—

OW: They don't look like their fathers, they look like their mothers! Lenny's really—I mean, he's developed this flourish with the baton, that he started a couple years ago.

HJ: His pinkie is up?

OW: Way up all the time. And he can't jump as high anymore. It's as if he's announcing to the world that he can still jump, but he doesn't really leave the floor! He used to leave the floor!

HJ: He did the most extraordinary thing. I went to a concert at Carnegie Hall and it started with Bernstein playing some Chopin. And he started crying in the middle of playing. I never saw him do that before—he just wept.

OW: Yes, he's very emotional—genuinely.

HJ: It was incredibly touching. It made the music stronger, in some way. He's so theatrical. Does he know? He must know.

OW: Of course he knew he was going to choke back the tears. He's a ham. I've known him since he started.

HJ: He's still a wonderful-looking man.

OW: Less so now. More and more like his mother. The last couple of years have been very cruel to him. Have really made him look like the old lady, you know. And, brashly, he's cut his hair shorter, hoping to look less like her.

HJ: And it doesn't work.

OW: No, now Lenny looks more like Gertrude Stein. It's a terrible fate that comes to men—and, particularly, very masculine men. And that's the cruelty, you see? You could see him in a dress, without any trouble at all, you know? . . . Oh, Kiki.

HJ: What's the matter?

OW: It's Kiki. She's forgotten herself.

HJ: She's farting?

OW: Oh, yes. Ooh, yes—oooh! Isn't that terrible?

Waiter: Shall we show you desserts?

HJ: *(To waiter)* It's not us—it's the dog. We just want you to know.

OW: Don't bring us a dessert for the next two minutes.

HJ: Oooh! That one came clear across the table.

OW: This is a real . . . like atomic warfare. Mmm, boy—that was one.

HJ: It's great to have a dog around in case one ever does it oneself.

OW: Well, in the eighteenth century, they always did.

HJ: For that reason?

OW: Yes. Do you know the *Arabian Nights* story?

HJ: No.

OW: A young man goes to a wedding feast, the most important wedding feast in the village. Everyone is on their best behavior. And just when the mullah is about to pronounce his blessing, and everything is quiet, he lets rip the loudest fart that's ever been heard. He is so embarrassed that he turns and flees. He steals a camel, and rides away from the village, out of the kingdom, and goes to the farthest reaches of the known world. And there, over the years, he prospers. Finally, as a rich old man, he comes back to the village with a great caravan. As he approaches it, a couple of women are working in the fields. They look up and say, "Look, there's the man who farted at the wedding."

HJ: Oh, God!

Part Two

1984–1985

Welles and Jaglom in Someone to Love, *Welles's final screen appearance.*

"I always acted as if everything was going to go great for him. I needed to act that way to feel that way, so that I could make him feel that way, and hopefully make someone else, or some combination of many someone elses, give him the money to work, to live. I was hustling me and him, and hopefully them, into a self-fulfilling prophecy. I told him deals were done, all that was needed was for so and so to fly in and confirm them, when it wasn't true. I didn't make it up out of whole cloth, but where things were iffy, I made them sound much less iffy."

—HENRY JAGLOM, e-mail, June 8, 2012

15. "It was my one moment of being a traffic-stopping superstar."

In which Orson recalls that director Carol Reed wanted him for *The Third Man*. He reflects on Joseph Cotten's career, and wonders what the excitement over Alfred Hitchcock was all about.

ORSON WELLES: You're eating already. Your mouth is full, which is a disgusting sight.

HENRY JAGLOM: And how are you today? You're late. That's why I ordered.

OW: Angry at a lot of things going on in my household. You know those wild stupidities that happen to everybody who lives longer than they should. I have a thing I have to put on my leg that compresses it, and I put it on at night. Somebody has to get me out of it in twenty minutes or I go nuts. But somebody went to sleep, and there was no getting out, and I had to fight my way out of this machine. It took me about forty minutes to get untangled. I'm a little out of breath from rage. You know, simple, quiet, domestic rage.

HJ: I saw *The Third Man* last night. I don't think there's another movie of Carol Reed's that's in its class.

OW: I think *Odd Man Out* is close to it.

HJ: That's a good movie. But James Mason's performance is weak.

OW: Well, Carol didn't think he was good enough. He talked me out of using Mason in something I wanted to do. He said, "Mason hasn't got the range. He drove me crazy in *Odd Man Out*. He can't do from here to there. He can only do from here to here." So I believed him, because he really knew acting. Loved actors.

HJ: The longer you look at Mason's performance—

OW: The less and less good it gets.

HJ: The character of Harry Lime fit you like a glove.

OW: It's a hell of a picture. Alida Valli. Boy, she's great. She's Austrian, you know, raised in Italy. She started very young.

HJ: What happened to her?

OW: She was the biggest star in Europe. She was huge during the fascist period, all through the war. In Rome. Then she was taken up by Selznick. Selznick destroyed her. He brought her to America, tried to make a big star out of her here, thought he'd have another Bergman, and put her in three—

HJ: After *The Third Man*?

OW: No, *The Third Man* was in the middle. He loaned her and [Joseph] Cotten to Alex Korda, who produced it. Alex had to have two American stars besides me to sell the picture. So he made this deal with Selznick, giving him all American rights. That's the only good picture she made here. You can't look at the others.

HJ: What else did he put her in?

OW: A terrible trial movie, Hitchcock, *The Paradine Case*. And something else terrible. She came back to Europe, and nobody would hire her. They said, "She can't be any good. She failed in Hollywood." After that, it was just, "A special appearance by Alida Valli." She should never have come here in the first place.

HJ: Carol Reed had never directed you before. Were you his idea?

OW: Yes. Selznick had bitterly fought against having me in it. He was so dumb. He wanted Noël Coward for the part. He was impressed by Noël. And not by me. Noël was a little mysterious, but he saw me around all the time.

HJ: Well, you did fuck up his charades.

OW: Alex held out, said it had to be me, and so did Gregg Toland. I took the Orient Express from Venice or from Paris, I don't remember which, and arrived in the morning in Vienna at about eight o'clock. I had my wardrobe. We went right out to the Ferris wheel, and by nine o'clock I had shot a scene. Then we shot for six days, five in Vienna and one in London. There were three complete A-film units shooting at once. Because Carol needed an entire crew to shoot one huge scene, where you saw down four blocks at night, and then, in another part of Vienna, the second crew was working. And a third was down in the sewer. That's how come we got it done so fast.

HJ: You don't appear until near the end.

OW: All the characters do is talk about Harry Lime. Until the last reel. Then I come on.

HJ: But it's not the last reel.

OW: Yes, it is the last reel.

HJ: No.

OW: I have one appearance—a silent appearance—in the reel before. I'm in shadow, and the light suddenly hits me when the window is opened. Jo Cotten sees the cat sitting on my shoe. That was the greatest entrance there ever was. We did it in Vienna, but not in a real location. Carol had a little set built just for that, on which we shot at the end of every day, towards dusk. We would look at the rushes, and then Carol would say, "Not yet," and we'd do it again, to get it perfect.

HJ: How much of *The Third Man* was Grahame Greene's, how much was Korda's?

OW: The real makers of that film were Carol Reed and Korda. Greene was nowhere near it. His authorship is greatly exaggerated. The idea for the plot was Alex's.

HJ: Really? Everyone assumes, automatically, that the Graham Greene novel came first, and then somebody adapted— It's not from Graham Greene?

OW: Korda gave him the basic idea. Said, "Go and write a movie script set in a bombed-out, nightmare city after the war, with the black market and all that. He just wrote a rough-draft sketch for the movie, and Carol did the rest of it. There's an example of a producer being a producer. Carol deserves much more credit than people give him. Graham wrote the novel *after* the movie was made. Also, he conceived the character as one of those burnt-out cases, one of the Graham Greene empty men, which was not my vision of him at all.

HJ: Maybe that's why Selznick thought of Noël Coward for the character that Greene wrote.

OW: Maybe. But I said, "No, he has to be fascinating. You must understand why he's got this city in his hand." And Carol took a flyer on that idea and changed the character completely. Greene's Harry Lime was nothing like the way I played it. Every word that I spoke, all my dialogue, I wrote, because Carol wanted me to. Including the "cuckoo clock."

HJ: I remember that verbatim. Lime says, "In Italy, for thirty years under the Borgias, they had warfare, terror, murder, and bloodshed, but they produced Michelangelo, Leonardo da Vinci, and the Renaissance. In Switzerland, they had brotherly love, they have five hundred years of democracy and peace—and what did that produce? The cuckoo clock!"

OW: I have to admit that it's unfair, because the cuckoo clock is made in the Schwarzwald, which is not in Switzerland at all! And I knew it when I wrote the line! And did the Swiss send me letters!

HJ: You have a generation of Swiss hating you because of that.

OW: But pretending to laugh. You know how the Swiss laugh, when they want to show they have a sense of humor? It's like the Swedes.

They go, "Ho ho ho. Ho ho—your joke about the cuckoo clock. You know, the cuckoo clock is not made in Switzerland." I say, "I know, I know." It was as misleading a statement as has ever been made for a laugh in a movie. I came to Carol the morning we shot it and said, "How about this?" And he said, "Yes! And so we did it."

HJ: Greene has script credit. Did he give you any problems about your writing your lines?

OW: No. Because he didn't take the movie seriously. It wasn't a "Graham Greene" work. He gave me a line that I was supposed to say from atop the Wiener Riesenrad, the Ferris wheel: "Look at those people down there—they look like ants." Well, that's about as clichéd as you can get.

HJ: So how much of *The Third Man* is Korda, and how much is Reed?

OW: It's full of ideas that everybody thought up on the set. Because Carol was the kind of person who didn't feel threatened by ideas from other people. A wonderful director. I really worshipped him.

HJ: How was *The Third Man* received?

OW: In Europe, the picture was a hundred times bigger than it was here. It was the biggest hit since the war. It corresponded to something the Europeans could understand in a way the Americans didn't. The Europeans had been through hell, the war, the cynicism, the black market, all that. Harry Lime represented their past, in a way, the dark side of them. Yet attractive, you know.

You cannot imagine what it was, a kind of mania. When I came into a restaurant, the people went crazy. At the hotel I was staying in, police had to come to quiet the fans. It was my one moment of being a superstar, a traffic-stopping superstar. The best part ever written for an actor. Had I not been trying to finish *Othello*, I could have made a career out of that picture. From all the offers I got. But by the time I finished *Othello*, the fever was over, you see.

Now, after this huge European success, it comes out in America—Selznick's version—saying: "David O. Selznick presents *The Third Man*. Produced by David O. Selznick." About three of those credits.

HJ: It was Chaplin all over again.

OW: I took Alex and David to dinner one night in Paris, right after it opened, and Alex said, "My dear David. I have seen the American titles." And David started to hem and haw, "Well, you know . . ." Alex said, "I only hope that I don't die before you do." David said, "What do you mean?" Alex replied, "I don't want to think of you sneaking into the cemetery and scratching my name off my tombstone."

When I was up for Best Actor for *The Third Man*, I was nearby, in Italy, a few hours away from Cannes. Alex called me and said, "If you'll come to Cannes, you'll get the prize." That's the way it works. I said, "Why don't I stay here and get the prize?" And he said, "If you don't come, they'll have to give it to Eddie Robinson, because he's been here the whole two weeks." I didn't believe him. And then I talked to [Robert] Favre Le Bret, who was president of the festival in those days, who said, "Yes, you come and you've got it. You don't come—" So I said, "Give it to him," and didn't go. And Eddie Robinson won.

HJ: Joseph Cotten is rather amazing in *The Third Man*.

OW: He was very good.

HJ: I've never particularly liked him, except in *Kane* and *Ambersons*.

OW: *Shadow of a Doubt*. He's awfully good in that.

HJ: Oh, my God! He's great in that. I completely forgot about it.

OW: That's the one good Hitchcock picture made in America. Hitchcock himself said it was his best. The English ones are better than the American pictures, the very early ones, like *The 39 Steps*. Oh, my God, what a masterpiece. Those pictures had a little foreign charm, because we didn't know the actors very well. But I've never understood the cult of Hitchcock. Particularly the late American movies. I don't recognize the same director!

HJ: He decided to become popular.

OW: Egotism and laziness. And they're all lit like television shows. About the time he started to use color, he stopped looking through the camera. I saw one of the worst movies I've ever seen the other night. Hitchcock's movie where Jimmy Stewart looks through the window?

HJ: *Rear Window.*

OW: Everything is stupid about it. Complete insensitivity to what a story about voyeurism could be. I'll tell you what is astonishing. To discover that Jimmy Stewart can be a bad actor. But *really* bad. Even Grace Kelly is better than Jimmy, who's overacting. He's kind of looking to the left and giving as bad a performance as he ever gave. But, then, you see, the world was so much at Hitch's feet that the actors just thought, "Do what he says and it's gonna be great."

HJ: If you think that one is bad, there's another terrible one with Jimmy Stewart and Kim Novak.

OW: *Vertigo.* That's worse.

HJ: And then the other one—what was the other one? His much praised comedy, *The Trouble with Harry.*

OW: By then it was senility.

HJ: No, it wasn't senility—that movie came earlier.

OW: I think he was senile a long time before he died. He was in life, you know. He kept falling asleep while you were talking to him. When I would go to Jo's, Hitchcock would be there for dinner. I'd go because Jo was fond of him, not because he was interesting. When he first came to America, I looked him up and took him to lunch at 21.

HJ: He must have been a different person then.

OW: No, he wasn't very interesting then, either. I was disappointed.

HJ: There's a movie I know you would hate that Jo's in with Jennifer Jones.

OW: *Portrait of Jennie*. He and I laughed at it when it was being made!

HJ: Jennifer Jones really could not act. Would you agree with me about that?

OW: Yes. She was hopeless. But the poor girl is nuts, you know. Something is wrong there.

HJ: So how did you know Reed could get that kind of a performance out of Cotten?

OW: Because I thought he was wonderful.

HJ: From something you saw him in?

OW: No, no. He'd been with me for years in the theater! He was a great farceur. His character was funny, and that's Jo's thing. He was brilliant at that! *Brilliant!* The problem with Jo was that he was never a romantic leading man. He was a character actor. Nothing could make him a leading man. And that's all he played in Hollywood. He looked stiff and wooden. Uncomfortable. It wasn't because he got bad, it was because he was doing something outside his range. And the fact that he was attractive and looked like he could play a leading man, made them think he must be one. Plus he had this big success in *Philadelphia Story* on Broadway, so they thought that would translate to screen. Jo's career was made not by *Citizen Kane* but by *Philadelphia Story*. Selznick picked him up and said, "We'll have another Cary Grant." But nobody ever wrote him another part like that, you see. So that was his career—doing what he couldn't do.

HJ: Did he know that he was unsuited for this?

OW: No. If he did, he wouldn't tell me. And why should he—he was a success. Remember, he started as a professional football player, and then became a stage manager for Belasco, and then a radio actor. We shared this one job—on a radio show called *School of the Air*. It was a show for children in the morning, and it paid $32 a week. So we were both living on this—both married. Then one day we did an episode that broke us up. It was on the Olympic Games. And we had to say things like, "Let me see your javelin. It is by far the biggest in all Athens." We couldn't stop laughing. The word went out that we couldn't be in the show at the same time. So that meant $32 every second week for each of us.

I had one radio job, a show called *Big Sister*—God, I loved it. I was the cad. And I had this girl in the rumble seat. And the suspense was, was I gonna make her? And it went on for about three months. That's the longest session in a rumble seat, you know. We had to do two shows, one in the morning, at ten, and one in the afternoon—for the different time zones. One day I was sitting in the barbershop, and I heard the theme song come on, and Martin Gabel was playing my part. I'd forgotten about the second show! That was the end of that job! But soon I got my own radio show and then my own theater.

HJ: What happened to Cotten when you made it?

OW: That was a difficult period for me, as a friend, at least, because suddenly I was making a fortune. Jo was still making those smaller salaries, and I was big stuff. I felt uncomfortable, because he hadn't got up there with me. Here I was in a country house, with a chauffeur and a Rolls-Royce, and Jo was still in the—you know. So I helped him, a good turn that many people would have regarded as an unforgivable thing to do. But he wasn't uncomfortable, he was delightful about it. I was the one who felt bad. So I was thrilled about *Philadelphia Story*, because it reduced the distance between us.

HJ: I think it's always harder for the one who's moving on.

16. "God save me from my friends."

In which Orson battles his reputation, talks about the importance of casting fresh faces in *Kane*. He explains that he never shot coverage so that the studio couldn't recut his films, although that didn't stop RKO from mutilating *The Magnificent Ambersons*.

———————————

Henry Jaglom: I just saw *Othello* again, in New York, in a theater, the Thalia, on the Upper West Side. The audience was standing and cheering. Kids, twenty-year-olds, thirty-year-olds. It's superb. It doesn't look dated, like so much Shakespeare does, because of the way you did it. It's not a costume fifties movie, or a sixties movie. I know that's why you didn't like Brando in *Julius Caesar*, for instance, because it looks like a picture that was made—

Orson Welles: At Metro in 1950, yeah.

HJ: The togas, and the haircuts and the makeup were . . .

OW: So Max Factor.

HJ: Exactly. But you so rooted your *Othello* in some imaginary ancestral land that—

OW: Because a funny thing happens in costume pictures. You sense the lunch wagon next to the set.

HJ: You should see *Othello* now. I think you'd feel very good about it.

OW: I'd rather hear about how good it is than see it.

HJ: Right. If you saw it, you'd find things you don't like.

OW: I know one thing that's no good, which is the first sequence in Venice after the crawl. I think it doesn't have the same authority as the rest of the film. It's because that's where we ran out of dough. That's the reel of "no dough." The film is good again the minute we're in Cyprus.

HJ: There's a soap opera—*All My Children*—do you know it? Your lady from *Citizen Kane* is in it.

OW: Which one?

HJ: The one who played Kane's first wife, Emily, Ruth Warrick. She's incredibly bad.

OW: She looked the part of Emily. And I'm one of those fellows who thinks, if they look it, then you can make them act it. Particularly a small part.

HJ: The breakfast scene, my favorite, she was wonderful in that.

OW: She was!

HJ: Wonderful. By the time it was all finished, the editing, and so on.

OW: There was nothing to edit. It was just cut from shot to shot. Because after each shot I went and changed my makeup, and she changed her dress. Then we came back again, and did the next line. They'd all been rehearsed. There was nothing to monkey around with. The camera never moved. It just waited.

HJ: Did you use master shots?

OW: I never shot a master in my life. Gregg told me that Jack Ford never did it, so I never did it, either. I stop where I know I'm going to cut. I don't ever shoot through it and then go back for cuts.

HJ: You stop shooting and do the close-up?

OW: Yeah, I stop. I don't give myself anything to play with.

HJ: How do you know what you're going to need?

OW: Because I decide what I want. In advance. In the areas I don't decide, then I shoot all kinds of things, but I still don't shoot a master. There's no protection, ever.

HJ: So the studio can't fuck with you, cut it without you?

OW: That's what Jack Ford told me. What can they do? They don't have anything to go to.

HJ: Is that why he did it?

OW: Sure. But of course he had a cutter. He never cut a picture himself. Never paid any attention to it. Could not give a shit.

HJ: How long did the breakfast scene take?

OW: Less than a day. Starting in the morning. I'd say we were done about three in the afternoon. Because there were no light changes, you see? Or only very slight ones. Ruth was a wonderful girl. And when she was young, she was quite sexy.

HJ: I didn't see that in her. In *Kane* you didn't emphasize it at all.

OW: No. Nor did I notice it. Only a couple years later when she came and visited me on the set.

HJ: You never noticed she was attractive when you were working together?

OW: I never allow myself to notice any of that.

HJ: Smart, yeah. That's not the time to let yourself be distracted.

OW: No. Particularly not if you're, by accident, successful. Because then everybody hates you. All the other girls, and their friends.

HJ: Dorothy Comingore, another fresh face, was so great as Susan Alexander, Kane's mistress and second wife, the one based on Marion Davies. How did you find her?

OW: Chaplin, you know, told me about her.

HJ: What was she in?

OW: Nothing. He just found her. He'd seen her in some little play or something. Her singing "Come and Go" was a real fabricated performance, because we sprayed her throat before every take with some dangerous chemical that made her hoarse. Her performance as the younger version of the wife was herself. The older one was chemical. That scene with her singing in the nightclub was the first shot I ever made in a movie. That's what we began with.

HJ: That's the first thing you shot? When she was supposed to be older, and her throat was sprayed?

OW: Yes, we began with that. Because we had the nightclub set which had been built for some B movie. So we pretended I was shooting tests, practicing how to make movies, for ten or twelve days.

HJ: That's great. And you learned everything you needed to know.

OW: Yeah.

HJ: And how much of that did you use, actually?

OW: Everything. We were really shooting the movie. It was a trick. We weren't testing anything. It was Gregg's idea. But I made one mistake. I was stuck with one terrible piece of casting that broke my heart, because none of the faces in the movie had ever been seen before on a screen. But in that nightclub scene they gave me a waiter from New York who had been seen in every movie for twenty years, completely ruining my dream of total . . .

HJ: I can't even remember his face.

OW: Oh, you wouldn't. But if you'd been going to movies at that time, you would have recognized him. He was *the* waiter, you know?

HJ: RKO's waiter.

OW: No, not just RKO's, he was everybody's waiter.

HJ: So what happened to Comingore?

OW: For two or three years she just refused everything, waiting for another Susan Alexander. Well, you know, those parts don't come along so often.

HJ: God, in a way, it's the worst thing that can happen, to get that at the beginning of your career, isn't it?

OW: It's the old, old problem in show business. Once you're a hit as the Irish busboy, nobody wants you as the gangster. Everybody loved her in *Kane*, so she was in a good situation. She had that pathos that could turn into bitchiness because it came from insecurity and vulgarity. She ended up, you know, being arrested for prostitution. She was picking people up in bars. It was tragic.

HJ: I recall she was married to screenwriter Richard Collins, who told HUAC he divorced her because she refused to name names. She was blacklisted in 1951, which ended her career.

OW: Speaking of Ruth Warrick, yesterday I was being interviewed by David Hartman, by satellite. For *Good Morning America*. With her and Paul Stewart. God save me from my friends.

HJ: Stewart played Raymond, the slippery valet in *Kane*, yes?

OW: Yes, and he's telling Hartman how much the picture cost. He's got it wrong, of course. And sounding as though he were associate producer, whereas he was brought in for a week's work as an actor. And Ruth Warrick is saying that I'm the greatest thing since Jesus, and that I walk on water, and all of this. And I'm trying to shut her up, because I know she's wrecking the show by going on and on. And after we're off the air she gives me her book, in which she writes all these wonderful things about me, like, "He was terrific to all the actors. And we all loved him—we were a family," and all that. "Except for Dorothy Comingore. He was terrible to her." So I said, "This is all invented." Because I hardly knew Ruth Warrick, but Comingore and I were great friends. And according to Ruth I was cruel to her. Now, this is one actress in a movie talking about another. It gets worse. A little later, she writes that I abandoned *Ambersons*, which I was editing, and went off to South America to make *Journey into Fear*, which Ruth was in, and *It's All True*. And that I had already begun that wastefulness which . . . And then she says, "Poor Orson." In fact, I went to South America right after Pearl Harbor, because Nelson Rockefeller, whom Roosevelt had named head of Inter-American Affairs, sent me down there. So here was Ruth Warrick overpraising me on the show, and then giving me the book to sign! What is interesting about her book is that the reader is likely to think that we had a love affair. She's practically saying it.

I don't know how many ways there are to direct a movie, but let's say there are a hundred. And mine happens to be, I direct a movie by making love to everybody involved in it. I'm not running for office—I don't want to be popular with the crew—but I make love to every actor. Then, when they're no longer working for me, it's like they've been abandoned, like I've betrayed them.

HJ: Do those last reels of *Ambersons* exist anywhere, do you think?

OW: Somebody told me the big scene in the boardinghouse with Aggie [Moorehead] and Jo has been found, but I've never tracked it down.

HJ: How many reels were missing?

OW: It would've played another fifteen minutes.

HJ: You know the guy who books the Z Channel is trying to get permission to show *Ambersons* without all that nonsense RKO stuck on to the end of the film.

OW: We had shot one complete reel—the party scene, without a cut. RKO chopped two minutes out of the middle of it, because it didn't further the plot. This little thing about olives, and people not being used to them. A cut in the middle of a one-reel shot. It's a very skillful cut—it plays all right—but the scene was much better before. And, of course, nobody can find the two minutes they cut out of the reel. It's a bit of sour grapes, because I did it before Hitchcock did it in *Rope*. The first reel in the history of movies made without a cut was in *Ambersons*.

HJ: And that's the only change, besides all the stuff at the end?

OW: No, there're other changes, but very few in the beginning and the middle. It's only when the story begins to get too dark. I don't know when I found the letter sent me by George Schaefer, who'd been to the preview in Pomona where they laughed at Agnes Moorehead. Half of her scene is cut forever, because the audience fell on the floor laughing.

HJ: That was the test in front of the Esther Williams audience in the Valley.

OW: And Schaefer said, "We really have to make it more commercial." Poor guy—he was in a terrible spot.

HJ: So they added their new ending.

OW: By the way, somebody's published a new *Kane* book and sent it to me, with a lot of essays and criticism written around the time it was being released. I realized that I've misquoted O'Hara all my life. He didn't say, "This is the best picture ever made. And the best picture that will ever be made."

HJ: Really?

OW: Yeah. He didn't say anything as good as that. I made it better. What he said was, "This is the best picture ever made, and Orson Welles is the best actor alive." I know why I changed it. Because he said the other to a lot of people at the Stork Club in my presence. So I pasted it onto the review, the way one does.

17. "I can make a case for all the points of view."

In which Orson waits on Jack Nicholson, looks for financing for *Lear*, explains why he dropped his knee-jerk contempt for Nazi collaborators and became friends with Oswald Mosley, and recalls that General Charles de Gaulle was a brave but pompous fool.

HENRY JAGLOM: I spoke to Jack about *The Big Brass Ring*. He was up in Aspen with Bob Rafelson. I said, "Have you read it yet?" And he said, "No." But with great cheeriness, despite not adding anything more; just, "No." It's clearly on the agenda, though. I just don't know when he's going to read it. I have my fingers crossed. I'm worried about Jack. He's the last one. Even if he says, "Yes," he won't want to reduce his asking price . . . Any news on *Lear*?

ORSON WELLES: Just to keep you up on all the different situations, we now have the French. This fellow sends me almost daily wires, saying, "If wanted, we'll give you a million dollars of our money, and then go into an arrangement with other people, and so on, anything you want to do." A million dollars! And begging me to take it. Begging me, wiring me.

HJ: Well, you were awarded the Légion d'honneur, after all. Did you see [James] Cagney receiving the Presidential Medal of Freedom from Ronnie?

OW: He didn't even seem pleased, you know? He looked like he'd been dragged screaming, out of bed. Very hard to have an award in a republic. A decoration really needs a king. It's like a title. You need a fellow up there with a crown on. The only reason the Légion d'honneur works is that it's old. It goes back to Napoleon. What was so smart about Napoleon was that he realized the necessity of creating a new aristocracy. And he set up the Légion d'honneur for that. He knew his Frenchmen.

HJ: You and Jerry Lewis are the two American film stars who the French have given this award to. I remember when you said, "They give you good reviews and then you see what else they like and it takes away all the value of it." They've given Jerry Lewis every award you can imagine.

OW: Yes, every award that I've gotten. And he got all the publicity. I got no publicity at all. But he didn't get his award from the president.

HJ: It's probably your Légion d'honneur, probably, that has finally awakened the French to your *Lear*.

OW: Yes. And for *Lear*—they want to be the patrons that make it happen. They say they'll do anything. I said, "There're two parts for French actors: the King of France and the Duke of Burgundy, but only if they speak English. That's all. The grips—head grip, head cameraman, sound, all of that—my choice. Any nationality." They said, "Fine, we don't care."

HJ: So what's stopping you from saying yes?

OW: The fact that I don't know all that goes with "yes." So I keep saying to them, "Wonderful! Delighted! We're willing to let you be the central producing outfit, but please remember that you have to agree in return that none of our key people are French, unless we want them to be," and so on.

We also have another firm offer of $350,000 from Italy. Of course that doesn't begin to make the picture, but it's a terribly good cornerstone. Because it's government money set aside for the *Com-*

media dell'Arte. If they don't spend it, the government takes it back. And the reason why it's so great is that we get it in dollars, and we get the tremendous exchange advantage against the lira.

HJ: So the total figure that you'd be most comfortable with is what? Can you give me that?

OW: Supposing that, as I think, the most efficient and cheapest way to make the picture, is in Italy or France, bringing in the whole English cast. It is three million four. Something like that. That includes money for contingencies. If you take out contingencies, it's a lot less. Nobody gets rich, but that isn't the point.

HJ: Right. At Cannes, everybody hears "Welles-*Lear*" and they go crazy. If I knew who to talk to, I know I could get a small fortune from China. It seems to me that the way to complete the picture would be to have an American nontheatrical sale in advance, cable and so on. And then put that together with a combination of Italy, France, and Germany, and maybe Spain, and maybe somebody else. But if Spain is only putting in fifty or seventy-five thousand, no opening night in Madrid. If Germany puts up a million dollars, and they want a big thing at the Berlin Film Festival, why not?

OW: A festival is not an opening.

HJ: Right. We reserve the opening for whoever gives us the most money.

OW: That's a very important distinction.

HJ: So, we should put all the energy now into getting *Lear*.

OW: My energy is being put into it. There's nothing I can do now, except react warmly to these people as they come in. I think we have to have every kind of gun cocked and ready now, so that one of them will go off. Otherwise, we'll just go on talking forever.

HJ: Not just one, we need three or four of them to go off, so we can get to three and a half million dollars.

OW: The French—there's no doubt that the French—

HJ: Also, there's no reason not to film in France. There are ideal locations.

OW: That is the great argument *against* it for me. That's why I wish we *didn't* have the French money. I don't want France to be so attractive. Because living in Paris is so expensive. Whereas if we shoot in Cinecittà, we don't have to live in Rome. Here is Rome, and here is Cinecittà—and we can live out here, outside of Rome. We just go to the studio and back. I dread spending four or five months of my life living in Paris and driving through the traffic to work and back. The thought of it gives me the willies, because it's forty-five minutes of hell before you get to work and forty-five more for the return. And where would the actors stay? We know what the hotel bills will be for everybody. You can't live in Paris for less than two thousand a week. So the actors will object, saying they're slaves. They'll get so angry that I won't be able to work with them. They'll work for five hundred a week—

HJ: But they won't put up with cheap accommodations.

OW: I see the whole budget going to hell. You blow it on hotels alone; that's what scares me. There's no use saying we'll get great prices, and Jacques Lang loves me and all that.

HJ: You're absolutely right. Jacques Lang may be the Minister of Culture and [François] Mitterand's favorite puppy, but even he can't do anything about the prices of hotels.

OW: That's why I have always been nervous about it, but they have been battering the door down. And there's no place else in France to shoot! There's a big studio in Nice, but it's built right next to the airport.

HJ: Which makes it impossible to record sound.

OW: The planes fly in every two minutes. You couldn't get through one Shakespeare speech.

HJ: Oh, you mean the Victorine studio? They built it knowing the airport was there? Knowing—

OW: No, Victorine is a very old studio. It was built years before there was an airport, or when the airport was very little—no more than four flights a day. And now, of course, people fly direct from New York to Nice. It's a great location, and you can make wonderful deals, but only if you're making a silent picture. Or else dub it afterwards which, if you do that with Shakespeare, it comes off as totally fake. You simply cannot do it.

HJ: Cinecittà is fine.

OW: Well, it's the best bargain in the world, and the best studio in the world. Built by Mussolini, you know.

HJ: The French deal doesn't prohibit shooting in Cinecittà, does it? Or it's not clear?

OW: We're trying to get that clear. I think they're hurt, because it seems to imply that Italy is better suited for movie production. And the Italians, who always despised me, are now for some reason particularly anxious to be nice. They want to give me the highest award known to Italy. Whatever that is. The something or other, that makes me an honorary citizen of Rome.

HJ: It could still be a French movie, because it'll open in France.

OW: Maybe we could just get on the train from Rome to France, and shoot there for three weeks, just to get that French money, even though it will cost a little more. But you see how all these things are interdependent. You can't nail down one without having the others in hand. I think I'll make another phone call to France, to see how everything stands. I've made all my conditions as tough as I could, on the theory that there's no use going ahead and then being disappointed afterwards.

HJ: I sent you something about the reorganization of Gaumont. They're saying they want to be the home for all the great international directors.

OW: Well, they were talking about that four years ago, in this restaurant. I say, "Let's see some action." They told me once, "We are aristocrats. We simply don't breathe the same air." It's impossible to talk to somebody like that. "We don't breathe the same air"! Another thing is a French deal would have to be in the Common Market. The Common Market, in my opinion, is about to collapse. I think, seriously. Thanks to Mrs. Thatcher and—

HJ: You're talking about two different—

OW: No, I'm not. I'm telling you the different things that I know.

HJ: Well, we'll hear from Paris within a week.

OW: We'll proceed with them or without them. In the meantime, we keep anybody who is cooking warm on the stove. I don't care who it is. Even the Chinese—we can do it in Peking. And we'd certainly have all the right equipment, and serious assistants.

HJ: You know, I'm going to meet the Chinese representatives in Berlin.

OW: Let's make a deal.

HJ: Who said to me that *Lear* is one of the few things they know they want. "We only charge twenty-five cents a ticket. But we have a billion people." He actually said, "Rear."

OW: Rear. King Rear! And his daughter Legan.

HJ: I don't know what they can give us. I'll listen.

OW: Who cares?

HJ: Huh?

OW: Who cares? Just to have it in Red China.

(The check arrives.)

HJ: Here, I've got this.

OW: No, you don't.

HJ: That means I'm next.

OW: What? What about your neck?

HJ: I said, "That means I'm next."

OW: I thought you said, "That means my neck." You know, despite all of the telegrams from France, I would be happier with the Germans in the driver's seat than the French. I just don't trust that whole Lang situation.

HJ: You think the French offer is gonna disappear?

OW: I think the government is gonna keep on cutting Lang's funds for the arts. Not the way Reagan is—

HJ: You mean for ideological reasons . . .

OW: But out of economic necessity. In other words, we're gonna find ourselves enmeshed in French politics, in situations we can't resolve. Whereas, Italy has somehow pulled itself out of near bankruptcy, and now they're in great shape again, making movies like mad! I would be much happier if this could be done without the French.

HJ: Really? Because I would love France to be involved. The film would get a real boost from opening in Paris as a French co-production.

OW: It'll still get that. I'm just scared. Because you don't make arrangements with the French. But the Italians, you can always make an arrangement with them. In other words, if I went in with dollars into Cinecittà—oh, boy. On the other hand, I must tell you an interesting thing about Italy. It's a country that has never had an old star. Never a Wallace Beery. Never. The Italians don't support anybody over forty years old. They're like America. Everything must be about young people. So they may change their minds about a movie about an old man. *Lear* is about old age. And France is actually the only country in the world where old, ugly actors are stars. Everywhere else, they have to become supporting players.

HJ: Raimu.

OW: Yeah, Raimu. And that awful actor that they all love. Michel Simon. Jean Gabin, even when he was too feeble to move. He was wonderful doing nothing. There's another one, earlier than him. Baur—Harry Baur.

HJ: Was Harry Baur any good?

OW: He had four eyebrows over each eye, and he could work each of them separately.

HJ: He was killed by the Nazis, right? In a concentration camp?

OW: He came to some bad end, yeah—because he always talked about how he was Jewish—so, of course, they grabbed him quick. The French police did it all. The Germans didn't have to lift a finger. Horrifying, when you realize that. The French made a lot of movies during the war. The Germans, too. And a lot of French actors who would rather not be reminded of it went to Berlin.

When I visited France and Italy right after the war, I was full of that righteous antifascist feeling that we all had in the safety of America. I didn't want to meet the people who had, if not exactly collaborated, certainly had not fought the Nazis. I was too prissy. And then, as I began to learn more about Europe under the occupation, and what it was like, and to compare it to us, I became less prissy about it. Because the people who were defending their children and their lives were in a different situation from the people who were defending their swimming pools and their contracts at Metro. They weren't brave enough to be partisans, but they hadn't sent any Jews to Auschwitz, either. I wasn't gonna be the one from America to tell them they were wrong. Of course, I never forgave the people who sent Jews to the camps. But I did get so I could forgive the people who entertained the German troops. What else were they gonna do—not entertain them? Not entertain, and go where? If you had no group, if you were a group of one, what could you do? I can make a case for all the points of view.

HJ: [Maurice] Chevalier entertained the German troops . . .

OW: That was mild. He was really very little tainted compared to the people who made propaganda movies. I don't think what he did was noble, I don't like him for it, but I wouldn't say, "I won't talk to Chevalier because he—" That changed in me. And then I found myself getting to know well so many famous villains from my earlier time. You know, I spent a long, four-day weekend at a country house in England, and realized only at the end of the weekend that this man I'd become so fond of and interested in was Oswald Mosley.

HJ: Did you know he used to be a leftist, a Fabian? Then he went all the way over to the right and founded the British Union of Fascists.

OW: A complicated thing. Louis Aragon was also at that house party.

HJ: He didn't mind being there with Mosley? He fought in the Resistance and was a staunch Communist his whole life.

OW: No. He just said Mosley was a damn fool.

HJ: A lot of the French fled, but some stayed and fought.

OW: Very few, very few.

HJ: There were two Frances, though. There was Vichy, and there was the group of French who were fighting.

OW: Not in Paris. They were all in the Southwest. An old radical stronghold.

HJ: Except that, if it's true, in all of Europe—aside from Denmark—proportionately, only one-quarter—"only" is a tragic number—of French Jews died. So the other three-quarters survived because of individual Frenchmen who performed great acts of courage.

OW: There were such acts in Belgium and Holland as well. And Italy—enormous quantities. You really can't give the French credit for that, any more than the other European countries.

HJ: I always have thought of it as two Frances, somehow, occupied and unoccupied.

OW: There's one France—and in a certain mood, collaboration happens.

HJ: What about the underground and the Resistance? There was Jean Moulin, as well as—

OW: I used to write them a newsletter every two weeks during the war. To the Free French, and to the underground. So I really know a lot about them. Very few of the French resisted. We didn't hear a moment of courage from the Communists until the invasion of Russia. And then they were as harmful to the underground as they were helpful. Because they were divisive. When the Freemasons and the Catholics were fighting side by side, the Communists wouldn't stand for it, and turned them against each other. It was only by the end of 1941, when Hitler was bogged down in Russia, and it was clear to the entire world that he hadn't a chance in hell. It was then that you saw these brave movements. Not just in France; I'm talking all over the place. What was surprising was the large number of aristocrats in the Resistance. More than the bourgeois. They weren't thinking Nazi, fascist. It wasn't political for them. They were thinking, "Here come the goddamn *Boche* again," you know, the Germans again.

HJ: Foreigners.

OW: Not foreigners—Germans in particular. From all the old wars with the Germans.

HJ: They're very nationalistic.

OW: No, aristocrats are never nationalistic. Because they're all related to one another. They never have a sense of nation. That's a typically bourgeois attitude.

HJ: But it's nationalism. The Germans, *Boche* or not, are foreigners.

OW: As I was saying, generally, the French were particularly bad. They had the worst history of resistance. And think about the last fifty years of French history? Leon Blum being neutral towards Spain? That was inexcusable. From a Socialist, from the Popular Front? So shameful, really. [Pierre] Mendès France was the exception, and he lasted all of nine months. I told you what de Gaulle said about Mendès France, who was his greatest enemy. De Gaulle said he was the other great man of France—besides himself. De

Gaulle was very hard to like. God, how Roosevelt hated him. Roosevelt spoke fluent French, but with an American accent, you see. Roosevelt said to him, *"Je suis très heureux d'être avec vous, mon Général,"* you know. And de Gaulle said, *"Comment?"* Constantly. He was so snobbish it was, "If you don't speak perfectly, don't attempt it at all." So they had to translate what Roosevelt said. And this was when de Gaulle was hanging by a thread! He was always a pain in the ass, and he ended very badly. He had plans to run to Germany—to *Germany!* with his paratroopers—during the so-called revolution in '68, which he took very seriously, too seriously. After all, the kids were just throwing stones, and all that.

HJ: He was going to go to Germany? How do you know that?

OW: It was in the papers. He was gonna go with paras, and two or three planes, escape the country. And this is the man who was known for being fearless. When they liberated Paris, he walked the whole length of the Champs-Élysées from the Arc de Triomphe to the cathedral of Notre Dame. With everybody on the roofs with guns. And he never ducked when they were shooting, and he was eight feet higher than anybody else in Paris. And yet, he was ready to flee to Germany. It just shows how easily you get disoriented once you are in power if the people seem to be turning against you.

Of course, Nixon also thought that the kids were gonna come and throw him out. I saw a little tribute to him on CBS the other night, saying he's coming back, becoming a great commentator and elder statesman. I wish they'd stop interviewing him on great world topics. Because Nixon is a sort of semicomic Dickensian villain. But he's become the only man who's making sense! It drives me *crazy!* Of course, it's easy to sound sane if you've got Ronnie to criticize.

All Nixon and Reagan do is make me revise my judgment of the Eisenhower years. The economy was great. Eisenhower made the right decision on Suez. And Korea. Got us out. And at the end said, "Beware of the military-industrial complex." And he turned over the country, at peace, in 1960. Despite that, we were all groaning, "Get us rid of this terrible president!" We've just got to admit that was a great eight years, you know?

HJ: There were all the jokes about Eisenhower going off to play golf.

OW: We underrated Eisenhower. We've got a president now who works much less hard than he did. Who doesn't even know what's going on. Unless it's written on a card.

HJ: I remember being shocked at the U-2 incident, Gary Powers, the pilot, remember? When Eisenhower said it wasn't a spy plane. I didn't think he would lie to the American people.

OW: Every president lies. The spy plane didn't bother me so much, because it seemed so obvious that we had spy planes. And it's not like shooting somebody. What I couldn't believe was the CIA stuff, the plot against Castro. In my innocence, I didn't think that America, as a nation, was capable of planning murder as an instrument of policy. I didn't think that was in our character!

HJ: Well, now we know. We've lost some serious innocence. Is it true you considered running for office?

OW: I have all the equipment to be a politician. Total shamelessness. But it's lucky I never ran. In the years from [Joseph] McCarthy to now, I would have either been destroyed or reduced. I was lucky that Alan Cranston discouraged me from running for the Senate.

HJ: Cranston discouraged you? I didn't know that.

OW: Yes. He was my man, given to me by Washington, to be sure that I could get the nomination in California. The year of McCarthy.

HJ: '52.

OW: And it was Cranston who told me, "Not a chance. You'll carry northern California, but never the Hollywood community." Then I found out he had ambitions himself. That's why, when I saw him run for senator, I always thought, "That's my seat!"

HJ: Now he's busily running for president. Who do you think the Democratic candidate will be?

OW: I would vote for John Glenn just because I think he'd win, and I believe in voting for who I think will win.

I've just read Caro's new biography of [Lyndon] Johnson, which will destroy him because it tells everything. It's exhaustive to the point of—you know, when he put on his left shoe on Thursday, the twelfth of May, 1946. But there isn't one good word about him in the book. He comes out of it a total monster. There's gonna be three more volumes. This one only takes him up to getting into Congress, and he's already a prick. He has very few defenders. There's me and somebody out in Kansas, who I don't know. But I think LBJ was a great tragic figure. That's what interests me. A very tragic figure, with his monstrosity, and his energy, and his desire to be a president who counted. He gets almost no credit for the things he did domestically, because of his gross behavior. After the Kennedys, everybody in Washington was so used to Casals scratching on the cello that Johnson's act didn't go over. And he was haunted by Jack. And then Bobby coming up. But what could he do, other than be president? It was the *only* thing for him.

HJ: I'm convinced Johnson would have made a great president had he run and won . . . Not like Roosevelt, but—

OW: I don't believe there could have been a great president in those years, only a good one. I think the presidential situation now is such that until there's a hopeless crisis, and you have a semidictatorship, like Roosevelt's, then we won't see what we call a great president.

HJ: Glenn is very Eisenhower-esque. But I don't think he's committed to very much. I mean, he's just moderate—he's just really moderate on everything.

OW: That's why I'm for him. I hate to think of myself as fighting for a moderate, but a moderate is what is desperately needed for this next period. We need antipolarization, you know. After Bonny Prince Ronnie.

HJ: Is it just the nostalgia that makes the Roosevelt years seem so glorious?

OW: No. They were glorious. Because you had a president who had made a hundred mistakes and never pretended he didn't, and who was ready to try anything. And you had a fascinating cabinet, great personalities—everybody around him. And it was a happy time, even with all the misery. People were starving, but he pulled the country together. That's when the labor movement really became a wonderful thing in America. We never crossed a picket line. Now the unions have no power. They're nothing. Reactionary, even, corrupt and weak. But then they were a wonderful thing.

You know Kissinger also believed that America was on the brink of civil war during the Vietnam years. Who was gonna make a civil war? How can an educated man permit himself to put that down on paper?

HJ: You think he really believed it? He's too smart to be so stupid.

OW: I hate Kissinger even more than I hate Nixon, because I just can't get over the feeling that he knows better, somehow. He must have talked himself into it. But he's a selfish, self-serving shit.

HJ: They've all forgotten Cambodia. They've forgotten the whole thing. It's really amazing.

OW: And the fact that Kissinger got free of Watergate, walked away without a scratch! Without a scratch! No wonder he worships Mitterand.

HJ: Metternich.

OW: Metternich.

18. Charles "Laughton couldn't bear the fact he was a homosexual."

In which Orson fondly remembers his friend, who lived in terror that he would be outed. He recalls that on London's West End, actors had to be gay or pretend to be gay to get parts. Orson would have liked to have made his own version of *The Dresser*.

HENRY JAGLOM: Tell me more about Charles Laughton.

ORSON WELLES: During the war, there was a great bond rally in Texarkana, Texas, with every known star in Hollywood. Charlie was going to do his well-known Gettysburg Address, which he made famous in *Ruggles of Red Gap* on the radio. I was the producer and director of that show. So I said to Buster—that's what I called him—"Is there anything special that you would like?" He said, "I want a divan." I said, "What?" He said, "Don't be ignorant. You know what I want, a chaise lounge."

HJ: That's great. He was so gay.

OW: I said, "Buster, you can't mean that. You're not going to lie down on a couch like Madame Recamier and do the Gettysburg Address in front of all these people. Do you know where you are?" He said, "Yes. But that's the way I feel." So out of vengeance, I said, "All right, I'll give it to you." So he came out, lay down, delivered the address, "Fawr scawr . . . fawr scawr and seven years ago our fathers brought forth unto this continent a new nation based on the proposition that all men are created equal . . ." and he killed it. When he was great, he was so great.

I was very fond of him. He was a sweet man. It was absolutely terrible what Larry did to him. Larry was sharing a season with him at Stratford. Larry was doing—what's that little-known Shakespearean play that Peter Brook directed with Larry and made a big success? Not *Timon of Athens* . . . *Pericles* maybe, and Laughton was doing *King Lear* and Bottom in *Midsummer Night's Dream*. And everyone said he was very interesting in both parts. But in front of the entire company in Stratford, Larry said, "Charles, you are an amateur actor and you have never been anything else in your life. Don't ask us to take you seriously." And Laughton went away and cried, wept like a child.

I told you what Larry did to Miles Malleson, the old character actor, in *Rhinoceros*. Larry put his arm around his shoulder and walked him up and down in front of the lights. And I heard him saying, "Miles . . . Miles, old boy, you know, you've had it. You're washed up." This defenseless old man. All so that Larry could take control and tell him how his part should be played.

HJ: This was his way of tearing them down, or something stupid like that?

OW: It was heartbreaking for him. Laughton never got over it. He was like a little fourteen-year-old boy, totally immature. Laughton couldn't bear the fact he was a homosexual, you know. He was so afraid the world would discover it. He believed in art, and all of that, always searching for something that went beyond what acting can be, or writing, or anything. Really, he was really looking for the bluebird.

HJ: He found it a few times.

OW: You bet he did. When he made that speech in *I, Claudius*.

HJ: For me, he was also wonderful in *The Hunchback of Notre Dame*.

OW: I can't judge that, because I am such a partisan of the Lon

Chaney performance, I just can't buy anybody else doing it. I think Chaney was one of the great movie actors. Everything he did I adore. To me, Charlie in *Hunchback* was the village idiot, the fellow where you say, "That's the unfortunate Perkins boy." You don't want to look at him.

HJ: Oh, no, he was much more than that. I felt he put all his feeling of not belonging into that role . . . And don't forget Laughton's Rembrandt.

OW: Laughton's Rembrandt has him pose as King David. He puts on this robe and he puts on a crown and he transforms himself. I still don't understand how he did it. Who played the beggar in that? I can't remember his name now. He was even better than Laughton and that's something.

HJ: Oh, my God! That's my favorite actor.

OW: He was a dear friend. He only died about four years ago. He was the leading man in a movie directed by Gregory Ratoff with Myrna Loy, *Intermezzo*.

HJ: I'm still trying to think of the man's name.

OW: He was a wild left-winger rabblerouser. He was on the barricades for forty years. So of course he only played degenerate aristocrats, and dressed like an awful-looking don at a small university with torn patches. When he arrived in Rome, Ratoff, in his Russian accent, says, "He can't play Myrna Loy's leading man looking like a bum. Take him to your tailor." So I take him to the tailor to the King of Italy. By this time, I'm speaking Italian. I say, "This is a distinguished actor from England and he is—"

HJ: Roger Livesey!

OW: Right. Mr. Roger Livesey. And I say, "He's going to play the leading role in this picture, and he has to be dressed like an English gentleman. Money is no object." The tailor looks at him like he is an insect, and he says—I'm loosely translating—"This establishment doesn't live for money. What can we do with these schmattas?"

I say, "Not what he's wearing—if you are an artist, you can make him look like a prince." So he begins to measure him. But then the tailor throws down the tape measure and says, "No I can do." So I say, "Look, you cannot put me in a position like this. I've brought you this distinguished man, and I've told you that no matter what he looks like, he's playing a principal role opposite Myrna Loy." He says, "Opposite Loy, what he play?" I say, "Her husband." And he says, "Do she betray him?" I say, "Sure, she betrays him." "She make horns on him?" "Yes, *cornuto*. He's a schmuck." And he says, "All right. I dress him!"

HJ: He's in the single most romantic movie I've ever seen. Which has the unromantic title, *The Life and Death of Colonel Blimp*. [Michael] Powell and [Emeric] Pressburger used him in everything. *Stairway to Heaven*, *A Matter of Life and Death*.

OW: Hated those guys. Not my cup of tea. To me, they never made a good film.

HJ: Did you know Pressburger?

OW: I know Powell better. I think Pressburger's the more talented of the two. But I don't share your admiration for either one of them.

HJ: *The Red Shoes* is kitsch to you?

OW: Yeah, total dreck. Total dreck. I even saw part of it again and switched it off.

HJ: *Stairway to Heaven*? *A Matter of Life and Death*?

OW: Awful.

HJ: *One of Our Aircraft is Missing*? Do you remember that? No?

OW: Yes, with Ralph [Richardson], who was very good in it, but the picture was abominable.

HJ: I'm in love with Powell. I saw all of the Powell-Pressburger films when I was a teenager.

OW: If you see them at the right age, you see them differently. You see the real value of them, what they really are.

HJ: It's true: how you feel about a film has to do with how old you are when you see it.

OW: In the theater, I can pretend that it's all happening right there in front of me. But I see movies through such a mist of years, I am incapable of feeling the thrill of them, even the greatest ones, because I cannot erase those years of experience. I'm jaded. I know I don't see movies as purely as I ought to see them. Before I started making movies, I'd get into them, lose myself. I can't do that now. That's why I don't think my opinions about movies are as good as somebody's who doesn't have to look through all those filters. I think all films are better than we think they are.

HJ: Maybe that's why Spencer Tracy is so fantastic to me, and Humphrey Bogart, too.

OW: Of course. Your age. I still see Lon Chaney as I saw him when I was eight years old. But I have had some disillusionment since I left movies, I must say.

When are you leaving for Paris?

HJ: Tomorrow night.

OW: I will give you two or three scripts. And you can drop them off where they need to go.

HJ: All right. Now, I want to be sure that I understand the sequence of—

OW: Still *Lear* first. If *Lear* collapses, *Dreamers* is always good. It doesn't date.

HJ: Is there anybody in particular you want me to see?

OW: There's a man who's head of TNF, French television. It's like the BBC. He said he would raise the three and a half million for *Lear* by selling it all over the place. But I don't know. He's no Henry Jaglom.

HJ: So this is three times the other French offer. And it has nothing to do with Lang, or the government, or anything at all?

OW: Nothing. He thinks this will be the jewel in his crown. But I still don't want to shoot in Paris. And they don't have anyplace except Victorine, although I've heard that it's been remodeled. It's now owned by Americans and is OK.

HJ: Despite the airplanes.

OW: Yes, because I now know when the air traffic is light. I would shoot from four in the afternoon until eleven at night, you see—something like that.

HJ: I can certainly find out what kind of reputation he has, what other people there think—

OW: He doesn't have a reputation. He's just got a position. I'm afraid he's never gonna sell *Lear* to anyone. Besides, he's demanding that French television must be the center of everything. And asking me to wait three months while you try to raise the money. And if he doesn't, you see, I've wasted three months. It's a real gamble. Also, I have to know that he's not going to make me cut the picture in France. And we need to negotiate how the profits are going to be dealt with. Instead of taking a salary out of the budget and taking some money after everything is paid off, I'd like to have two or three territories. In fact, I would even like to have my company or a company associated with me be a minor co-producer. He may not like it, but I don't like to have a monolithic boss.

HJ: Absolutely not. Because he could end up owning your picture and—

OW: I won't do it. And I think I can break him now, because he has nothing else. He's so hot for it that I think he'll give in.

HJ: What about England?

OW: You're big in England. I was never big in England. I'm dreaming of when I will be.

HJ: Every time I mention *Lear* to them, they say, "Oh, wouldn't that be nice." I was worried that Olivier's *Lear* would hurt us. It was on TV. But I think it helped. They don't like Olivier in England.

OW: No, they don't. They've never gone to his Shakespearean movies. 'Cause they never go to any Shakespearean movies. They want to see Shakespeare on the stage, not in a movie theater . . . You know, everybody may be interested. But are we really going to carry the movie around by bus from country to country so we can make it a national event in every country?

HJ: Do you know who Victoria Tennant is?

OW: Who?

HJ: Victoria Tennant.

OW: A member of the Tennant family?

HJ: She is a daughter of the Tennant family. Quite a beauty. Her most famous role here was in the miniseries *The Winds of War*. She played opposite [Robert] Mitchum. Anyway, she lives with Steve Martin. He's not your favorite, I know. She begged me at a party Saturday night to tell you that she believes that there's no one who could do Cordelia as well as she.

OW: Not a chance.

HJ: All right, good. I like clear answers. They make things very simple. I don't have to tell you all about her, and what she did and didn't do, and what she said and didn't say.

OW: Too bad about Steve Martin. The Tennants controlled the English theater for forty years. They had the whole West End by the short hairs. When there was a West End, that is—it was totally Tennant. But very hard to get a job there if you weren't homosexual. Really. A real Mafia working against the few straights who were around. Even Donald Wolfit couldn't get on the West End stage. Everybody, unfairly, made fun of him because he was the only non-queer actor alive in the golden age of acting.

HJ: Wolfit was Sir in *The Dresser*, [Ronald] Harwood's play. But Harwood was actually his dresser.

OW: You'd have to pretend to be homosexual to get ahead. Either be queer or act like you were queer. Larry kind of did that.

HJ: And you think it was a political move.

OW: Absolutely.

HJ: Richardson was certainly not homosexual.

OW: Well, you see, they didn't really take to him until his old age. Not when he was at the Old Vic. Not until he did his great hit, *Dangerous Corner*, written by [J. B.] Priestley. He was one of the very few straight actors flying the flag for the heteros. As was Jack Hawkins. I wanted Hawkins to play Iago for me in the theater.

HJ: That was in '51? When you were Othello?

OW: Yeah. And I would have had him. Jack would have loved to do Iago, as anybody would. But Larry didn't want him.

HJ: Because he was straight?

OW: It was Larry's theater, and the leading actors had to be approved by him. So I had to use [Peter] Finch.

HJ: He was straight.

OW: But he was fucking Vivien.

HJ: Did Larry know that?

OW: He knew it, sure. He wanted to go away on a yachting trip with Vivie, and keep Finch busy on the London stage. And Finch was a wonderful Iago. But not as good as Hawkins would have been. He played him as eaten up with bitterness. I'd rather play Iago than any part in Shakespeare, but I'm not built for Iago. That's the part, though. Not Othello. You know, everything Iago says is in prose, and everything Othello says is in poetry. Now, look at the advantage that gives the actor right there. And—did I tell you this? [Henry] Irving and [Edwin] Booth played Othello on alternate nights in London. One night Iago, one night Othello.

Booth was famous for his Iago. So they expected him to steal it. Then Irving did the same thing. Each of them stole the play as Iago. Stole it, no matter which one played it. But you need great, big actors like that.

HJ: I saw the film version of the *The Dresser* last night. At one point, Wolfit or Sir, says, "Lear is the greatest tragic part of all time."

OW: Of course. *The Dresser* is a parody of *Lear*. The dresser is the fool—

HJ: Oh, my God. You know, I never even got that. I feel stupid.

OW: It's a little clumsy, but that's what it is. The writer, Harwood, is trying to say a lot more than he needed to say to make a very good vehicle play. You mustn't look too closely at it. But that's what it is.

HJ: Albert Finney is magnificent.

OW: Stick a dagger in me! I tried so hard to get the rights to that play. You've ruined my lunch.

HJ: You'll be even more upset when you see it, because you'll think about what you could have done with it.

OW: I have no intention of seeing it. I know it'll be good, and I know Finney will be great in it—that's why I won't see it. Why should I make myself sick? If I had any hope that it was bad, I'd go. Do you know how I screwed it up? I had the idea of having the dresser played by Michael Caine, not Tom Courtenay. I thought Michael would be something. Instead of Courtenay's flagrant queen performance. But Courtenay had a kind of lock on the property. And that's how come I lost it.

HJ: The money guy who put it together was a friend of mine. I remember, he said, "It has to be Courtenay." Because he played the role on the stage.

OW: If only I had said, "Courtenay is all right with me," I might have got it. Courtenay was a friend of mine. But I was so keen on it being Michael Caine, because I don't think anybody had *any* idea how good that play would be if it were *not* played the way Courtenay plays it. If it had the kind of richness and comedy and warmth, furious tenderness mixed with bitchiness that Michael would have brought to it. Because he's maybe the best actor on the screen now, he's so good. I'm sure Finney is great as Sir, but that part should have been done by any one of a number of actors who are the right age, and don't have to act it. It would have been wonderful with Richardson. Can you imagine Michael Caine and Richardson in that thing? And it would have been a great way for Richardson to go out, you know. Because he never made it in Shakespeare, except as Falstaff, which is written in prose. It would have blown the roof off. It would have broken your heart! There wouldn't have been that slightly mean feeling that you get.

HJ: I thought you didn't see it. Oh, you've seen clips from it, you said.

OW: Long clips.

HJ: What I thought was wrong with the movie was that Finney was too good playing Sir playing Lear. He couldn't resist grabbing you, when he's supposed to be the epitome of every bad actor's need for the audience.

OW: Just like Larry was too good as *The Entertainer*. But, you see, I didn't read it as a play about a bad actor. Sir had to go on tour because he wasn't queer, you know. But *The Dresser* absolutely annihilates any possibility of my doing my movie, which is about a very different kind of actor. They wouldn't like it as much.

HJ: It doesn't annihilate it, Orson. As you say, it's completely different. Yours is an Ameri—

OW: No, in mine, Sir is not American. He's Irish. It was based on [Anew] McMaster, who was the most beautiful man who ever lived. He looked like a god! He had blond hair, and he had the most marvelous voice you ever heard in your life! McMaster really was gay. So I couldn't play him. I could only direct it. And when he was about twenty-three years old, he got panned in the West End, went back to Ireland, and played pinups—little platforms built in church halls, and so on—for the rest of his life.

HJ: So he didn't tour because he was straight, he toured because his feelings had been hurt on the stage in Lon—

OW: And each year he could go to fewer and fewer places, because he would have fucked more and more choirboys. So his tour was increasingly reduced. And then he would play four or six weeks in Dublin. He played Othello with nothing but a little G-string. Mac Liammóir, who was his brother-in-law—

HJ: Mac Liammóir was married to his sister?

OW: His sister was a bull dyke. And these two wild queens were known in Dublin as Sodom and Gomorrah. I beg your pardon, I ruined that joke. Sodom and Begorra.

HJ: I've heard about Mac Liammóir all my life. I never heard of McMaster.

OW: Nobody heard of McMaster, nobody, 'cause he stayed in the smalls of Ireland. And he had all these famous people who worked with him at one time or another, including [Harold] Pinter, who was his stage manager. And when he died, Pinter wrote a book about him. I would love to get a copy. I've never met Pinter. I saw him at the guild hall this last time when I was speaking. And he was near, and I wanted to go up to him, but no way could I push my way past His Royal Highness and say, "Mr. Pinter, how can I get a copy of your book?"

19. "Gary Cooper turns me right into a girl!"

In which Orson argues that Cooper and Humphrey Bogart are stars, not actors, and goes on to explain the difference. Bogart thought *Casablanca* was the worst picture he ever did while it was in production.

———————

HENRY JAGLOM: Is Bogart as good as I think he is?

ORSON WELLES: No. Not nearly as good as you believe. Bogart was a second-rate actor. *Really* a second-rate actor. He was a fascinating personality who captured the imagination of the world, but he never gave a good performance in his life. Only satisfactory. Just listen to a reading of any line of his.

HJ: What about *The Caine Mutiny*?

OW: I saw Lloyd Nolan play it on the stage. He was hair-raising. He made Bogart look sick. There's no comparison. Bogart in the thirties did the worst thing with Bette Davis, when he had that Irish accent, that I've ever seen anybody do.

HJ: I think that was *Dark Victory*. To me, he gives the perfect performance in *Casablanca*. And he was good in *In a Lonely Place*.

OW: Oh, come on, he had that little lisp. Bogart was a well-educated, upper-class American trying to be tough. You didn't believe him as a tough guy. Anybody who knew him as I did . . .

HJ: Do you always have to add "as I did"?

OW: I knew him in the theater, before he went to Hollywood as just another out-of-work leading man. We were so glad he got a job, you know.

HJ: You didn't like him in *The Petrified Forest*?

OW: Well, I didn't hate him. I was glad he got by with it, but Warner Brothers had five tough-guy actors who could've done it just as well.

HJ: They had that horrible guy they offered *Casablanca* to. George Raft.

OW: Yeah, he was a terrible actor, too. What's interesting is that George Raft knew he was the world's worst actor. He told me that all the time. He'd say, "I'm just lucky, you know. I can't say a line."

HJ: I know you love Gary Cooper, but to me, he was just a very pretty George Raft. All I see is a man stumbling over his lines, trying to remember what's going on. But you're queer for him.

OW: I am. Gary Cooper turns me right into a girl! And you love Bogie. Neither one of them were much good. But we're in love with 'em.

HJ: And yet, you tell me Gary Cooper is great, and . . .

OW: Well, no, just that he's a great movie star, a great movie creation. That's the thing about a movie star. We really don't judge them as actors. They're the creatures that we fell in love with at a certain time. And that has to do with who we want to have as our heroes. It's absolutely impossible to have a serious critical discussion about enthusiasms for movie stars. Because a movie star is an animal separate from acting. Sometimes, he or she is a great actor. Sometimes a third-rate one. But the star is something that you fall in love with . . .

HJ: We don't have movie stars like that these days. I agree Bogart was lousy in *Dark Victory*.

OW: *Dark Victory* was the first Broadway play that I lit.

HJ: Lit? I didn't know you did lighting. You were a lighting director?

OW: That's why Gregg Toland wanted to do *Kane*, because he had seen my lighting and—

HJ: You always gave Toland the credit for lighting *Kane*, for being the greatest lighting director ever.

OW: Yes. But I lit it.

HJ: All right, but you have to admit Bogart is phenomenally good in *The Maltese Falcon*.

OW: Somehow we always get back to Bogart. No, for me, [Sydney] Greenstreet is the great performance. I had seen Greenstreet all my life in the theater. He was the most extraordinary supporting actor in the Theatre Guild. A short, little tubby man just right for small drama. Then, in *The Maltese Falcon* I suddenly saw this gigantic screen-filling personality, and from then on, for the rest of his career, he was wonderful in every part he did. I adored him as a person. Adorable. Adorable man.

HJ: What about that movie with [Lauren] Bacall, her first movie? *To Have and Have Not*?

OW: It's a wonderful Hemingway story that they screwed up badly. So ridiculous compared to the story.

HJ: The hurricane one was *Key Largo*, wasn't it?

OW: I like that movie better.

HJ: Do you have that in the theater, too, stars who don't necessarily act?

OW: Oh, yes. The Lunts. The last play they did was so embarrassing I didn't know where to look. When they were good, they were—you saw *The Visit*?

HJ: Yes.

OW: They were among the greatest actors I've ever seen in my life. Truly, truly. They were unbelievable.

HJ: In what way? I wish I could understand.

OW: It was like having roses thrown at you. But the Lunts got too old. They were sour toward the end. They got bad. Actors either get better or worse as they get old.

HJ: And while we're talking about this, you're not crazy about Ingrid Bergman.

OW: No, she's not an actress. Just barely able to get through a scene.

HJ: But when she and Bogart get together in *Casablanca*—

OW: I admired *Casablanca* very much. I thought it was a very well put-together piece of *Schwarmerei*, with just the right measure of every ingredient and all that crap, and of course, tremendous luck, because they were making it up as they went along. They were playing it not knowing how it was going to end. They didn't know who she was going to end up with, or why. And all of them wanted out. Bogart used to tell me, "I'm in the worst picture I've ever been in."

HJ: You liked him personally?

OW: Very much. And once he made it in movies, I saw he was a real star. Ingrid Bergman, too. And when you start to dissect a real star, one person will say they can act, another person will say they can't. What is indelible is the quality of stardom. And whether it's acting or not is a useless argument. Because the star thing is a different animal. It breaks all the rules.

HJ: Are you saying Bogart never took himself seriously as an actor?

OW: I think Bogart thought he was as good as anybody around.

HJ: And he was a decent man?

OW: I wouldn't say decent. He was a brave man. He was amusing and original. Very opinionated, with very dumb opinions and not very well read and pretending to be. You know, a lot of people who aren't interesting on the screen were very bright. Paul Henreid is very bright. He was supposed to be the star of *Casablanca*. The antifascist hero. Bogart was the second guy. The fellow who owned the restaurant, you see. But *Casablanca* ended Henreid's career.

HJ: Because everybody remembers Bogart, Bergman—and oh yeah, that other guy. After that movie, Henreid played a supporting character for the rest of his life.

OW: You know the mean joke played on him by Walter Slezak, and a bunch of other actors on a subsequent movie? Henreid is sitting there, in his chair, waiting between takes. And the other actors get into a conversation—that he can hear—saying: "It was Ralph Bellamy in *Casablanca*. "No, no, it was . . ."

HJ: Who directed *Casablanca*? Michael Curtiz?

OW: No idea about dialogue, but a very, very good visual sense. Very Hungarian. You can't imagine how Hungarian he was.

HJ: Jewish, I'm sure.

OW: No, Hungarian. Real Hungarian. One of the stories about him was when they had an extra call with some blacks in a group, he says, "All the whites over here and all the niggers over there." There was a terrible silence and the assistant director says to the director in a low voice, "Mr. Curtiz . . . you say 'all the *Negroes* or you say *colored*." So Curtiz says, "All right, all the colored niggers over there." Tracy told me that story. He was on the picture.

HJ: What's handled so well in *Casablanca* are those big scenes in the casino where all the French are milling about and the Germans come in.

OW: Awfully well done. Curtiz used to be an assistant to Max Reinhardt, so he knew what he was doing.

HJ: Did Reinhardt deserve the reputation that he enjoyed in Europe?

OW: He deserved it. I regarded Reinhardt with awe. He was a great, great director. A great master of spectacle as well as intimate comedy. He could do anything. I saw his production of *Merchant of Venice* and *Romeo and Juliet* with Elisabeth Bergner, who was superb.

HJ: You saw *Romeo and Juliet* with Elisabeth Bergner? Oh, my God!

OW: My father took me, as a child. I also saw an [Arthur] Schnitzler comedy that Reinhardt did in a small theater in Vienna. Marvelous performances. Wonderful.

HJ: But was he as great a force as you say?

OW: You can't imagine. Nobody, before or since, has ever had such a commanding role in the theater in as many countries at once. He had four or five theaters he ran at the same time. Hugely successful, *The Miracle* made a fortune.

HJ: *The Miracle*?

OW: *The Miracle* was a huge piece of pageantry, in which the theater was totally transformed into a cathedral. In Vienna. He collapsed the proscenium long before anybody else did. He had a theater at his castle in Salzburg, and the greatest actors in Europe would come to play there every year. Bill Dieterle was one of his assistants also. And [Ernst] Lubitsch.

Reinhardt came to see my production of *Danton's Death* when he arrived in New York. I was playing a small part, about eight lines—Saint-Just. *Danton's Death* had been one of the biggest successes of his career. He did it in a sports arena with an audience of about five thousand people each night. [Vladimir] Sokoloff played Robespierre for him in Berlin and he also played it with me in New York. I was very nervous because here was a production totally unlike his, you know. Reinhardt came backstage, sat with the director, talked for a while while I waited, and then said to me, "You are the best *Schauspieler* in America. You must do the great parts."

Nothing about the production. So all he could do was tell me what a great actor I was.

HJ: So he didn't like the production.

OW: Of course not. Couldn't blame him.

When he got to Hollywood, he couldn't come to terms with the fact that he was a nobody refugee. He was lost. Probably didn't have enough respect for the medium, either, I think. Although he had the sense to know that Mickey Rooney was one of the most talented people in Hollywood and to cast him as Puck. So this man ruling over everything in *Mittel* Europe had no chance in America. None of the refugees did. Only the writers, who could just sit and write. Think, what did Brecht do? What did Kurt Weill do? What did any of them do?

HJ: Well, Weill had another career. I mean, you may not like it, but it was another career.

OW: Not much of one until just at the end. He was out of work most of the time. So was Thomas Mann, ruling over everything. You don't know what America was like during the war. It was the pits. The stage died. People flocked to the theaters, but the movies died, too. Because all you had to do was turn the projector on. No movie failed. But they got worse and worse. The war flattened everybody's taste in a very curious way. The best thing they could do in the movies was some delirious piece of fabrication like *Casablanca*. That was *the* great work of art, during the whole period of the war. Nothing else.

HJ: Why has that picture taken on such a—?

OW: It has nothing to do with anything except Hollywood's dream of the war. But that's its charm. To me, it's like *The Merry Widow*, which is a great work of its kind. There never was a Vienna like the one in *The Merry Widow*, and there never was a Casablanca like the one in *Casablanca*. But who gives a damn, you know? It was just commercial enough, so everybody was happy. And it had a wonderful cast of actors. But a great film? You can't call it that. It's not a great film. It's just great entertainment. The person who loved it when it opened, who persuaded me to take it more seriously, was Marlene. She's the one who said, "They'll be showing that thirty years from now. You listen to me." So then I had to think, and say, "I guess you're right."

20. "Jack, it's Orson fucking Welles."

In which Jack Nicholson finally responds to *The Big Brass Ring*. Orson voices his admiration for Jacobo Timerman, considers the paranoia of Jews, and laments the destruction of Paris by the automobile.

––––––––––

HENRY JAGLOM: I have good news and bad news. I'll tell you the good news first. Jack said yes to *The Big Brass Ring*, but he won't reduce his salary. I said, "Jack, it's Orson fucking Welles. Imagine it's 1968!" He said, "If this were 1968, I would do it for nothing. I really want to do it, but it will totally throw me into the art movie world again and I've been working to get out of that into the big, mainstream things, where they pay me millions and millions of dollars. If I do a picture for half that, how do I explain to the next person that I'm demanding four million?"

ORSON WELLES: I should have known better. They all said no, and each kept me waiting weeks before each "no." And every "no" hurts me more than I let on. They always want earth-shattering from me. They want *Touch of Evil* from me. And I'm not ready with any *Touch of Evil*. They're thinking, "Orson is old-fashioned. He's lost it. He used to be an innovator." But I tell you, every script I've ever written, if you read it before I made it into a movie, it would look straight and conservative. I've always felt there are three sexes: men, women, and actors. And actors combine the worst qualities of the other two. I can't go on waiting for stars.

HJ: I'm afraid you may be right. And it's a shocking thing to think this about my friends, you know?

OW: But that's the way friends are, if they're stars.

HJ: You said that from the beginning—and I didn't believe it. I just thought everybody would be so excited at the chance. I'd like to kill the bastards.

HJ: What about Jack Lemmon?

OW: He's old-looking.

HJ: Really? I was just thinking that he looks good. Because he's actually not. What is he? Fifty-five?

OW: Yeah. He looks good in this restaurant, under these rosy lights. But you see him on TV—he's always giving long interviews, he loves to talk, as we know—and he looks every minute of his age because they blast him with light, so we don't recognize him. Fifteen years ago, Lemmon would have looked credible as a young candidate, but Kennedy changed the image of how a presidential candidate should look.

HJ: If we don't get the response we want on *Big Brass Ring*, would you sell the script?

OW: Well, before I went to Europe, I started improving it, and I got a third of the way through. And my improvements were so great that I was sure that I should continue in case it should ever be made. I do still have doubts about it, but I would like to see Jack play the candidate, the guy who throws himself in front of the car running against Reagan. Jack is a great loser character, you know.

HJ: What about Al Pacino, Dustin Hoffman? They are two of the greatest actors of my generation, both highly respected, and excuse me, they're a lot better than Burt Reynolds and a lot of the others on your list.

OW: Not your friend Dusty Hoffman. No dwarfs. Besides, they're ethnic.

HJ: They're what?

OW: They're ethnic.

HJ: You mean, they're not Irish leading men? Aren't the Irish ethnic?

OW: You know what I mean. No dark, funny-looking guys. I want an Irish leading man like Jack, or at least an all-American WASP.

HJ: Why?

OW: It's the president of the United States. Were you born yesterday?

HJ: That's all changed. Everyone said a Catholic couldn't get elected president, then Kennedy got elected. Everyone said a divorced guy couldn't get elected, and then Reagan did.

OW: This will never change. Never. You can't do a story like this and have some Italian play that role: "Cazzo, you gotta respect-a the president, and that's-a me."

HJ: That's disgusting.

OW: Oh, you want Dusty Hoffman? "Oy, vey, don't be such a putz, kill 'em."

HJ: You've got a very fifties, fucked-up idea of what looks American.

OW: You're my bleeding heart. I was more left than you'll ever be.

HJ: What about Paul Newman?

OW: Paul Newman would work.

HJ: Newman's Jewish.

OW: He's not ethnic. I don't care if they're Jewish; I don't care if they're Italian, but they can't be ethnic. Hoffman is ethnic, Pacino is ethnic."

HJ: So no Jews, no Italians . . .

OW: No. This has to be a guy from the heartland of America. Or we don't have a movie.

HJ: The one who was totally willing to do it was De Niro, without even reading the script, and you just—

OW: Don't try to sell me on De Niro. I don't care how great you think he is.

HJ: He's too ethnic also?

OW: Not just ethnic, though that's part of it. More, it's that the great things he does on the screen . . . none of them look to me like the qualities of a candidate. You're writing off an awful lot of the country with him. My candidate is a fellow who's got to carry Kansas. I really don't see De Niro carrying Kansas.

HJ: OK. Here's more news. I don't know if it's good or bad. I had a call from *Love Boat*. They want you from May twenty-first until June twelfth, that's twenty-one days. I said to them, "Well, are you going to make an offer?" "No. We want to know his availability." I said, "Mr. Welles's availability depends on whether you make an offer. I'm not telling him anything, honestly, until you come up with a concrete offer." I also said, "You know, I'm sorry, I've never watched your program." Complete silence. They had the main man call me, because I was dismissive of the first person. So the deal is, you fly to London—shoot in London—they then fly you to Paris—shoot in Paris for a few days—then you fly back to London. And then you board a ship to Stockholm! He said, "Have you ever been through the Kiel Canal?" I said, "No." He said, "It's meant to be fabulous!"

OW: Oh, boy! You'd have to *pay* me to go through the Kiel Canal.

HJ: He was like selling a cruise. He was a cruise director. But it's not a heavy shooting schedule. In other words, it's a party—that's what it is.

OW: One big party.

HJ: I wonder what they'll offer for that?

OW: Maximum twenty-five, probably twenty. It's amazingly small money.

HJ: I assumed $100,000 for a big-name guest.

OW: Yes, well . . . Let me tell you the history of American television in a few well-chosen words. As soon as CBS and William Morris and NBC and MCA—those four—saw what television was, they made a secret pact. I don't believe in conspiracy stories, but this one is true! Which was that nobody in a series was ever going to get anything like movie money. Nobody. So that when Henry Kissinger came on, they gave him $5,000 for one day. And even if you're a top actor, and willing to do *Love Boat*—there's always somebody— for a long time the top salary for *anybody*, for any length of time, in any hour show, was $7,500. That was broken by the Beatles, when [Ed] Sullivan paid them twenty-five, or something, for their first appearance on American television. But despite that, the fee has remained low all this time. You'll find that most of the guest stars on shows like this are getting $2,500, $3,000, $3,500. And glad to get the exposure.

HJ: Why would June Allyson want to do that? Or why would—

OW: Why not? Who's hiring her for anything else?

HJ: They ask you to go on a cruise—

OW: And they think that's the payment. They don't know that I can go on any cruise in the world free, if I'll lecture, or do magic one night, and then sign autographs.

HJ: *Love Boat* has been on the air forever, hasn't it?

OW: I'm unable to watch even one segment. Because I don't like the man who plays the captain. From *Mary Tyler Moore*. He has a kind of New York accent that gets my hackles up. I can't stand it! I liked old boring—what's his name—Lou Grant. What's his real name?

HJ: Oh, Ed Asner. He's wonderful on *Mary Tyler Moore*. I spent a very interesting evening with him and Jacobo Timerman the night before last at Michael Douglas's house—it was a fund-raiser for El Salvador. Timerman wrote a book critical of Israel's invasion of Lebanon, and now he says he can't stand it in Israel anymore. He said, "They were spitting at me in the streets." I said, "If you're gonna be a conscience, you're gonna have to suffer some of this."

OW: Timerman is a real conscience.

HJ: What he's lived through—jail, torture, electroshock—in Argentina where he grew up, for speaking up against the generals during the Dirty War. Now he's a man without a country.

OW: Isn't everybody? He's got a country, and it's wherever he is.

HJ: I said, "Where are you gonna live?" He said, "I'm going to see what is going on in Argentina. I want to make sure that every one of those criminals is tried."

OW: I am really in awe of him.

HJ: At Michael's, he was talking about how upset he was at the American Jewish leadership and the American Jewish community for supporting Reagan's reactionary policies in Central America. Because Israel provides arms, at America's behest, to Honduras. It was a living room full of progressive Jews, but a lot of them were very uncomfortable with being singled out. It got them worrying about anti-Semitism. And Asner did a wonderful thing. He talked about the fact that the Jews have become part of the establishment to the point where they've forgotten their whole liberal humanitarian tradition.

OW: They won't speak out about Lebanon. Or Central America. You know, there are large sections of that community who don't like the word *Jew*. *Jewish* or *Jewish persuasion*, or *Jewish culture* are fine, but not the word *Jew*! Don't call a Jew a Jew. That's really strange. And sad.

HJ: I didn't read Timerman's Lebanon book, so I don't know to what extreme he went. Is it fair? Reasonable?

OW: To me it is. From my point of view, it's saying what I would say as a non-Jew. America has missed absolutely no opportunity, not only during the Reagan administration, but in my lifetime, to render it impossible for us to be anything but the deathly enemy of all Arabs, and, of course, all Latin Americans. We can never polish that image. I don't care how much money we pour into it.

HJ: Timerman is going to cover Central America for the *New Yorker* now.

OW: Nobody's written well about Central America. Well, there's Joan Didion. She spent seven days in Central America. Wrote a best seller. It should be called *Seven Days in Central America*.

HJ: Here's Patrick [Terrail].

PATRICK TERRAIL: What's do you call a pole with a twenty-five-million-dollar mansion? The Pope.

HJ: What?

PT: The Pope.

HJ: That's a rather bigoted joke.

PT: It's sweet.

OW: What it has is that it's clean. I expected some filthy punch line.

PT: I would never tell a filthy joke to Mr. Welles. Not coming out of my mouth . . .

(PT exits.)

OW: You have no idea how close I am to signing for *Lear*. And I've got, I think, a deal in Mexico for *The Dreamers*. I don't dare believe it—you know what it's like. The world is too full of disappointments to celebrate these kinds of things till they happen. They'll probably all collapse.

HJ: They won't all collapse.

OW: I think my future is in advertising. I did Carlsberg beer in England for five years. Then they decided they could do it cheaper by getting a man who could imitate my voice. They had him for

two years and I've been back for the last three years. I did one yesterday.

HJ: Have you seen [John] Gielgud's ads for Old Spice?

OW: Yes. They're not using him well at all, you know.

HJ: He plays a sort of strange butler or something.

OW: That's because of the thing he did with Dudley Moore, *Arthur*.
Well, they thought, if that went well with the movie, that'll go good
with Old Spice . . . Gielgud used to play Shakespeare as though he
were dictating it to his secretary. I told him that myself.

HJ: You did?

OW: In *Hamlet*, when Fortinbras is marching by, it sounded partic-
ularly that way: "Witness this army . . . 'Have you got that, Miss
Jones?' Such mass and charge, led by a delicate and tender prince . . .
'Am I going too fast for you?' "

HJ: Funny!

OW: I'm exchanging telegrams during the next three days with the
French TV guy I told you about.

HJ: And do you have a better inkling about his capacity to raise
that money?

OW: If he can't, nobody can. He has to. His job kind of depends
on it. And Jacques Lang has come in on it with some government
money. So let's hope it works.

HJ: Well, I heard a story in Paris, from the people who seem to
know what they're talking about, that Mitterand has seven or eight
cassettes that he puts on at night, over and over again. Five or six of
them are about very complex intellectual subjects of some sort.
But there are three movies, and two of them are yours—*Kane* and
Touch of Evil.

OW: You know that the president in France is not like a president
in America. He is more like a king, you know? As somebody once
said, de Gaulle established a monarchy in a republic, because the

president makes the decisions. When everybody said, "We don't like that, a pyramid in the middle of the Louvre," he said, "I like it," and that's the end of it. There's a pyramid in the middle of the Louvre.

HJ: How do you feel about that pyramid?

OW: I hate it.

HJ: I'm wondering if I hate it only because I want to hold on to the past.

OW: My answer to myself, when I ask myself that question is, "Balls. It looks ridiculous!"

HJ: But maybe it's just because we want a more traditional look.

OW: But it *is* a traditional look. I just don't believe in mixing up traditional materials that way. I think if you have to have a shape there to let the light in, a box would have been less offensive. There is something assertive about that pyramid. It's making a statement. Everybody said, "You're gonna think the [Georges] Pompidou thing is beautiful. You just have to get used to it." But the more you look at it, the more impossible it is. It's a big piece of junk. But I remind myself that half of aesthetic France threatened to leave Paris when they started to build the Eiffel Tower. So maybe I'm just as reactionary. If I am, it doesn't bother me much, though. I'm perfectly content to be reactionary—to belong to my own time.

HJ: Everybody thought the Eiffel Tower was a piece of junk. Now it's something so beautiful—

OW: But, you see, the Eiffel Tower is marvelous because it has an historical meaning. It is the last great work of the Age of Iron.

HJ: Still, at the time, you can imagine people who wanted the vista uncluttered being—

OW: But now it's destroyed anyway because all the good views have been ruined by the Tour Montparnasse. If you stand and look through that small Arc de Triomphe—that little miniature, which is in front of the Louvre, and look up the Champs-Élysées, you used to be able to look right through the Arc de Triomphe into blue sky. Now what you see looks like Detroit.

HJ: But I'm curious. Is taste objective or subjective?

OW: Subjective, basically. But it's an interesting question. I remember my darling Louise de Vilmorin, who always swore that Paris was one of the ugliest cities in the world, a terrible nineteenth-century atrocity. She could only stand the things that dated from before then, and there were few enough of those. If your taste is back there in the seventeenth and eighteenth centuries, then Paris is an ugly city. The automobile did it, with all those underpasses and the highway by the Seine. Do you remember what the Seine was like when you could stroll along it with your girl? God, that was another world.

I've been asked to write some little thing in *Paris Vogue*, along with a lot of other people who don't know anything, about why I love Paris. And I can't think of anything to say. It should be "Why I Loved Paris." When I could walk on the sidewalk in Paris, I loved it, but now I have to climb over automobiles. Taking down the Halles was the beginning of the end. Les Halles was a good building. The new one is already falling apart. It looks older than Notre Dame! The paint is peeling off it. Soon there won't be any real Paris left, you know. Or real London or real Rome. Because a few untouchable monuments are not gonna keep a city . . . I think all the cities of the world are in decline. Because the idea of supporting cities has ceased to be part of world culture. We're all moving into shopping malls . . .

HJ: The old concept of the city as a cultural magnet has been abandoned. And they're overcrowded.

OW: And, of course, the traffic has ruined the sex life of the French. There's the famous *cinq à sept*. You know what that is? The businessmen, when they finished at five, before they went home to their wives had a *cinq à sept*, which was with a mistress. Now, you can't do that and get back home by seven. You can't *move* in the city. I think architects are bums nowadays. I'm convinced of it.

HJ: I. M. Pei is a bum?

OW: A show-off, anyway. I'm very interested in architecture, and I'm absolutely persuaded that I'm right. I don't have a moment's doubt. Architects have achieved marvelous theatrical effects with their mirror-glass buildings. But then you realize that they're built over volcanic earthquake faults. And that they depend on high-energy usage. You cannot open a window on a spring day. You could be locked up in there with no heat, or no air-conditioning, or whatever it is. And, therefore, these are bad buildings. For a moment, a group of people in Brazil was making interesting modern buildings with big louvers that you could open to the air, which gave them a kind of human feeling. I don't believe buildings should dehumanize us. By definition, they have to belong to us, on some level. Otherwise, they're just monuments to greed.

HJ: I love the older New York skyscrapers.

OW: I don't think that most of them are any good, either. I think they were only good at the very start, with [Louis] Sullivan. And those buildings weren't skyscrapers.

HJ: You don't think that the Chrysler Building—

OW: I like the Chrysler Building, but it's a little kitschy. A little Art Deco.

HJ: I love Art Deco.

OW: I hate it, you see? I deeply hate it.

HJ: So does my mother. She always said it was the maid's furniture.

OW: The maid's furniture is what it is. I knew that Deco was bad—let me be modest—when I was as young as fourteen! And I was so happy after the World War, when people started building other things. I said, "Oh, thank God! You know, there goes another one of those awful things down!" Deco was what I had against all the great ocean liners. I loved going on those ships, but I used to say, "What a shame that they aren't like the ones they made in 1890," you know? The older ships were wonderful to look at.

HJ: But you like Lubitsch. And he uses the Deco look.

OW: All the time. But I don't think Lubitsch has a strong visual sense. He wasn't interested in the sets. I watched him shooting, and it was all about the actors and what they're saying.

21. "Once in our lives, we had a national theater."

In which Orson is offered a job directing a feature about the contretemps over The Cradle Will Rock. But the script, by Ring Lardner, Jr., is awash in Old Left pieties, and he wonders if he will be able to control the film.

———————

HENRY JAGLOM: So what's new?

ORSON WELLES: There is a young man, thirty-three years old, handsome, tremendously intelligent, and rich as hell, who financed a terrible picture called *Wide Blood*.

HJ: Not *Wise Blood*?

OW: *Wise Blood*, I guess, whatever it is.

HJ: Huston's film. I know who you're talking about, Michael Fitzgerald.

OW: Yeah, for $900,000. So he tells me, "We have a script written by Ring Lardner, Jr." And I read it. Not because I really wanted to, but because I'm in it—there's a leading character named Orson Welles. It's about the night we moved *The Cradle Will Rock* from the Maxine Elliott to the Venice Theatre. It's got a very simple MGM plot. The kind with Mickey Rooney and Judy Garland, you know: What are you gonna do when the bad guys close the theater? If you knuckle under to the bad guys, aren't you gonna throw everybody out of work? The hell with that—the show is gonna go on.

Rent a theater, find a piano. Open the show. That's all the movie is. But I am shown in the worst light of any character, because the guy's source is Houseman. Offensive. I said, "This is terrible." My problem is, should I direct it?

HJ: Was Lardner's script true to what happened, aside from the fact that you're presented in a bad light?

OW: Yes, it's accurate, in fact. And they propose to start as soon as they can. I said yes, because in the last analysis, I am the hero, and a glamorous one. I sat them down at this table, and I said, "Would you sit still for my beginning the movie as I am now, saying, 'There was a young man called Orson Welles, age twenty-four, and I don't know him at all. I know his memories—the ones that have survived—but I really don't know this guy. He may have been the biggest pain in the butt, and I know what the other people who were in this story are going to tell you about him, or I think I do, but I'm going to show you what I think happened. The basic facts.'" So they agree to everything, which is a great problem for me, because I'm having second thoughts. I'm saying to myself, "This is terrible. I cannot, in my old age, live off pieces of my youth."

HJ: What budget are we talking about?

OW: Four million.

HJ: Four million! Wow! You should do it.

OW: My other problem is Ring Lardner. I don't know if I can cope with him as the author. Because I have to have a free hand, including rehearsals and everything else. I like the way the story is constructed, because it's such a clear-cut heroic story. But not the way it's written. As the movie stands now, it has a great fault. Very easy to fix. Ring Lardner's membership in the Communist Party is leaking all over the pages. People are talking about what defying the government means for the revolution of the world, and so on. And I think all that needs saying is that once in our lives, in America, we had a national theater, and that padlocking the doors was the end of it, and the end of the Depression as a subject for the American theater.

HJ: Who's the cast?

OW: Amy Irving, David Steinberg, and Rupert Everett.

HJ: Of course! Amy is married to Spielberg. What's his first name?

OW: *You* need Reagan cards.

HJ: David Spielberg? No.

OW: Steinberg—yes.

HJ: Spielberg, not Steinberg.

OW: Spielberg! . . . It's David Spiel—Steven! It's Steven!

HJ: Amy is playing Virginia Nicholson, whom you were still married to then. And Steinberg as Blitzstein, and Rupert as the young you.

OW: The starting date will be the first week in February, next year. I have no problem with Amy's pregnancy. Because I suddenly remembered that Virginia was pregnant. So if she starts to show, I'll put a line in about it. I could easily fall in love with her. But as you know, I don't believe in directors falling in love with their leading ladies. And I'm glad that I'm at an age when it would be indecent.

HJ: So you don't need any other casting for *The Cradle Will Rock*? You'll shoot at Cinecittà? And do exteriors in New York?

OW: Yes.

HJ: And what about the march?

OW: If I come back to America, I'm going to do only their feet. Because I began thinking of how these extras are going to react, and how one bad face, out of the hundreds, could be—I'm just scared that I cannot control the expressions of so many people. So I thought I'd make a little Eisenstein montage.

HJ: Are you going to be able to get the contract you want?

OW: I'm assured of it, but I haven't gotten it yet. I talked to Fitzgerald and said, "You know, your letter says I have absolute artistic control. But your two other producers are not friendly to me."

HJ: Who?

OW: You know, the asshole from *Animal House*, a real shit.

HJ: John Landis. Well, let me be of some help here. He's a person I can influence.

OW: Kill him.

HJ: No, no, I don't want to. He's a really decent guy. What's he done?

OW: Won't leave me alone. Keeps phoning me and giving me advice on how to make the movie. In a very patronizing way. Everything he says is dumb!

HJ: And who's the other? Not Folsey, George Folsey. His father shot a lot of Minnelli musicals—*Meet Me in St. Louis*. They're not coming to Rome, are they?

OW: Oh, yes, they're coming with their wives. To shop and all that. Unless they're in jail.

HJ: Oh, right, that *Twilight Zone* thing. The Vic Morrow thing, killed by a helicopter blade.

OW: You know that both of them phoned me to give me advice on the script the day they were indicted? On the *day* they were indicted!

HJ: You would think they would have better things to do than to call—

OW: Exactly. Well, anyway, I said to Michael Fitzgerald, "Pretty soon I'm going to have to have a contract, because you're making your deal. And artistic control in a note from you is not the same as a contract. I must have final cut." And he says, "No argument. I've told them." Apparently, when he told Paramount, they said, "This is a collaborative art form." And Michael said, "Not with Orson

Welles. Final cut or nothing." He claims we're set. But there may be a question about *his* authority. I have to have a commitment from everybody. I will not make the movie without it, and I know that I've got them by the balls, because of all the money they've put into it already. But unless it's in the contract, they have tricks.

HJ: I'm telling you, Landis is a good guy.

OW: I already know I'm gonna have Michael on the set from early morning till late at night every day. There was already a moment when he got mad at me. He asked me a useless question, and I said to him, "Why do you ask me that question?" So I got a letter from him saying, "I am not John Houseman. I can ask any question I want."

HJ: If he's turning it all over to you, why does he want to be on the set?

OW: Because he has nothing to do. It's fine, just as long as he doesn't sidle up to me and say, "Wouldn't it be better if you did it this way? Walk that way? Emphasize that a little more? We don't quite feel—" The answer to that always is, "That's very interesting. Yes, I'll have to think about that." Nobody has told him that the real producers, in the old days, never came on the set. Ever. Because on the set, the director is the boss. It would make the producer look like nothing. You went to their office. That was their way of showing they were somebody.

HJ: What's the status of it now?

OW: Ring Lardner is sending me, on Monday, a rewrite of his first twenty pages, based on what I've said. I, in the meantime, have knocked myself out writing the first twenty pages. And I hope my twenty pages crosses his twenty pages in the mail, so mine don't seem to be an answer to his. I cannot get the producer to understand the delicacy of a situation in which I am *not* the coauthor.

HJ: But why can't you be the coauthor?

OW: In a sense, I have to be. Having been witness to these events, and never in my life having made somebody else's script. But I can't get that through to him. And Ring with me would be like . . . you know.

HJ: So you don't want him at all. Well, what does Fitzgerald say when you talk to him about it?

OW: "Anything you want. And Ring will be there with you, and so on." What am I gonna *say* to him?

HJ: You have to persuade the producers that Ring is superfluous, without hurting his feelings.

OW: No way I can do it without hurting his feelings. I shouldn't be put in that situation. I really shouldn't.

HJ: Did you say that to Fitzgerald?

OW: I sat with him the other night, alone, and he just wouldn't listen. All he wanted to do was beg me to have Ring there. As though, just having the screenwriter and the director together, somehow—

HJ: The movie would magically come into being?

OW: Yeah, 'cause that's the way John Huston did it. In *Under the Volcano*, which Fitzgerald also produced. And I said to him, "You must understand that John and I are two different kinds of directors. He has been gainfully employed, without interruption, for all these years. Because if he doesn't get what he wants, he goes ahead with the picture anyway."

HJ: And gets what he wants on the next one.

OW: Yes. But I can't, you know?

HJ: Because there may not be a next one.

OW: The only thing I can say for myself is that I do not have on my record a single clear-cut artistic failure. And that can't be said of many people. This situation is so unfair to me! They didn't ask me who should write the script. Ring is ready to do anything I say, but, really, he ought to be paid off and leave. And they want to start now, you see. They're pushing me: "Where are your pages?" So my alternative is to have three weeks' rehearsal and improvise an awful lot of things. But it's the kind of story that I think is better planned, even if you then depart from the plan.

HJ: Can't you get them to use your twenty pages?

OW: Well, I'll see what he's done. But the first twenty pages have to be my twenty pages, unchanged. I think there's little question that mine are going to be better than his. It *must* be my picture. I cannot allow a piece of my own life to be told by somebody else. I don't even *approve* of using a piece of my life, because of my own peculiar prejudices in that regard. And here I am, being frankly autobiographical, and depending on my memory, which may be unreliable.

HJ: Why are they averse to a cowriting credit?

OW: That's been suggested. That he should come and work with me—in the traditional way of the writer with the director, you see. And I've got a great way to counter that, because I can say, "These things concern my memory of a real event." I mean, Ring Lardner? An ex-Communist, who still has his heart in the party, and a WASP. This film should be filled with Jewish-Italian ambiance. It's New York. Let's have a latinity in it, a little salsa.

HJ: They ought to be giving you a contract, because you're now actually writing without one.

OW: Or any explicit agreement on my part I want the picture made. Because if I can't correct the script and casting, I don't think the picture should be made. I started to say, "Well, to save money we should get rid of Lardner." And they said, "You mustn't think about money." And I said, "You want me to make a picture under four million. I have to think about it. No matter how smart the producers are." "You just be the artist, and direct, and Ring'll write the script." Of course, I have no idea what Ring is gonna say about my pages.

HJ: What if he says, "No, I don't like them?" Now they're confronted with the writer they've hired saying, "Orson's pages are too, uh, subjective. You need an outside—"

OW: Or he'll say, "Orson is trying to make himself look more sympathetic." I'd say, "You're goddamn right I am!"

HJ: You told me a very good thing, which you should emphasize with them, that you'll make yourself unsympathetic in those areas where it will be good theatrically.

OW: My crime, you see, according to this script, is that I was willing to risk these people, who'd been out of work for all this time, put 'em on the street, for the sake of my principles.

HJ: It's economic immorality, an artist's self-absorption.

OW: You know, at the time, everyone involved with the production expressed the automatic knee-jerk reaction of the progressive: "Free speech cannot be stopped," and so on. Marc [Blitzstein], my wife, and myself were biting our fingernails. I was saying, "We're all for moving it but are we being cruel? Nobody's stopping to think that all these people are gonna be out of work." I kept thinking we could save the situation, somehow. I said, "We don't have to make a big drama out of this. Remember, I can go to Harry Hopkins, and we can arrange something, I'm sure. The administration doesn't want this to happen. This is the Justice Department and the Congress. They're out to kill the Federal Theatre, and they're going to do it." But they padlocked the theater. And we decided.

HJ: So padlocking the theater was the last straw. You figured they were going to kill it one way or another anyway, so why not blow the whole thing up by moving the play.

OW: I have to explain, in the script, why Houseman agreed to all of this.

HJ: You mean moving the play to the Venice Theatre and—

OW: Without telling the truth, that he saw this move would make him a Broadway producer. And the hell with everybody. Because that would be really cruel. But I have very interesting proof of his thinking, because some fans have been sending me old programs of my plays. Just recently, I got one for the *Voodoo Macbeth*, in which you can only find Houseman's name on the back page, with the man who turns on the lights. All Houseman did on the original production was take care of the box office.

HJ: You mean he thought that the publicity would make his reputation.

OW: Recently, some producers who wanted me to do something or other, wrote me a letter. They planned to do a handful of plays for Home Box Office. And they said, "One of our plays for the year is the Houseman-Welles *Cradle Will Rock*." And I can't bring myself to answer them. It stops me, every time. Because I want to read them a little lecture. And I can't do that, you know. After we had moved *Cradle* to a commercial theater, we were making a fortune—we financed the Mercury Theatre with that money—you suddenly had on the first page: "Mr. John Houseman."

HJ: So his goal was really what you were accused of, exploiting the situation to forward your career, making you seem like a ruthless person.

Getting back to your contract or lack of contract, it is inevitable that what they will try to do—it's just the nature of the beast—is get you to work as long as possible without signing you. Orson, you're going to have to be a little hard-nosed now.

OW: We're talking. Fitzgerald says, "Well, I want to do what I've done on my other two pictures. Everybody who's important to the picture—sound, and executives, and the art director—will get a piece of the picture proportionate to his effort, and so on." And I said, "That's a beautiful idea. But I make a lot of money doing other things, and I have to give them up to do your picture. And I don't have any money, I don't have any assets at all. And I have an enormous amount of tension, obligations, human beings who depend on me. So I have to ask for my money up front. I'll happily lose the five million dollars that I could have made on the back end." I think he's bought that, agonized his way through it, even though it spoils his beautiful symmetry.

22. "I smell director."

In which Orson complains about the onerous demands made on directors, and helps Henry with his movie *Always*, understanding that his approach requires the illusion of transparency.

———————————

HENRY JAGLOM: I've just come from a three-hour meeting that totally drained me. The worst kind of boring—trailers and ads and teasers and posters. Having to pretend to listen to a lot of people's opinions. That's the thing I hate. Having to try to not get a reputation right off for being an impossible dictator. Even though I'm in the position, fortunately, where I can say no.

ORSON WELLES: In my dealings with Hollywood, I was always in charge of the trailer. I made it myself. In fact, in *Kane*, I wrote the outline of the trailer and shot stuff for it while we were still shooting the movie. Because you see something that you're doing, and you say, "That would be good for the trailer, you know?" Even if it wouldn't work for the film.

Making a picture is always a tremendous strain on a director, who is supposed to be the source of energy. And being the source of energy, he must also be a monument of patience. But I'm so impatient on a set, I always announce at the beginning, so that it's clear, that no assistant director is allowed to ask for silence, or to talk to sound, and sound is not allowed to say anything except, "Rolling," after I say, "Camera." Not another word. So then, after you get through with that, you have to wait for Joe with the hammer, or Jill with the curl—or whatever it is.

Then, after you're done with the shooting, you go into the cutting room. And that's a tremendous nervous strain, too. Editing is the other great pain of being a director, how much of your life is spent in a dark room, not creating, but waiting for someone to do something. Waiting, not for yourself to think of an idea in front of a typewriter or behind a camera, but for other people who do dumb things. And the dumber the thing is, the longer it takes. You advance the film to the place you want, then make the note and hope the cutter understands, and wait till he executes it. Because he has to roll back the film, or he puts it in backwards, or it's upside down, or there's a break in the film, and he has to go and find it.

I hate those great huge rolls of film in stacks of cans. And I have a system, which is, I always make what I call a source, for every scene. Which is another reel that includes every fragment of what I've picked out that *might* be good. Because in a bad take, there may be something I like, so I put all of them on one reel. And before I'm finished with a scene, I always run the source, to be sure I've squeezed everything I can out of it. But I have to run through the whole reel to find that one bit, so it takes forever. I spend all my time handling film. The new editing machine, which I've seen now, is the greatest step forward since I don't know what.

HJ: The flatbed?

OW: It means that three months' work can be done in ten days.

HJ: Why do I fear that something about the creative process will get lost by that expedition? I like to go back and forth, looking over everything again and again.

OW: I don't look over everything again and again. You know that I never wait until after I've looked at the rushes to begin the editing. I cut them as I'm looking at them. But I suffered agonies spending twelve hours a day on the old machines. Why not spend six?

Before, my ratio was, I figure, three days cutting to one day of shooting. Now, at most I would spend a fraction of that on the cutting. What that means is that I no longer have to be the great organist at the console, which drove me nuts. Now I can behave as if I were painting a picture or writing a script or a book. If I want to think, I just stop and think. It liberates you. Frees you from taking months out of your life, just sitting around. Now, I don't wait for the tool. The tool waits for me.

(Zsa Zsa Gabor enters.)

ZSA ZSA GABOR: How are you, darling? How wonderful to see you.

KIKI: Arf! Arf!

ZG: Whose dog is that?

OW: That's my dog, who bites.

ZG: No, no. *(To Kiki)* You bite?

OW: Yes. Especially Hungarians. How are you?

ZG: Fine, darling.

(Zsa Zsa Gabor exits.)

HJ: I see your point. I'd love to speed up my editing process, especially if I gained more time to think.

OW: But of course, it's going to be the end of the director controlling the cutting. Because the cutting will all be done by the time he gets off the set, by the editor. Who will have worked very hard for an hour and a half every day. Then the cutter really will get a credit with a card for himself for great editing. But how will anyone know who edited what? Who made what cut? It's hard enough to know what's directing, what's acting. You really don't know, in any single instance, whether it's the actor or the director. But you never can tell that to a critic.

HJ: I need help with the script of my new movie, which I'm calling *Always*. I'm going to act and direct, and I always have trouble with that. The first day is insane, every time, because I'm sitting there, in the scene, trying not to be there, so I can see what is going on.

OW: You have to be able to press a button and become the director for a certain length of time, and then become the actor. Say, "Fuck all the rest of it; now I'm gonna act."

HJ: Let me tell you the story line, which is based on my real relationship with my ex, Patrice, who's going to act in it. Prior to when the movie starts, she has come back from Santa Fe, where she's been for six months. I've called her up and asked her to come back to the house that was our house—now my house—to sign the divorce agreement. In honor of the occasion, I've decided to cook her dinner. I don't know how to cook, and I do something wrong, which results in her getting food poisoning. Either I pick mushrooms from my garden, stupidly, or I leave the fish out too long, or—

OW: May I stop you right on that point, with food poisoning?

HJ: Sure.

OW: Mushrooms are too dangerous. Mushrooms—that's like life or death. Don't call it "food poisoning." She's told you, over and over again, that she's terribly allergic to something, and you forgot it, and put it in the stew, where it's unrecognizable. It could, in a Freudian way, be interpreted as deliberate.

HJ: So, I surprise her with this lovely dinner that I've made myself. She's pleased, touched. And in the course of our two-person dinner, with elaborate silverware—

OW: Beautiful napery—it's obviously not only more than you'd ever do, but more than you could ever *conceive* of doing. It looks like a page out of "Home" in the *Los Angeles Times*.

HJ: With flowers on the table—everything.

OW: *Comme il faut.*

HJ: She's stunned, and touched and everything. In the course of the dinner, the audience learns a little bit of the background, which is that she left me two years ago, that I was devastated because I thought this marriage would last for the rest of my life. We didn't break up because of fights or arguments or incompatibility, like most people. It had more to do with today's world, where women are told, "It's not enough to be happy, it's not enough to love somebody. You've gotta find out who you are," and all of that. The point is we really love each other, despite her having done this thing. In the course of the dinner the bell rings. It's the notary who has to witness the signing of the divorce papers.

OW: Now, why did you do that? Because that's essentially gross.

HJ: Is it poor taste? I wondered. I can prepare her by saying, during dinner, "Listen. We have to sign in front of a witness who is a notary."

OW: If you say that right away, it's all right. As long as it isn't a surprise. As a surprise, it's gross. You can't really have cooked her this marvelous dinner, and then say, "And now we have the man with the notary stamp."

HJ: This is exactly what I'm asking you for, so this is marvelous. Thank you, Orson. I hope you don't mind doing this.

OW: No, I love it!

HJ: I own an old Wurlitzer jukebox. I put on a Fred Astaire tune from the thirties, and we dance. And it is during the dance that she starts feeling ill. She has to stop. I take her upstairs to bed—my bed, which was our bed—and put her to sleep there. I quietly tiptoe out and into the cutting room, which is a room around the corner in the upstairs of the house. I am a man who makes documentary films on science and science-allied fields for public broadcasting. And I'm working on a film either on time and memory, or on the relationship between men and women. Or on the chemistry of love, that pseudoscience that tries to investigate the emotional condition.

OW: What worries me about everything you've said just now about the three subjects, is they all sound like they might turn into allegories for your story. And that's bad. Bad, bad, bad.

HJ: Perhaps, more than anything else this afternoon, that's what I have to ask you about. Naturally, I admit I am tempted to use—

OW: Don't do it.

HJ: Not allegorically in an intellectual way, but in an emo—

OW: Not in *any* way.

HJ: Too heavy-handed? Too schematic? But stuff about memory, and the past, and time and loss—that's the kind of thing I've been thinking about, and I'm quite obsessed with my childhood, my past, and so on.

OW: I just don't know about the documentary.

HJ: All right, let's leave that open. I forgot to mention one thing. The very opening of the movie you're probably gonna hate. Which is, I sit in a chair, in my living room, speaking into the camera. I say I was completely happy, I was positive that I had the best relationship in the world, and there was nothing that I wanted. Then one day she came home from yoga class. And the camera whirls to the door, and Patrice comes in. This is a flashback. I see that she is worried. "What's wrong?" "Nothing." "What's wrong?" "Nothing." "Something is obviously wrong. You look upset." I keep probing, which is what actually happened in real life. And she says, "I'm thinking that I don't know if we can live together anymore."

Then the camera comes back to me in a chair—present time— and I say, "After that came the most devastating two years of my life. I cried, I experienced the most incredible pain that could be imagined. Eventually I felt better, I got stronger, I went about my life. And tonight she's coming over to sign the divorce agreement. I've gotta cook her dinner." I get up and go into the kitchen, and the doorbell rings. That kind of thing. Basically, to try to cover, in perhaps a minute and a half, the whole two years we were together. And bring it from when she says, "I can't live with you anymore," to now. Any thoughts on that?

OW: I don't like it at all.

HJ: Why?

OW: I smell director. I smell director. It's getting too neat. You're setting yourself up for a terribly tight, well-constructed piece of clockwork. You see how the whole movie could be like that.

HJ: Oh, I would hate the whole movie like that.

OW: So, don't lead us to expect it. Don't set us up for something we're *not* gonna get, and that looks cleverer than its content. The content should be more important than the ingenuity of the director.

HJ: I didn't mean to make the shot too smart. I wanted to take care of the past that way, quickly, in one setup.

OW: Now, I would suggest that the past—I don't think this is too precious—the past should have her coming in with a Chinese dinner in buckets—or you doing that. In other words, so we see how they lived. You know, they're kind of intellectual gypsies. "I went out to the Imperial Palace and got all the stuff you like." So we've seen that the happy past consisted of takeout food. And the dinner and the notarized divorce is, you know, Lubitsch. And I would suggest—only because you asked—that if you do do that dinner, when she is expressing her appreciation and surprise at this effort, that you turn against what you've done, and condemn it as a piece of Lubitsch nonsense. So, in effect, you start arguing with her about her appreciation of what you've done for her.

HJ: That's very good—very, very good.

OW: Sure. You say, "All I lack is, you know, three fiddles and a cimbalom."

HJ: Three fiddle players and a what?

OW: And a cimbalom.

HJ: What's that?

OW: That's the thing that—*(sings a few notes)*. Pronounced ZIM-ba-lom. It's a funny word.

HJ: But what about my jukebox?

OW: You shouldn't say, "I've got the jukebox." She should say, "You've got the jukebox." And she stands there. Not asking you to dance, but with her arms out. So it's the easiest thing to go and take her . . .

HJ: Now, the next day we wake up together in the same bed. I fell asleep next to her, close to her. And she wakes up shocked that I'm there.

OW: Has it been made clear to us that there's gonna be no rising magoo in the bed?

HJ: That there wasn't any what? Oh, sex, you mean? That would be clear.

OW: She sits up, maybe, because she's gotta go to the can. And she says to you, "I know that you fed me"—whatever it is—"papaya," you know? "It's all gone, and it wasn't fun getting rid of it. I've told you at least nine hundred and ninety-nine times that I'm allergic to papaya. I think I should go to the office."

HJ: She's just taken a job in Los Angeles at the Yoga Center which, in fact, is where Patrice now lives. She likes it. She feels it's part of the search.

OW: The search, the terrible search. Wait a minute. I have an idea. You must let me tell it. It has nothing to do with the plot at this point. It's an argument for you to give her, somewhere. This great search is mainly being conducted on the West Coast. And it is because people, pioneers, have been fighting their way to get here for one hundred and fifty years. Finally they're here, and there's nothing here.

23. "I've felt that cold deathly wind from the tomb."

In which Orson refuses to embrace Henry because he is afraid of catching AIDS. *Lear* is going forward, but he thinks the political situation in France is unstable. He fears *Wind* is dated. *Cradle* is stalled.

HENRY JAGLOM: You look troubled? What? No hug?

ORSON WELLES: If we could figure out a way to hug without kissing, that would be fine.

HJ: Why no kissing?

OW: You know, we could have AIDS.

HJ: Well, neither of us, as far as I know, has AIDS. Is there something I should know about you, Orson?

OW: They don't know how it's transmitted, and saliva is one of the responsible parties.

HJ: We don't drool on each other when we kiss.

OW: I'm not kissing anybody. I'm not even sure about shaking hands. But I can hug you in such a way that we each face in opposite directions.

HJ: Orson, what is this, a comedy routine?

OW: I'm deadly serious. I haven't gone through my life to be felled by some gay plague. We might be carriers. You never know.

HJ: Oh, my God. Oh, my God. If people are going to start doing that . . .

OW: I might be a carrier. For every thousand guys with AIDS, five thousand are carriers who will never have it.

HJ: Yes, but those are people who have homosexual relationships, the carriers.

OW: There are 6 percent of the people that have it for which there is no explanation.

HJ: I'm going to pee.

OW: Then what are you going to do?

HJ: Zip up, wash my hands, and come back.

OW: That's not good enough. Are you going to touch the knobs?

HJ: Orson, you're becoming a fanatic.

OW: Yes, a fanatic to save my life. Did you touch Kiki?

HJ: Yes, I petted her.

OW: I don't know if dogs can catch it.

HJ: If dogs could get it, they'd be dying. All gay guys have dogs.

Waiter: *Qu'est-ce que vous aimez manger?*

OW: *Rien.* I'm not too well. I don't think I'm going to eat.

W: Do you want a little turnip soup? Very nice.

OW: I don't like soup.

W: OK, then. Maybe a salad or something mild?

OW: Never salad in a restaurant . . . *(To HJ)* I'm determined never again to eat a salad in a restaurant. Because I've watched them in the kitchen, and I've been told that's how you get hepatitis. It's the dirty-fingers disease. The first courses are only salads. There must be something else they could come up with for a first course. God-damn nouvelle cuisine; they only think in terms of salad. They make salad out of every goddamn thing in the world—salad of roast beef. What salad generation do you belong to?

HJ: What?

OW: This emphasis on greenery, and all that. The 'sixties. The Great Health Movement. Oh, I'm sure it's done everybody good. And it's probably good that people don't drink the way they used to. Everybody was drunk when I was young. It wasn't fun. It was boring. You just got used to dealing with your drunken friends.

HJ: I came from a generation where everybody was high all the time.

OW: Equally boring. Although I think that more middle-class Americans and fewer show-business people are stuffing it up their nose these days.

HJ: What's that painting on the wall?

W: A David Hockney.

OW: Patrick asked me to do a drawing as well, and I'm ashamed that I didn't do it. I have a bad hand. For the last three months, I can hardly sign my name. I have this pinched nerve. I got it in Paris, for no reason at all. Agonizing pain. I'm crippled—these two fingers are almost dead. Oh, boy, I'm scared.

HJ: Chiropractors are good for that.

OW: Or acupuncture. I got into the hands of a fake acupuncture man in Paris who came with incense. And he said, "What house are you?" And I said, "What house?" And he said, "Astrologically." I was, already, "Goodbye." And he wasn't even Chinese or anything. On the other hand, I also think that there are many areas in medicine where the proper quack is the right fellow to go to. But I have a foolish prejudice against anybody who isn't a doctor, because my father believed in everyone who wasn't a doctor. He lived his life by his horoscope, which was done for him by very expensive people. He believed in everything—

HJ: But science.

OW: But God, you know? It's often the people who are not religious who are the most superstitious. There are more clairvoyants in Paris than in any city in the world, four clairvoyants to one doctor, even though the French don't believe in God. It's the old Chesterton remark, "If you don't believe in God, you'll believe in anything." It's true. Because if you don't believe in God, you will substitute every mystery that is outside of yourself, however nonsensical it may be. And, of course, astrology is so maddening, because it was all laid down at a time when the planets were in another position. An Aries is now actually a Pisces, and so on. I'm old enough to remember when everybody had their palms read, the way they now have their charts done. And in palmistry as practiced in the West for the last two hundred years, every line is different from the old palmistry of the Hindus. The lifeline was here, the love line there, but it's still supposed to work. The place with the greatest number of believers in this sort of thing is the Soviet Union, supposedly ruled by dialectical materialism. The hunger to believe has not been filled by Lenin, mummified in the Kremlin. The time may come when we'll be able to live without mystery, but then we'll have to question whether we'll still be capable of poetry. It's pretty hard to imagine—a world or an art without any kind of deception.

HJ: There was that rock that you brought on *Carson*.

OW: I went to a shop that sold exotic minerals. I got one of those funny-looking stones. And I came on *Carson* and I said, "There are only seven of these in the world. And I have permission, just for tonight, to show it on television, because these stones are being studied at leading universities. The writing on the spine of this stone is extraterrestrial, and we have no idea how either got there. But if you have a watch or a clock which doesn't work anywhere in your house, or on your person, this stone will make it go." At that moment, when I held up the stone, the clock in the studio at NBC, which had gone on the blink, started to tick.

HJ: Love it! . . . Bogdanovich called. He told me—

OW: Wait a minute! I'll tell you what he talked about. He talked about Bogdanovich!

HJ: He said, "I'm having a problem." He was using Springsteen for the picture he's finishing, *Mask*. "The studio made me take all my music off . . ."

OW: Yeah, I read about that.

HJ: So he's suing the studio for a couple of million dollars.

OW: It's a great thing to do after you've been out of work.

HJ: So I said, "Peter, do you really think this is a good idea?" He said, "Well, I've done it." Apparently the boy that the movie is about loves Springsteen. So he sent a letter to Frank Price at Universal, where the film is set up, demanding that he not interfere with his creative rights, that filmmakers have the right to put any music they want in their movie, and he would like you to—

OW: Fat chance.

HJ: To sign it!

OW: No.

HJ: I have to find a graceful way to decline for you.

OW: No. Ask him to call me and I'll tell him. You know, if we were in France, he'd have the law on his side. According to French law—

HJ: He'd own the movie.

OW: Here a movie is the property of the people who are hiring you. And you cannot invoke a right which doesn't exist.

HJ: They gave him final cut, so they promised him a certain kind of—

OW: A promise! Where is a letter like that gonna get you, you know? Everybody'll say he's a pain in the neck. Who'll want to work with Bogdanovich?

HJ: He can't win this. The movie's out. There're hundreds of prints going around.

OW: And good notices. First good notices he's had in years.

HJ: The movie relates to the book Peter wrote about Dorothy Stratten. You know, the Playmate he met at Hef's. Who was murdered by her husband. Peter is very emotionally involved with this material.

OW: I read that book.

HJ: I think it's called *The Killing of the Unicorn*, or something like that.

OW: For a man to betray himself that way, in front of the world, is really disturbing. She was a semihooker, you know.

HJ: Which is not Peter's thing at all.

OW: And he implicates himself as a stooge of Hefner.

HJ: He says he owes it to Dorothy.

OW: Oh, no. After I finished the book, I don't believe he was in love with her. He was in love with himself being in love with her.

HJ: You're being too hard on him. I think it's part and parcel of the *Kane* thing, the great man thing, which has been fed to him by *you*. It's all your fault.

OW: A little bit, yeah.

HJ: And it's not just him. Von Sternberg with Marlene, Hitchcock with Grace Kelly, Woody Allen with Diane Keaton, Fellini with Giulietta Masina, Bergman with Liv Ullmann. People think that part of their job now, to be a great artist, is to find one of these young ingénues and mold them. It has entered his subconscious. Because he did the exact same thing with Cybill [Shepherd]. And now he—

OW: He's never gonna get over Cybill.

HJ: Dorothy was the great romance of his life. She was a nineteen-year-old who had a brutal husband, and for the first time she was being treated nicely—by Peter.

OW: It's all so Ernest Dowson—the last of the romantic poets—who spent his life mooning around because he was hopelessly in love with a girl who served him beer in a pub. "I have been faithful to thee, Cynara! in my fashion." You know? "I called for madder music and for stronger wine, /But when the feast is finished and the lamps expire, /Then falls thy shadow, Cynara! the night is thine." And this is all about Adelaide the barmaid. Who was bored to death with it, you know? It always has to be with an unworthy object. That's a necessary part of all this. It's never with some marvelous girl who's clearly worth it. It's always somebody that you just happened on. He's gonna spend his life on this.

HJ: *Mask* is about a boy born with a deformed face. He apparently picked this subject because the first play he took Dorothy to see was *The Elephant Man*. She identified with it, because her great beauty was similar to the grotesque ugliness of the Elephant Man. In that the extremeness of each of them—extreme beauty and extreme ugliness—separated them from the common folk of the world.

OW: Shit!

HJ: This is his movie for Dorothy. It's the myth of how horrible it is to be beautiful. But despite it all, I'm very fond of Peter. He's uniquely gifted. And he's as much a victim as everyone else.

OW: But he mustn't go writing manifestos. He certainly isn't doing himself any good.

HJ: Then why is he? Why?

OW: Well, I think the chief reason for most self-destruction is the death wish, which almost everybody has, to one degree or another. And people who are actively creative, or actively and fruitfully in love, or involved in the living world, escape it. But it's always there. And people who assume attitudes of a romantic nature, that have to do with ego, are particularly prone, I think, to the death wish. Like Narcissus who drowned in his own image. The ultimate act, in some way, of self-love. I can choose the time and manner of my death. Romantic suicide. The world will be sorry it didn't treat me better. I think it's very common.

HJ: Are you conscious of it in yourself?

OW: Oh, yes. Two or three times I've thought I had a fatal disease. And I've thought of it with a certain relief. In other words, no more obligation to take care of people. I've felt that cold deathly wind from the tomb blowing over me. It's the real voice of the devil, you know? It's why people invent the red guy with the horns. It's the death wish, the opposite of life. It's surrender. Which is, I think, a very egotistical thing to do. I turned that voice off quickly, when I heard it and felt that.

HJ: Did you happen to see this six-part thing on Freud on the Arts and Entertainment Channel? Wonderful, wonderful program. And a very well-written script by the son of Rex Harrison and Lilli Palmer.

OW: Lilli Palmer is very good in *The Other Side of the Wind*. She plays Marlene. But don't let's go into that this lunch.

HJ: Well, can we just mention one thing about that? *California* magazine wants to know if you'll tell the story of what happened with *The Other Side of the Wind*. I thought that to have all of that out might help the situation in France.

OW: The opposite. It's just *because* of France that I wouldn't do it. I cannot tell the truth without attacking the French judicial system. But I am in no position right now to get the French angry at me.

HJ: But can't you give an account leading up to how it got into the vault in Paris? Pending arbitration with the Shah's brother-in-law, who is claiming he owns it, the French refusing to release it to you, all that.

OW: No, I can't. If *Lear* is off for any terrible reason, I'll do it instantly. You know, it's just a scandal . . .

HJ: I thought that you had won the rights to *The Other Side of the Wind*.

OW: Yes, I did.

HJ: But then I heard just this week that there was somebody new assigned—

OW: Yes, a new arbitrator. And it has to be all done all over again.

HJ: If you got it away from the Iranians and the French, could you finish it? The cast is dying off.

OW: Yes. Edmond O'Brien just died. Tony Selwart is blind. John Huston can't move. I don't want to think about it now. The film has become strangely dated. But in an interesting way. I'd have to turn it into an essay film on that period. Because that's when all the young movie people wanted to be *auteurs*. And not to be Spielberg, as they do now. It was a different time.

HJ: Speaking of France, Gilles Jacob, who's now the head of the Cannes Film Festival, wants to stop by and say hello to you.

OW: Sucking up to the Cannes Film Festival people, eh?

HJ: I don't have to suck up to him. They love me. Now I just want you to be nice, Orson.

OW: He's a member of the "criminal class." Anybody connected with the Cannes festival is a crook.

HJ: Please, Orson, don't be ridiculous.

OW: Don't worry, I'll be gentle. You have no idea. I'm a hypocrite. A sellout.

HJ: Michael York asked, did I convey to you what he said about his indefinite availability. Especially for *Lear*.

OW: I like him very much.

HJ: Oh, he's a fine actor. And a truly modest actor. You can do with him, more or less, what you want.

OW: English actors are more modest than Americans, because they've never had Lee Strasberg to teach 'em that they know better than the director. I'm always making fun of Method, but I used a lot of that Stanislavski stuff in my work with actors, making Iago impotent, for instance, and giving that to Mac Liammóir to "use" in *Othello*. Othello is destroyed easily because he has never understood women—like Lear. Shakespeare was clearly tremendously feminine. Every man who is any kind of artist has a great deal of female in him. I act and give of myself as a man, but I register and receive with the soul of a woman. The only really good artists are feminine. I can't admit the *existence* of an artist whose dominant personality is masculine.

HJ: So what is the status of *Lear*?

OW: They are passionately anxious to make it. But after having promised me that *I* would be the producer, I have been given, with no choice in the matter, a French producer they want, a successful and intelligent man who I dislike intensely. Very cold. The only thing in his favor is that he's producing a lot of different things— he'll be awfully busy. What I don't have yet is a contract, and that's what I have to have. I'm not just demanding that I have artistic say-so, but also that I have production say-so—if I stay within the budget. I don't want somebody telling me, as he already has, that this or that costs a lot of money. They are shocked by the fact that I want to know everything about the production. They want me to be the artist and not concern myself with all of that. Well, the first thing they did with me as the artist not concerned with all of that was to take me to an enormous studio outside of Paris and say, "This is your studio." It's the biggest studio in Europe. It was filled with a set. I said, "When is the set gonna be out?" They said, "Well, maybe in August, but we don't know." So I said, "Well, I can't make the picture in one studio. I must have two studios, because while we're shooting one scene, they have to build what's gonna be the set for the next scene." Obviously, two studios. They'd never thought of that. That's the kind of leave-it-to-us mentality.

HJ: Just like Michael Fitzgerald. Is there anything to be done about that situation, in terms of—

OW: Not with him in the Bahamas. I don't dare deal with *Cradle* without Michael. I don't want to seem to be speaking for him. But he's not gonna be trying very hard in the Bahamas.

HJ: Do you get any feel from him about where he is on *Cradle*? Is it—?

OW: He claims he's got it all together, which isn't true. He's got it all together if we're willing to shoot in Berlin, because Berlin is offering a million dollars. But it's ridiculous to shoot this picture in Berlin. I'm not gonna do it, until I've done at least one other picture. Nothing can convince me otherwise.

HJ: Is there a reason?

OW: I've told you, and you don't agree. And that's the end of it. I don't think the first thing I should do after being absent from the business for ten years should involve mining my own past. There's an inherent weakness in this as a comeback movie. Politically it's wrong.

HJ: Because it looks like, instead of plunging forward—

OW: That's right. I'm going backwards. My feeling about *Cradle* is that I'd like to do it. But I would be perfectly happy to sell the script.

HJ: It's such a brilliant script, now that you've reworked it. I'd hate to see anyone else directing it.

OW: I wish you'd be more complimentary. The truth is I haven't got anything unique to offer it as a director. I've done it as a script.

HJ: So you feel good about *Lear*? I mean, it looks good?

OW: I don't dare say. But I fear they'll never come through. They all want to have dinner with me, but when it comes time to fork over the money, they disappear. It's always the same thing—I'm unmanageable, I walk away from films before they're finished, et cetera, et cetera, et cetera. So boring. I don't want to hear about it. More disappointment. Lang, who last year was receiving people in his office in an open-necked shirt, is now dressed by [Pierre] Cardin. Has bought an apartment on Place des Vosges, which costs about a million and a half. The *Socialist* Minister of Culture! On the other hand, he's talked about *Lear* again to Mitterand, so from that point of view, it looks good. There's nobody fighting it. It's just me trying to make sense of the deal. I don't want to sign a deal in which I discover that there's any possibility of disaster, of miscalculations which put it over budget, or anything. That's why I've been difficult, because I want to know the ground I'm gonna walk on.

HJ: Have you made it clear to them that that's the reason you've been difficult?

OW: Yes. But they don't listen very much. They listen to themselves. I hope I have a contract with the *Lear* people in the next week or two. If it doesn't go first, it'll never happen. But I think the French situation is very delicate. If the people who are now in the government and television change . . . There's a real fascist element rising in France. And because this is a socialist government—and of course, it's nonsense to call him a socialist—all the centrist conservatives are afraid, as they always are, that it is the weak wall through which communism will break. The French always put the blame on their president for everything that could possibly be wrong. So they may join them, even though the Communist Party has become a joke.

HJ: *(Calls out)* Excuse me—Hello!

OW: He's not our waiter.

HJ: Oh.

WAITER: Here is your kiwi.

OW: My God, that's beautiful. It's not as beautiful as a plain peeled one, but it's beautiful. Thank you. I made a discovery about the kiwi.

HJ: Which is?

OW: That it's the greatest fruit in the universe, but it's ruined by all the French chefs of the world who cut it up into thin slices. You cannot tell what it tastes like unless you eat it in bulk. Then it is marvelous. And it has the highest vitamin content of any fruit in the world.

HJ: You look much better than when you went to France. I mean, you're looking particularly well, and healthy and fit.

OW: What's that?

HJ: That's my mint carrier. As others might have cigarettes or toothpicks, I carry mints for my coffee. It's a little eccentricity, I suppose.

OW: If Ronnie can have his jelly beans . . . God, I'm worried. I hope that his checkup turns out all right, because I'm more worried about [George H. W.] Bush than I am about Reagan! I want Reagan to live! Bush is a creep, a real creep. Especially compared to Gorbachev. Bush thinks if he doesn't ignore Gorbachev he'll lose the Jesse Helms group, so he has to kowtow. What's amazing is that not one American Kremlinologist . . . Krem . . . Krem-lin-ologist . . . had a word to say about Gorbachev. He popped out of a box.

HJ: The great thing that Reagan has is a sense of personal security about himself. God knows based upon what.

OW: But he has it, and it's absolutely genuine. He comes bouncing into the room. You know Tom Wicker's line "My favorite thing about Reagan is that he's a genuine phony." And that's what he is. But he has this security, which we haven't seen in a president in a long time. Even Eisenhower was stuttering around, not sure what it was to be a politician, you know?

HJ: People have always liked him. He knows he's a nice guy.

OW: Yeah. He made one funny joke not long ago. In the cabinet room he says, "We ought to have a plaque saying, 'Ronald Reagan slept here.'" He can make any kind of mistake. He could promise anything and have it fall apart, and the public goes right on adoring him. Anybody who could get out of that retreat from Lebanon, with two hundred eighty Americans killed for nothing, without a scratch on his popularity or anything, is amazing.

24. "Jo Cotten kicked Hedda Hopper in the ass."

In which Orson recalls his affair with Lena Horne, who was black, gifted, and radical. Hopper warned him against it. When the owner of the 21 Club told him Horne was unwelcome, he played a nasty joke on him.

Orson Welles: I have to go to a social event that I . . . dread.

Henry Jaglom: What is that?

OW: A surprise party for Jo Cotten's eightieth birthday. It's in Santa Monica, at seven thirty. Black tie. Jo has had a stroke, you know. The last time I talked to him was about four days ago, and I said, "Well, what are you reading?" He said, "I can't read. I can follow conversation; I can talk; but I cannot read." Now, that's awful. I thought you could still read after a stroke.

HJ: Depends what kind of a stroke.

OW: Every kind of a stroke.

HJ: Why can't he read? It must be—

OW: I don't know. Somehow the process of turning letters into words is blocked. You have to help him with words. And he has to have therapy four times a week to keep that up. But he has something in Pat, a very devoted, attentive wife. He's always been very lucky. He had one other wife, who died, who worshipped him for twenty-five years. He's been coddled all his life.

This evening just hangs over me now. With his stroke, and with all the people who are going to be there that I don't know, I don't really want to— All those socialites from Palm Springs and Santa Barbara. And they all hate me, because I'm the oldest friend. What I'm really gonna be doing is entertaining them. It'll be just ghastly. If I could just go and visit him on another day. But how could his best friend not be there? The feeling is not how nice that I come, but how could I *not* come.

HJ: Did you see that made-for-TV movie *Malice in Wonderland*, where Elizabeth Taylor plays Louella Parsons and Jane Alexander plays Hedda Hopper? There are two characters named Orson Welles and Joseph Cotten.

OW: You know, they sent the script to me and Jo, and they said, "What do you think of it? Do you like it?" And he said, "No." So then they called me and said, "Do you approve of this?" I hadn't read it, so I just said, "No."

HJ: There's this scene where the Cotten character gets furious, because Hedda said something about his wife.

OW: Well, no. What Hedda was doing was printing that he was balling Deanna Durbin, which he was. In cars, in daylight, where everybody could see!

HJ: There's also this wonderful, strange scene where Cotten pushes Hedda's face in a plate of food.

OW: No, he kicked Hedda Hopper in the ass. The truth is that Jo Cotten was a Southern gentleman, with extremely good manners. That's what makes this story so good. He came up to her at a party and said, "Hedda, I just want you to understand, if you say that again, I'm going to kick you in the ass." She didn't believe it. She kept talking about it, and he just came and kicked her in the ass. The last man in Hollywood that you'd think would behave that way to a woman.

HJ: They made you the more reasonable one. Which is also not your reputation.

OW: That's true. I did say, "You mustn't kick Hedda in the ass." I told him I would kick her in the ass instead. But he insisted.

HJ: And in another scene, Hedda walks in on you when you're about to screen *Kane*, and you say, "What are you doing here?" And she was the one, according to this, who tipped off Hearst. She's portrayed as this insane woman running roughshod over the whole town, terrifying everybody.

OW: She was. And she destroyed Louella. Hedda had always been my defender, because I'd hired her as an actress when she was out of work. She always said, "I know you're a dirty Commie Red. But you were good to me and good to my son, and I won't—" Then she added, "But you've got to stop fucking Lena Horne." And I said, "I don't take instruction about things like that." And she said, "You *have* to, if you care about your career, and care about your country!" Nobody who knew about it gave a damn that Lena was black. Except Hedda, you know. But what was she gonna do? Write it in a column? I didn't give a damn. So I said, "Hedda, you can go boil your head." She always laughed when I insulted her. That's show business.

HJ: She was that reactionary, that she really believed these things?

OW: Violently, much more than Louella. She was wittier. She was smarter. You know what Jack Barrymore called Louella Parsons, who was terribly ugly. He said, "Louella—that queer udder."

HJ: "Queer udder." What a horrible description!

OW: This great truck used to come up to your house, just before Christmas with gifts from her. And you must never have given the news of your divorce to anybody but Louella. She would never forgive you. She always had to have the divorce. That was hers. You don't know the *power* those two cows had in this town! People opened the paper, ignoring Hitler and everything else, and turned right to Louella and Hedda.

HJ: How did she know about things like you and Lena?

OW: She offered fifty dollars for information and people called her up. Not friends, but waiters or valet-parking people, anybody. Somebody reported that I went into Lena's house or something. She and I never went out. In those days, you didn't go out with a black woman. You could, they wouldn't stop you, but things were delicate. And I didn't want to hurt her feelings. I once took her out to the 21 Club, thinking it was safe. Jack Kreindler, who looked just like a baked potato, and owned it then with his cousin, behaved correctly. But he took me aside afterwards and said, "Next time, it would be better not to come here." So when I got back to Hollywood, I told Charlie Lederer what had happened, and said, "What are we going to do about it?" Well, Jack Kreindler used to come to Hollywood on a holiday, and everybody would entertain him. So Charlie and I stopped what we were doing for two weeks and worked night and day on this prank. I gave a party in the private room of Chasen's, honoring the "Maharani of Boroda," and invited Jack. Now, we got the Maharani from Chicago. She was a hooker. I said she couldn't be local; it would have gotten around. She couldn't even know who the people she'd be meeting were. Everybody you ever heard of was at that table. It was very grand, so that Jack would be at ease, and not get suspicious. I sat him next to the Maharani. And she began giving him a little knee thing. And then the hand on the knee, and all that. And finally she says to him, "You know, I'm here without my husband—he's coming later. But we have a special religion, and it forbids us to stay in a hotel. So we have to buy a private house wherever we go. I'm going to slip you the address. You come there at two o'clock in the morning. Scratch on the window." So he took this piece of paper. Now, for the previous ten days, we had been searching for a house down on Central Avenue. And we found a big black mammy, like Aunt Jemima, a Hattie McDaniel type, you know? Coal-black, and this big. And we had been sending her obscene letters. Calling obscene things through the window. Generally annoying this poor black woman. By the time dessert was served, the Maharani got up and said she had to leave. And she was taken by a limousine to a plane.

HJ: She was taken by a limousine to a plane from Chasen's?

OW: To an airport, so she'd be out of town and couldn't talk. Now, at two o'clock in the morning you've got Jack Kreindler, man about town, all-around American, scratching on the window of this woman's house. Ten cops rush up and grab him, because she's been complaining. They take him downtown to the station house, where they take photographs. Which were never printed, but he thought they would be, so he went through all that. Of course, his high friends got him out, and kept him out of the newspapers. He never knew who did it to him. I think it's the best practical joke I've ever played.

HJ: This is really true? How did you know, for sure, he would show up? The whole thing wouldn't have worked if he hadn't shown up.

OW: He had to. She was the greatest hooker you ever saw. You would have shown up, too. *Anybody* would have shown up. We were very sad that she had to leave. And she was very funny. She knew exactly what she had to do—she'd been pretty well educated. It was a lot of work. Very expensive, too—the dinner, everything. But we thought Jack had it coming to him. I never told Lena. I never wanted her to think that anything had ever happened. She's half-Indian, you know, red Indian. If you were black, nobody was ever luckier.

HJ: For being able to hide the fact that she was black?

OW: That was never hidden. She was black from the minute she stepped on the stage. I told you what Duke Ellington said about her to me when he introduced us. He said, "This is a girl that gives a deep suntan to the first ten rows of the theater!"

HJ: She struck me as tremendously repressed.

OW: Well, no more than any other black, except that she's the one that received storms of applause for forty years. Come on. I'll accept that any black had a rough time, but she didn't, not particularly. Nobody urged her to pass for white. She was a famous black singer her whole career, and nothing else, no matter what she says now. And her marriage, a mixed marriage, was the first famous mixed marriage. Everybody wrote about it as such.

HJ: But she said that they put makeup on her to look darker in the movies. Because they didn't want her to look white.

OW: She's leaving out the truth. The movies that they made her look darker in—those were the black movies, the race movies. You know, made only for black audiences. I was on the set, waiting to take her out to lunch, when she was doing *Cabin in the Sky*. And she was made up like she would be with her own skin color. But when she was fifteen, and sixteen and seventeen, she made a lot of those race quickies.

HJ: It's amazing, those two women, Hedda and Louella, could get that strong.

OW: And in New York, [Walter] Winchell. Winchell was terrible, but I was very fond of him, because he had great charm. And he was such an egomaniac that it was funny to be with him. As you know, after the *Kane* thing, my name was never, ever printed in a Hearst paper. The Hearst paper in New York was the *Daily Mirror*, and Winchell was forbidden to write my name. So he called me G. O. Welles, George Orson Welles, and nobody ever noticed it. He deliberately put me in almost every day, just for the fun of it. That was his idea of being cute.

HJ: "George" being your actual first name.

OW: Of course. And he was such a prominent character in the Broadway of that time that not to be friends with him was to miss a whole side of that life. And you know, it was better to be his friend than his enemy. I had a big enemy among those guys, Lee Mortimer, a sort of second-rate Winchell, who used to print awful things about me every day. And I always greeted him effusively so that he would think that I'd never read a word he wrote.

25. "You either admire my work or not."

In which Orson encounters Mrs. Vincente Minnelli. He tells stories about John Barrymore, and gets a nibble on *The Dreamers*, but his prospects for financing any of his projects are growing steadily dimmer.

HENRY JAGLOM: I am just reading this book on RKO which you are prominently featured in. It's the one that Jesse Lasky's daughter wrote, *The Biggest Little Major of Them All*.

ORSON WELLES: I've heard about it.

HJ: There's a picture on the back of you and your lady of the time, and Schaefer, I guess who was head of RKO when you made *Kane*.

OW: Dolores del Rio.

HJ: Dolores—at the premiere of *Kane*.

OW: That was actually in Chicago, the one with Schaefer. The real opening was in New York. That was in the days when the crowd were still screaming, "Here comes Norma Shearer!" The days when there was that kind of opening. Jack Barrymore made the famous joke. A radio reporter announced, "And here come Mr. John Barrymore, and Orson Welles, who made this picture! What have you got to say, Mr. Barrymore?" And he said, "Now it can be revealed. Orson is, in fact, the bastard son of Ethel [Barrymore] and the Pope!" On the air, across the nation. Cold sober. Just sheer mischief.

You know, Jack was quite mad. His father died at forty-five, in an insane asylum. Jack would get drunk in order to be the drunk Barrymore, instead of the insane Barrymore. He would suddenly realize at the table that he didn't know where he was or how he got there. A tragic situation.

One day I got a call: "Jack is in Chicago, dying. Get on a train and go there." So I got on a train, went to Chicago. Went to the Ambassador East, where Jack was staying, but he wasn't there. But Ethel was there and Lionel was there. Ethel and Lionel and I went around Chicago looking for Jack. We finally located him in a whorehouse on the South Side. He wasn't dying, but God knows, we could see he was going to. And then all of us were stuck in his hotel for the weekend. I just sat there and listened to them talk, because they hadn't been together, the three of them, in forty years. Or very seldom. They began reminiscing about their childhoods, and so on, these three extraordinary people with their gargoyle laugh, like creatures on the front of a cathedral. It was unbelievable.

Did I ever tell you the story of the love affair between Jack and Katharine Hepburn? Now I've checked this story with both Jack and Katie, and it's true. Her first picture, *A Bill of Divorcement*. He was still a top-of-the-bill star. He hadn't yet descended to, you know, "Swing and Sway with Sammy Kaye." After a day's shooting, he said, in that Barrymore voice, "Miss Hepburn, would you like to come to my dressing room for lunch?" She said, "Well, I, I, I . . ." So she did. She arrived at the door and is met by Jack in a dressing gown. He opens the door, and she comes in and she looks around, and there's a couch, and nothing else. And she says, "Well, I, I think, you know . . . there must be a mistake." Jack, all very proper, said, "Oh, yes, I made a mistake." He went to the door, opened it, bowed, and she went out. That's the whole affair!

HJ: A real gentleman.

OW: Not gonna fumble around. He went on making those terrible movies, in order to pay his creditors. If he'd gone into bankruptcy, he wouldn't have had to make them. I saw *Grand Hotel* again the other day. They had it on the cable. It was almost the last picture he made, where he was still highly considered, was still "John Barrymore." You know what Garbo did the first day of shooting? When he came to work in the morning, she was waiting outside the stage. To say good morning to him, to escort him to the set. It is the only nice thing I know about her.

(*Lee Minnelli enters.*)

LEE MINNELLI: Orson, you're one of my favorite people in the whole world. Such a beautiful voice.

OW: Aren't you nice? Here's Mr. Jaglom . . .

HJ: How do you do. Please sit down.

LM: You know Vincente is home now.

OW: Yes, I'm so glad he's out of the hospital. Well, send him my very best wishes.

LM: The doctor said in a few weeks, he could have some friends visiting . . . If you were free?

OW: Oh, I'd be delighted . . . if I'm still in the country. We're leaving in a couple weeks . . .

LM: May I give you our address and number?

OW: Would you please? Yes. Absolutely.

LM: Because it would mean so much to him. It would be good if he could see his friends. I don't want him to think he's forgotten.

OW: Of course not.

LM: It's a right turn at the Beverly Hills Hotel.

OW: Yes.

LM: But please call me. I would be flattered. We have tea about four thirty. When will I call you?

OW: Well, I can give you my number. If that doesn't answer, I have left for Italy. Lovely to see you.

LM: Well, thank you very much. It would mean a lot to Vincente.

OW: All my best.

LM: Goodbye.

(Lee Minnelli exits.)

OW: The difficulty with this sitcom is that I've never met Vincente. Never once. Even in the golden days, even at a party, I have never met him. Maybe we may have met back in the—but no, I remember very well the people I have never met before.

By the way, some people have appeared saying that they love *The Dreamers*. First time I've ever heard that from anybody aside from you and me. Two girls and two guys. The gentlemen are 100 percent. The American girl is 100 percent, but the French girl is a bitch.

HJ: I know. I know. I don't know if it's worth it even if they come up with the money. She's the one who was looking at Oja and said, "Yes, but can she be cold?" I replied, "I didn't know *you* were casting this. Are you questioning that Orson Welles can get the performance he wants out of this person? Are you assuming the right to tell him who's right for—" I was furious at that.

OW: Now that having been settled, my dear Henry, back they came and said, "We're worried about the other parts." And I said, "We really have our choice of the best English actors of that age group, but only if they're free at the time we shoot." I'm in no position now to give those people contracts and deliver them in a package.

HJ: I told them Rupert Everett . . . Jeremy Irons . . . Michael York . . .

OW: They said, "We would like an option." And I said, "My dear friends, you pay for an option. An option means you have exclusive rights to something. Nobody in the world gets an option without any recompense." I added, "What I could do for you, if I decided it was the right thing to do—*if*—would be to write a letter of intent. I'll only do that when you give me the feeling that you're close to the money. And you are not giving me the feeling that you are close to the money, only that you would like to get close to the money. In which case, a letter of intent ties my hands.

HJ: Because you don't know that next week somebody is not going to—

OW: Drop out of the sky. Now, in fact, another group loving *The Dreamers* has shown up. And one of them is a horse's ass who lives in Hollywood.

HJ: Which horse's ass?

OW: How to distinguish? If they turn around and show their heads, I can tell better! But well meaning. And the other is an investment consultant, who has intimate contact with big money, but does not pretend to have it himself. But believes that he can raise it in short order. And they sat here and this is what the conversation was like: The horse's ass said, "I hear all these different stories." I said, "Do you expect me to sit at this table and prove to you that I'm . . . you know . . .

HJ: Stable?

OW: I said, "The biggest madman in the world could be very convincing. You either admire my work or not." And after an hour and a half, it emerged, he doesn't believe he can raise the money, pretty much because the rich guys won't like *The Dreamers*. Then the horse's ass said, "You must do *Lear*; that's the thing," so on and so on. "And have you anything else?" And I said, "Are we in a souk? I'm going to put out all my things on a rug and then you'll decide what you want to buy?"

26. "I'm in *terrible* financial trouble."

In which Orson vainly pitches a project, complains about friends who disparage him, reviews several books about his life, and bemoans the fact that he can't make a living while his bête noire Houseman, thrives.

———————

(Susan Smith, from HBO, joins them.)

ORSON WELLES: I've been working on a book, and I've only got it in outline form, with some scenes blocked in. And as I was getting excited about it, my friend Henry here told me about you and your interest in miniseries. I have two ways I can go with what I have. One is to do it as a novel, and then sell it, and let the network development system do its thing—

SUSAN SMITH: You mean, do an injustice to the mat—

OW: Without me having anything to do with it. Because I could not stand to work under that committee system. I'd just take the money and run. But when I heard about you, I thought even though it might be economically suicidal for me, maybe I should do it directly for HBO.

SS: Tell me what you have in mind.

OW: In one sentence, it's a miniseries set in Majorca or San Tropez, where the richest people in the world go. Or better, a dictatorship in a Central American country that is overthrown by a coup d'état, and there is a revolution. Much of it offstage, but some of it is in the story as a background for all the things that happen to people in a kind of Acapulco-type place. There are two cities on the island. One is the port, and the other is the resort. The resort is on the Atlantic side, and the story is basically the life of a resort. The kind of people who are there range from [Robert] Vesco to a presidential candidate. Everybody who is anybody.

SS: I'm very interested in doing something about the Dominican Republic. Because I think that it's kind of an interesting—

OW: I wouldn't be remotely interested.

SS: Why?

OW: Because I have my own story, in my own Dominican Republic. I've *invented* my Dominican Republic. I'm not interested in real history, because I know Latin American politics to an unbelievable degree. I'm an expert on it. And you cannot tell that story using any individual country. You must combine them to do it properly, and it must be fictional.

SS: Oh, I only said Dominican Republic more than Acapulco, 'cause—

OW: I don't understand why you don't understand it, frankly.

HENRY JAGLOM: There's a resort like Acapulco in the Dominican Republic.

OW: We're not getting anywhere.

HJ: No, no. Wait, wait, wait—wait! We're just trying to understand—

OW: I'm not gonna go on. 'Cause if a resort doesn't immediately interest her, it won't, even if I go on for an hour.

HJ: Wait a minute, I don't agree. I don't agree.

OW: She doesn't like rich people! Doesn't want a story about rich people. That's what doesn't get anywhere with her, is that it?

SS: I think you should go on. I want to hear it.

OW: I can't sell it. I'm a bad seller.

HJ: No, it's not a question of selling.

OW: I quit.

HJ: Tell it, rather than selling it.

OW: No, I can't.

HJ: Okay. Well, then maybe if she could read something . . .

OW: I haven't got anything. It'll take me six months. It just didn't ring a bell with her, so no use talking about it.

SS: Well, it does interest me very much. I think you're wrong.

OW: *You're* wrong. You're really wrong! Boy, are you wrong.

HJ: You're not being fair. You're not being fair.

OW: Her eyes went dead when she heard *resort.*

HJ: Her eyes didn't go dead.

OW: Sure they did.

HJ: You're being too sensitive about that.

OW: I am, yes. I can't sell a thing. Forget it. We'll think of something else. You don't see what a resort— You didn't like *Grand Hotel?*

SS: I loved *Grand Hotel.*

OW: Well, then, that's it.

HJ: Instead of a hotel, it's in a resort.

SS: I understand that. I just want to hear the story.

OW: There isn't *a* story.

HJ: Wait a minute. Orson, there is a story. I mean, there is a story about a presidential candidate; there's a story about the revolution going on outside. The opening on the airplane.

OW: There are a lot of stories. But when I get that dead look, I'm dead! I can't do it. I begin to wonder what I'm talking about. I have to get a little spark from somebody. If I don't get it, that's it. I'm lost. Because I have nowhere else to go with it. You're my only market. You're the only game in town.

SS: There are a number of different alternatives. As I told you earlier, there are basically like six or seven half hour—

OW: I couldn't work in a half hour. You didn't tell me that.

SS: Maybe I didn't. That's why I'm telling you now.

OW: I thought you said that you told me.

SS: You're not listening, because you're so angry.

OW: Yes, I am. Oh, yes.

HJ: That's not fair, Orson!

OW: I don't like to be iced off like that.

(Smith exits.)

HJ: I'm changing the subject. The *New York Times* called me to ask me what I thought of Charles Higham's biography of you. Higham got slammed in the reviews.

OW: Higham has given interviews in which he's said that I pushed him away from my table. But I've never even met him. I did dip into his book, and I couldn't find one page that didn't have a glaring factual error, you know? So I didn't read the book. *Everything* is wrong. But who remembers anything correctly? That was what *Citizen Kane* was originally going to be, the film that Kurosawa finally made, *Rashomon*. It was going to be the same scene, played over and over from different points of view. Higham's is a book made by a crew of underpaid research people. He didn't write it. He just pasted together clippings. I don't know why they're digging it up now.

HJ: Because it just came out. It's his second book on you.

OW: I know why—because they're furious at Barbara Leaming for being so successful. And at me, because I'm the first person who has ever been on the cover of the *New York Times Magazine* who is not a personal friend of the editor-in-chief.

HJ: I hate the title they used for her excerpt: "The Unfulfilled Promise." It emphasizes the negative.

OW: They made it up before they read her book. And they wouldn't change it. There will be a review of Barbara's book in *The Saturday Review of Literature* by Houseman's boyfriend. He'll lash out at me.

HJ: The reviewers are blaming her for falling in love with you. They say that you completely captivated this woman. The only criticism I've heard of the book is that she lost her objectivity.

OW: Well, I told her that. And I warned her against exactly what the publishers wrote on the back of the book. I said, "You must not emphasize my collaboration. You must underplay that, because it's—"

HJ: She couldn't help herself. She wanted them to know that it was authorized, and that she really—

OW: It was *not* authorized. An authorized biography is when she hands me her manuscript, and chapter by chapter I say, "No, no, no, yes . . ." and I get the last word on any point of fact. But I never read a word of it. I said, "I'm saving that pleasure for my old age." But the truth is, I don't want to read it, because there'll be some things I don't like, and I don't want to feel quarrelsome. I only read the captions of the pictures. And one made me so furious that I decided that— You know, that my memory of Dolores del Rio is her underwear.

HJ: Yeah, that was a good line, something like, "It was so erotic it was indescribable."

OW: But I've got a good piece I want to write, which is a refutation of the reputation she gives me as the great lover. I'm gonna tell about all my failures.

HJ: The thing that's really great about the book is that she puts the lie to the myth of your self-destructiveness, dissecting—film by film—what happened, and really making it clear. That's something they wouldn't believe coming from you. And she does it not sounding like you.

OW: That's also something I wouldn't want to do myself. It's whining. But the other important thing is that Barbara's book kills the "Houseman-Welles production" canard, which you've read a million times. Because at the time the plays were done, they were never called the "Houseman-Welles" productions. Apparently, Houseman is trembling with rage. I think he's deeply wounded. And that's a good thing, too, after all these years.

HJ: People are saying, "I didn't know that Houseman was that insignificant."

HJ: The only thing I objected to in the whole book was the Joseph Cotten involvement—complicity, by implication—in the cutting of *Ambersons*. Where she says RKO used him to persuade you.

OW: It's going to be terrible, because he's my oldest friend. He'll never forgive me. I kept saying to her, "Put on your thinking cap. Think about my friends who are alive, and don't hurt them." The Cotten thing is very serious. I call him a "Judas," and so on. It's very unfortunate. Because Jo was acting in my best interests. But I say, "So was Judas." It's too tough. I'm going to write him about it. I can't talk to him about it, because he'll cut me off and say it doesn't matter. But it does.

I don't want to start picking at Barbara's book, you know. I'm enormously grateful. She did a nice job.

HJ: She really captures the truth. So you become this demystified . . . human, instead of all those terrible— The mythology is so destructive.

OW: Alex Trauner, the great production designer who I am very fond of, who did *Othello* for me, was quoted in a review of Higham's book, saying, "The trouble with Orson is, he's self-destructive. As soon as the picture is ready to go to the lab, he invents a reason not to send it," and so on. But Trauner wasn't around. He was only on

Othello the five weeks that we were in Morocco, not on the rest of the picture. But he saw that the picture stopped and started, so he came to a conclusion that this was my caprice.

HJ: As somebody who's been spending time going around trying to get financing for your projects, I know just how destructive that particular line is.

OW: Especially from a man of his position—he designed for Marcel Carne, Billy Wilder—*Hôtel du Nord*; *Le Jour Se Lève*; *Les Enfants du Paradis*; *Kiss Me, Stupid*—and there he was, knocking me down.

HJ: And then he's saying it with love, which is even—

OW: Worse. And admiration, which is worse yet.

HJ: Yeah, because it makes it sound like it's true!

OW: He actually told me that he's always admired me. And I said, "I believe that, but it's not the point."

HJ: He's so apologetic.

OW: An apology for something like that is worthless. He should have shut his mouth. Even supposing it's true. Say you believe it's true. That's your right. But you should shut up about it, that's all. Because my point to Alex was not, "Is it true or not?" But rather, it's not for a friend to say. *I* may be self-destructive, but I don't expect my friends to destroy me. That's the reason I got mad at Peter Brook, who gave a long interview about how I lack the epic sense in my movies. I said to Peter, "Probably I *do* lack the epic sense, but even so, I think we should leave it to the critics. We've got enough of them." If some other filmmaker says it, all right. At least I don't know him. But not my close friend. "You were the best man at my wedding! Why are you doing a long interview about my lack of epic sense?"

Now Gallimard is publishing all of Trauner's paintings for movies and they want me to write an introduction. I don't want to write the thing. So I said, "I really don't see, Alex, what I can say about you. It's not that I'm cross—we're still friends—but I can't do a heartfelt tribute to your work after what you said about mine." And that got me out of two days' work. Because introductions, to me, are the hardest things to write.

HJ: Robert Wise stood up at this big Directors Guild thing for you, and said how wonderful you were, how you had a huge impact on his life and so on, and then made some kind of negative remark, "What a shame that—"

OW: Who needed that? He was shaking when I ran into him afterwards. He wouldn't have had to shake if he hadn't said that. It's like Chuck Heston, who still claims that *Touch of Evil* is a minor film. Over and over, every time he's asked to speak, he says, "Let's not talk about *Touch of Evil* as though it's a major work." He sincerely believes that. And he's a horse's ass, because he's in a film of mine that other people think is important, so why doesn't he shut up and pretend it's important? What besides that has he made that's important, you know? He speaks wonderfully about me. He's full of admiration. But he says, "There's some side to him, that I've never seen that we must assume is very abrasive to producers." That's his other line. I've heard that over and over again. Then, when he's completely relaxed, he says, "Well, of course, we have to remember that, as it turned out, it's really Orson's film as an actor." He has a bad conscience, too, because he refused to come back to the studio and do the reshoots. He phoned me and told me, "I signed on to do a picture with Willie Wyler, *The Big Country.*" So he's got that little guilt. That makes *Touch of Evil* a minor film.

HJ: He called Ed Asner "a continuation of what's been going on in Hollywood since the days of Paul Robeson." That's quite a quote. Racist, to boot.

OW: What the hell is he talking about? The left in Hollywood today is the feeblest—Heston once marched with Martin Luther

King, you know. It's a long way from marching with Martin Luther King to "a continuation of what's been going on since Paul Robeson." What a horse's ass.

HJ: You know, *Touch of Evil* is playing on cable this month.

OW: It's got all the lost stuff in it! I saw a reel and a half of it last night. And I had to quit. I got too excited. I had forgotten those scenes. I thought they were gone forever. It was such a joy. And it's so beautiful in black-and-white. Oh, my God.

HJ: What did you think of Robert Carringer's book *The Making of Citizen Kane*, the professor in Indianapolis?

OW: Houseman has claimed for twenty-five or thirty years that there *was* no second script—my script—only Mankiewicz's. He was always a jealous son of a bitch. He never got over the fact that I gave him work to get him money once when he was struggling. But this fellow Carringer found the smoking gun, the telegram from Houseman to me, telling me that my script is better than Mankiewicz's. Carringer was given the opportunity to go into the RKO archives, and he read everything. And that satisfied him that my version of the controversy is right.

But I was kind of disappointed in Carringer. He is just as harmful as Higham. He has a description of me putting my arms around him as we sat at a table. Now, I am a nontoucher. It's just a dream of his. His great discovery is that *Kane* was made by a number of people, not just by me. He begins his book by saying that "I said to Orson something about movies being a collaborative art. And he immediately flew into a tantrum." I don't fly into tantrums. It's not in my character. I simply said to him, forcefully, that the use of the word *collaborative* is no more true of films than it is of the theater. Sometimes it is, sometimes it isn't. You know what I'm saying. And as far as the credit goes, I hadn't seen the beginning of *Kane* since I made it, or the end—I had forgotten where the credits are—and I saw it yesterday morning. I saw that I shared the director's title card with Toland. It says: "Directed by Orson Welles; photography by Gregg Toland." On the same card. I don't think many people have done that. The cameramen were always listed with the make-up department. And I'm supposed to be the one who wants credit for everything? Carringer pads out his book with a little half-baked chapter on *Ambersons*, making the point that it's a failure because I didn't have the same people with me, the same art director, and the same cameraman, and so on.

HJ: You know, Houseman was Higham's source.

OW: Yes, he thanks Houseman for his collaboration. Higham is really unspeakable. He lists seventeen major untruths in a *Vogue* piece that I wrote. What are the lies that he's exploding? I was telling how hard it was for anybody to get a room in my father's hotel, that it was one of the most exclusive hotels in America. And he says, "The hotel in Grand Detour was not one of the most exclusive hotels in America."

HJ: The level of trivia is truly wonderful. Why do you suppose he hates you so? Because you are Orson Welles and he's not? I think envy of the gifted colors all these books. He's just jealous. Like Houseman.

OW: You know, in the beginning, when I should have been playing Hamlet, Houseman kept saying, "These plays are not vehicles for you. Remember, we're an ensemble company, not the Orson Welles Players." So Martin Gabel plays Danton, instead of me. And so on, you know. But in the profession which I have chosen, my only real disappointment is that I feel I've never been properly appreciated as an actor. Mostly my own fault, for giving my energy to the production, rather than to my performance. Also, my own fault for pretending I wasn't a star actor and was just there.

HJ: I've wondered about that, why you didn't capitalize on your great notices. So it was mainly Houseman, then?

OW: All Houseman. But I had no argument with that, you know? That seemed right to me.

HJ: The spirit of the times dictated a kind of group, or collective mentality.

OW: You know, Houseman's become so famous now that Rich Little does an imitation of him.

HJ: A terrible comic. Houseman is so pompous and pretentious.

OW: That's what he's like. Pomposity is his basic characteristic.

HJ: Where did that absurd accent come from?

OW: He's a Rumanian.

HJ: Jewish, right?

OW: Yeah. But a Rumanian who was born and raised in Buenos Aires.

HJ: What about that accent?

OW: In Buenos Aires, there's this whole population of people who have been speaking English for generations and have never been back to England. So they've developed their own English accent. Besides being Rumanian. Which, as Alfonso XIII said, "Being a Rumanian is not a race. It's a profession."

HJ: In the past years, have you ever found yourself in the same place with him?

OW: No. If I know he's going to be someplace, I don't go. Not because I don't want to speak to him, but because it's uncomfortable.

HJ: He's made such a reputation off you, in a way. It's infuriating when history is revised. It's not only the Stalinists in the Soviet Union. He's rewritten his whole life, using his memoires, so that he's become central to everything you've achieved. And now he's enjoying his senior citizenship as a grand old actor. He is dreadful. As an actor he can't read a line.

OW: Absolutely dreadful! And he got the Academy Award! It drove Cotten mad with rage. But he laughed all through the show. Laughing mad, you know? He was in some movie with Houseman and he said, "Jack made a tremendous fuss about where his dressing room was going to be." And Jo couldn't look at him! If a gypsy had told us, "One of you will get the Academy Award. Who will it be?" he would have been the last one any one of us would have chosen. My first wife, who was a very clever lady and understood people awfully well, said from the beginning of my partnership with Houseman that there was something of Iago in him. She said, "He's destructive! He's trying to destroy you. Listen to me!" And I said, "This is pure mischief! The malice of a wife! Houseman is my valued partner." But she was right! About three weeks after we met, he said to me, "I keep dreaming of you riding bareback on a horse." And I should have taken that more seriously. But I just laughed. Before he rose to his present eminence, he had about twenty years when he wasn't doing much of anything, except dining out and knocking me. And then he slowly built himself up to what he is now: elder statesman, Academy Award–winning actor, and leading salesman of anything you have.

HJ: Life is full of amazing turns.

OW: Houseman has had twenty commercials on camera. I've had one. I'm in *terrible* financial trouble. And I keep trying to make a decent movie that will also make me money.

HJ: I know this irritates you, but I keep getting back to the fact, Orson, that I don't fully understand why, with all the frustration that you have to deal with, you don't invent a film like *F for Fake*, which you know you can do brilliantly, while you're waiting for these projects to go forward.

OW: I need money. When I had *F for Fake*, I had money.

HJ: How much did *F for Fake* cost?

OW: Very little, but I had it. And *F for Fake* was such a flop in America, you know.

HJ: I keep thinking that whether they get it or not at the exact time that you make it, eventually, they'll get it!

OW: We don't agree, you see. Essentially, I don't believe in a film that isn't a commercial success. Film is a popular art form. It has to have at least the kind of success that European and early Woody Allen movies had. People should be in those tiny theaters, lining up to see it. And they didn't do it with *F for Fake*.

HJ: So why don't you—I hope you don't mind my bringing it up—cut one of your unfinished films and release it? Or why don't you do some commercials again?

OW: No personal essay film will make any money, you know that. *F for Fake* proved it. If Wesson Oil would let *me* say that Wesson Oil is good, instead of Houseman, I'd be delighted, but nobody will take me for a commercial. It's just a closed door, and I don't understand why. He must have made five or six million dollars. I don't understand that man's continued success. And when he isn't making a big commercial, he makes a small one. He's now selling automobiles for a local automobile dealer in New York. While I cannot seem to crack it. Why I can't, I do not know. A real mystery: why they prefer Houseman, with his petulant, arrogant, unpleasant manner. I don't know what is the matter. It's a very weird and terrible situation. I don't know where to turn. Except I can't . . . I can't . . .

HJ: During the period when you're preparing for *Lear*, or for *Dreamers*— Orson, I'm not— Please don't be mad at me.

OW: No, I'm not mad at you. I'm explaining to you that it's not like I'm just sitting around doing nothing. I'm working on scripts that might make some money. And they take all kinds of time. I've been fighting the income tax people for a long while now. The deals for *Lear*, even, include very big salaries for me that would get me out of trouble with them. And that's what I need. I can't afford to sit down in the cutting room with my old films. I have the cheapest competent editor, who's willing to work as a kind of favor for eight hundred dollars a week. But I haven't *got* eight hundred dollars a week to give the man. And I have big obligations, so that—that's the awful thing—I'm not a free soul. I'm doing the impossible thing of trying to make money off the kind of movies that don't make money.

HJ: Please understand, I don't mean to minimize your situation. I've told you that I'm working on this problem now. I know you're taking care of a lot of people, and—

OW: You know, I had it made with that damn brandy company, the French cognac.

HJ: You had it, and then it went away.

OW: Do you know why? The owner went to Hong Kong, checked into his hotel, turned on the TV, and saw an old commercial, which they were not supposed to show anymore, by contract, of me talking about Japanese whiskey. The local station figured, "Who's gonna catch us at this?" and put it on the air.

HJ: Oh, God! So they fired you.

OW: And that was five years, that contract.

HJ: Okay. We'll get another one. We'll get another one.

OW: I've worked with advertising agencies all my life. In the old days in radio, you worked for them, because they were the boss, not the network. And I have never seen more seedier, about-to-be-fired sad sacks than were responsible for those Paul Masson ads. The agency hated me because I kept trying to improve the copy.

HJ: Whoever heard of Paul Masson before you—

OW: And now we have John G.

HJ: Who is that?

OW: John Gielgud. He's doing his butler, from the little dwarf's movie.

HJ: From *Arthur*.

OW: That's one of our profound disagreements—Dudley Moore.

HJ: I don't have anything against short people.

OW: Nor do I. I just know what they have against me. There's never been a tall dictator—never.

HJ: Oh, my God.

OW: Name one. They're all under normal height.

HJ: Was Mussolini short?

OW: Very short.

HJ: Franco?

OW: Short. Hitler was short. Including those that you might feel more sympathetic to. Like Tito—tiny. Stalin—tiny.

HJ: The height theory of history.

OW: Remember that the melancholy freaks are all giants, not midgets. The midgets and dwarfs all have delusions of grandeur.

HJ: How tall are you?

OW: I used to be six-three and a half, and I'm now about six-two. Six-one and a half, maybe. My neck keeps disappearing. Gravity, you know? Like Elizabeth Taylor. She has no neck left! Her shoulders come to her ears. And she's still young! Now, look, imagine where her face will be when she's my age. In her navel, you know?

HJ: They'll have a special man in Beverly Hills who pulls—elongates necks.

OW: She had a neck like a swan when she was in *Jane Eyre*. That's how I understood *Lolita*, when I read it later. I used to offer to read lines with her. "Wouldn't you like to go through that with me?"

HJ: How old was she?

OW: Oh, something disgraceful!

HJ: You had a touch of . . . a touch of . . .

OW: Your Polish fella.

HJ: A touch of Roman. And Chaplin.

OW: More Roman. Chaplin was like that only in his old age.

HJ: Getting back to your financial situation—

OW: I'm a wage earner who— You know, I live from week to week. My wife and her establishments cost me six thousand dollars a month, apart from anything else. And I've got a daughter—one of my daughters, who has to be helped all the time, and I have, you know, every kind of obligation. And that's the hell of it. If I were free of any financial obligation, I would have done essay films, because that's what I would rather do now, more than story films. It's what I think has not been done. But essay films are like essays. They are never going to compete with fiction features, just as books of essays have not been able to compete with novels, ever.

If I got just one commercial, it would change my life! And that's why my failure as a performer in commercials hurts me so much, because of the difference it would make in my life. I don't even get the radio ones anymore! My whole income has gone from—three years ago, I made a million seven hundred thousand dollars . . . You know, I could comprehend it, in this youth-oriented world, if my ex-partner wasn't getting so rich on it.

HJ: Let me try to do what I can to find out about that. I really didn't understand. I have to assume that people don't know that you're available. In the meantime, you could—

OW: There is no "meantime." It's the grocery bill. I haven't got the money. It's that urgent. That's what drives me off my . . . nut. I can't afford to work in hopes of future profits. I have to hustle now. All I do is sweat and work. I'm imprisoned by a simple economic fact. Get me on that fuckin' screen and my life is changed.

HJ: Okay, I understand the priorities.

OW: The priorities are personal; they're not an artistic choice. For some reason, there are people all over the world who think Welles-*Lear* is a great idea. So I'll get paid big money for that. And, you know, there are five or six people scattered all over the world who think *The Dreamers* is a wonderful script. Then there's *The Big Brass Ring*. They're all things that, if they come through, there's money up front. But we haven't got the deals.

27. "Fool the old fellow with the scythe."

In which Orson realizes that his prospects will most likely evaporate, contemplates the evanescence of fame, which ebbs and flows with the regularity of the tides, and peers into the future.

HENRY JAGLOM: Now, what is with *Lear* today? What's happening?

ORSON WELLES: Dead.

HJ: Well, it's not dead, because this producer is trying to come up with terms.

OW: No, no, it's dead.

HJ: Why?

OW: No way of doing it in France. He's changed every single point in the agreement that we made.

HJ: So there's no use communicating with Jacques Lang?

OW: I'll tell you all about it, if you'll give me the time. Rather than answering—

HJ: Okay. Sorry.

OW: I'd rather do a monologue than submit myself to an interrogation. I have a problem with Jacques Lang, of course, because he thinks his producer is the best producer in France. He'll believe the producer's side of the story, and not mine. And Lang is not putting up enough money to make the difference anyway. He's just giving his blessing. The producer, as described to me by my old cameraman, is indeed very successful and very intelligent, but he's a weather vane. He'll tell you one thing at ten in the morning, and another at noon.

The budget was five million dollars. Then they began to talk about how it was hard to get the last million. I said, "I'll give up three hundred thousand up front, and defer it." Then they wanted me to do postproduction, all the editing, in Paris. I explained to them that I have back income tax that I have to pay for another year, and that I can only do that by finding some money in America. I cannot spend a year in France cut off from my other sources of income. And since we are doing it on tape as well as film, I said I'll give them a very good rough cut before I leave, but I'll do the final cut and mix in America. They agreed to that and the compensation, so then I said, "In all of your correspondence, you have called me the producer, but now you're giving me this man." They said, "We have to, by French law." I said, "But I must have the right to decide how the money is spent within the budget. Not just artistically. If I want to spend one day on one thing and ten days on another, it's my decision. That makes me the producer." They said, "All right."

Yesterday came the telex—yesterday! My entire compensation is seven hundred thousand, instead of a million plus the cassette rights we agreed on, and I am not to get one cent of that until the entire film is delivered. Which is the first I ever heard of that. And I must do all the postproduction in Paris—a total violation of our understanding. So, there's no way of patching it up in France. My immediate problem is public relations. How is this bombshell going to go off in the French press? All the newspapers in Paris are ready to say, "He doesn't really want to make a movie. He's running away after we—a million dollars isn't good enough for him." So what I want to do is to tell Jacques Lang, and the French press, that it's not that I'm walking away from *King Lear*. It's that my producer has changed the conditions under which I am to make the picture, unilaterally. It's a diktat. The telex is not, "We regret that we are forced to change—" Rather, it's take it or leave it. Now, the big money from French television had been earmarked for a miniseries called *Ali Baba*, and they had to take a big hunk from *Ali Baba* for *Lear*. So I suspect that this producer *wants* me to say no, so he can get the money back for *Ali Baba*. How do you like those apples?

HJ: Those are bad apples. Have you heard from the English about *Lear* at all?

OW: This morning I talked to the daughter of the producer, who is my liaison. She said, "Well, we have the money in London, but we have to move it to Switzerland. And until it gets to Switzerland, we'll be unable to give you a starting date." Which is about as unlikely a story as I've ever heard. Just a bad lie.

HJ: Look, this might cheer you up. Do you know about the video-disc of *Kane*? With the narration and the explanation?

OW: No, I don't know about narration and explanation. I don't like that. Why didn't they invite *me* to do it?

HJ: Every single cut you made is validated now by this professor who comments on the film. This is why you couldn't have done this.

OW: Well, theoretically, that's good for teaching movies, so long as they don't talk nonsense. "Do you see why this camera's in the wrong place? Do you see why this cut is bad? Do you see why the pace drops here?" That would really be teaching people. I could do it with somebody else's film—but you're right, I couldn't with my own. You can't say why it's good. You can only say why it's bad! You could teach the ordinary grammar of moviemaking using a fairly respectable bad film, you know. Cukor would be a very good director for that. Because he doesn't stand up under a hard look.

I noticed that the new movies for television, which are obviously made by young directors out of film school, are technically much better than they were five, six years ago. And inventive. They're just, of course, doomed, because they're for television, and these directors are being clever with garbage. But you get to a point—I have, all my life, not just now—when you make something that's really quite good, not wonderful, but a very good mediocre play or movie, and you settle for it.

HJ: The great thing about what's happening with these laser discs and video things, is that it gives film permanence. As opposed to when you started working, when you could easily expect that film would be gone twenty, thirty, forty, fifty years from now. Now you know that they're gonna last.

OW: I regard posterity as vulgar as success. I don't trust posterity. I don't think what's good is necessarily recognized in the long run. Too many good writers have disappeared.

(Gilles Jacob enters.)

GILLES JACOB: I just saw you on the French TV talking to students.

OW: It was all a little too reverent for me, you know?

GJ: You know, we have not too many people to revere. So we are not so used to revere someone.

OW: I don't know. I think it is a French instinct to revere or to neglect, with nothing in between.

GJ: Probably.

OW: The giants of French culture suddenly don't exist anymore. Nobody has attacked them; they just aren't there, you know. Look what happened to Anatole France—disappeared. Malraux—vanished.

HJ: But they're dead.

OW: Well, look at Scottie Fitzgerald here, in America. He disappeared in his own lifetime. For the last five years of his life, none of his novels was in print. You could not buy a Fitzgerald novel. Faulkner is vanishing. He used to totally dominate the whole world, not only America, but the Continent, particularly. My God, he's starting to become invisible. Steinbeck, poor fellow. He was a bigger talent than anybody gives him credit for. But his faults have over-shadowed his talent to such a point that he's vanished, you know? He was a terribly sweet man. Writers are not necessarily the sweet-est people in the world. Robert Frost was an angry man—but who knows—maybe just rude to bores. When someone came up to him, he'd say, "Yes? Get out." My trouble is that I say, "Stay another ten minutes," and people still say I'm a shit!

HJ: Their natural lives exceeded their creative lives.

OW: It's no wonder Fitzgerald and Hemingway and O'Hara hated the fact of aging. They simply couldn't bear to be forty-two years old. The fear of death. They wanted to fool the old fellow with the scythe.

HJ: Filmmakers disappear all the time.

OW: René Clair was a good friend of mine. He was very bitter at the end of his life. He used to say to me: "You know, there has never been a movie which isn't out of fashion after fifteen years. It's like journal-ism where you write on sand. It disappears; it's nothing." He was really revered, in the English-speaking world particularly. My God, René Clair was, you know, what Fellini was twenty years ago.

HJ: What was the reason for Clair's decline?

OW: He made some commercial movies at the end, which were not "René Clair" movies. So that hastened the deterioration of his reputation, until it disappeared entirely. Because we all had a picture of a "René Clair" movie. Then he began to make amusing sort of . . .

HJ: Entertainments.

OW: You couldn't tell the difference between those movies and any other well-made films. It's like Olivier choosing to make *Dracula* rather than disappear from view. That hurt him very much. If you make that choice, your reputation is gonna suffer.

GJ: Also, I have the feeling that some directors have only ten years, fifteen years, before they're finished. Don't you think so?

OW: Directors are poor fellows, carrying not much baggage. We come in with only our overnight bags, and go out with nothing. There are names in those old lists of the greatest movies that have totally vanished, you know? Now, when my career is only a memory, I'm still sitting here like some kind of monument, but the moment will come when I'll drop out of sight altogether, as though a trapdoor had opened, you know? Although I'd prefer a Verdi ending.

HJ: What's that?

OW: Verdi did great work when he was young. Very early. Highly acclaimed. Spent his middle years overseeing productions of his music, orchestrating his earlier work. Trivialities. Then, in old age, one day someone came and told him, "Wagner is dead." He lit up. Did his greatest work in the following years, after decades of nothing.

HJ: Who would your Wagner be? Who would have to die to set you free?

OW: I'm not going to answer that.

Orson Welles died on October 10, 1985, five days after his last lunch with Henry Jaglom, in the middle of the night, with his typewriter in his lap. It was a heart attack.

Epilogue

Orson's Last Laugh
by Henry Jaglom

Saturday afternoon, Oct. 5th, at lunch, Orson told me that the attacks were beginning to come in, in response to the books out on him, especially Barbara Leaming's wonderfully supportive—to his mind, largely accurate—biography. The success of the book as it was about to go into its second printing had cheered him, setting the record straight on Houseman and so many things, and he was philosophical about the attacks: "Once they decide they're for you or against you, it never changes. Hope and Crosby they always loved. Me and Sinatra they decided against early on, and they never let up." He talked of *Time*, *Newsweek*, the *Washington Post*.

He complained that in a year and a half, Ma Maison would be moving into a new hotel, and "What will we do then?" Kiki growled and he fed her a small cookie, while warning her that if she kept on crying he'd never take her out again.

He told me that Paul Masson wanted him back to endorse its "terrible wine again," but on a one-year contract instead of three, at lesser money and with required performances-cum-appearances around the country. He'd turn it down, but slowly, seeing how good he could make the deal.

Welles never let anyone capture his likeness, but made an exception for Jaglom, provided his friend use a grease pencil on black paperboard that Welles sent a Ma Maison waiter to procure.

We talked of Israel's raid on Tunis and Gorbachev's public relations talents as evidenced in Paris, how "Reagan was going to be made to look like an amateur," and how the French bungling of the Greenpeace ship business in New Zealand was "going to cost Mitterand his job." And what a shame that was. He made me have dessert by dramatically reading the menu and we laughed at stories of people's odd pomposity and pretensions and he let himself have a dessert plate full of lime sherbet.

A typical few hours—in short—some stories, some hopefulness, some creative ideas, some anecdotes, some sadness, some old memories, much shared understanding, many communicative smiles. As always.

But for some reason I didn't have my little tape recorder on in my bag. I remember thinking as I drove over that I'd done almost every lunch for a few years and I didn't feel I had to anymore. I remember wondering if he'd notice that it wasn't there, and what would he think it meant if he did.

The tape recorder was one of the only two things we didn't speak about. The other was his weight and its health implications. The closest we got was, "You're looking well," or "I swam my laps," or "I can't eat that anymore; you have to eat it for me and describe it to me." We did a lot of that in the south of France.

In fact, he looked a bit tired. He said, "Time is passing," but he said it lightly, sadly but lightly, in relation to our ongoing inability to get a film financed for him to direct.

This morning my phone rang; it was my office. There was a rumor he was dead; the press was calling. I called him on his private number. His man, Freddie, answered, said how sorry he was, yes it was true, he found him on the bedroom floor at ten this morning, and he couldn't rouse him. Freddie called the paramedics. He apologized to me (in lieu of Orson) for calling them, as if he had violated the trust for privacy that he still somehow felt he was expected to honor, even now.

Orson was dead.

All day the hypocrites got on radio and TV and eulogized him. I kept wanting to call him and tell him, "You won't believe what Burt Reynolds said, what Charlton Heston came up with." One by one each of those who wouldn't help him when they could, now stepped forward to praise him. I cried and tried to hear his laugh.

Even in death he did his "dancing bear" act for them. I got furious and gave a few angry interviews of my own.

Then I watched him on my editing machine in *Someone to Love*, which I am cutting together, saying that you are born, live, and die alone.

"Only through love and friendship can you create the illusion that you are not entirely alone," he said, in what turns out to be his last appearance in a movie, his last acting job.

I'm having a harder time now, creating that illusion.

"You have your ending now," he says to me, on my screen.

"Can't I have an ending after the ending?" I ask, essentially.

"No," he says.

"Why not?" I ask.

"Because," he finishes, with a smile, "this is The End."

And he blows me a kiss.

And to the cameraman he shouted, "Cut!"

And the screen went black.

Appendix

Welles had so many unfinished or unmade films, scripts, treatments, and pitches, in addition to trailers, tests, shorts, fragments, and filmlets of every sort, it's nearly impossible to determine how many there were at the end. According to Jonathan Rosenbaum's meticulous inventory of Orsoniana, *Discovering Orson Welles*, when he died, Welles left approximately nineteen projects in various states of completion. What follows are thumbnails of the four that figure in his conversations with Jaglom, as well as a partial cast of characters.

NEW OR UNFINISHED PROJECTS

Don Quixote

Welles transposed Don Quixote and Sancho Panza to Franco's Spain. The juxtaposition of the two throws into stark relief both the pathos of their quest, rendered anachronistic by the march of history, particularly the rise of fascism, as well as its timeless significance. Child actress Patty McCormack played a little girl visiting Mexico City who encounters Welles. Soon after he tells her the story of the two windmill tilters, she meets them herself. The shooting began in 1956 in France, and continued, fitfully, until the late 1960s, early 1970s. Welles kept running out of money. Over the course of lengthy production delays, McCormack grew up, and Welles had to drop her from the film. He repeatedly changed the concept, at one point exposing Quixote and Panza to a nuclear holocaust, and at another sending them to the moon. Welles claimed he originally shelved the film because he was waiting for Franco to die, saying, "It's an essay on Spain, not Don Quixote." He worked on it on and off until he himself died.

The Dreamers

The Dreamers was a script written in 1978 by Welles and his companion Oja Kodar based on two short stories by Isak Dinesen, "The Dreamers" and "Echoes." In the course of his years-long attempts to find financing, Welles shot two ten-minute segments around his home. In the first, fully made up and costumed as a nineteenth-century Dutch-Jewish merchant, Welles tells the story of Pellegrina Leoni, an opera diva who loses her voice. It was shot in black-and-white. In the second, shot in color, Leoni, played by Kodar, appears herself. She bids the merchant farewell, explaining that she is off to seek a new life.

King Lear

Welles was also anxious to put his version of *King Lear*, for which he had very definite ideas, on the screen. "Up to now, everybody, myself included, felt we had to extend the visual elements of *Lear* instead of doing what the movies make possible, which is reducing it to its essential so it becomes a more abstract and intimate *Lear*," he explained. "It's about old age and it's not about somebody trying to outsing the Metropolitan [Opera] and outshout the thunder." He intended to do a less-is-more production, shot in 16 millimeter black-and-white, mostly in close-up. He continued, "I believe the key to *Lear* and his extraordinary behavior at the beginning of the play, which is the toughest thing to swallow, is the fact that he probably had three wives, anyway probably two, and his last wife died in childbirth and he has lived for at least 25 years without the company of women. He lives with his knights, he's going to pieces. The absence of women, of the civilizing element of life, is the thing that blinds him and makes the tragedy."

The Other Side of the Wind

The Other Side of the Wind was cowritten and coproduced by Welles and Kodar. Shot between 1969 and 1976, it is Welles's satirical take on the state of film, circa 1970, and a film à clef in which he skewers his enemies, including John Houseman and Pauline Kael. It features John Huston as Jack Hannaford, an over-the-hill director trying to make a comeback with a New Wave-y film-within-a-film called *The Other Side of the Wind* that parodies fashionable European directors of the moment, such as Michelangelo Antonioni and Jean-Luc Godard. Guests are on their way to Hannaford's seventieth birthday party, staged in all its extravagant, Aquarian glory, but he is killed in a car crash immediately thereafter. The movie is a mash-up of stills; various film gauges and formats—Super 8, 16, 35 millimeter, as well as video—black-and-white and color; and different genres. Before *The Other Side of the Wind* could be completed it became embroiled in a legal fight over ownership between Welles and the brother-in-law of the Shah of Iran, who invested in it. It has not been released to this day. Henry Jaglom, Peter Bogdanovich, Oja Kodar, Susan Strasberg, Paul Mazursky, Lilli Palmer, Stephane Audran, Cameron Crowe, Dennis Hopper, Claude Chabrol, and more make appearances.

PARTIAL CAST OF CHARACTERS

Joseph Cotten, one of Welles's oldest friends, hooked up with him for the Federal Theatre production of *Horse Eats Hat*. Cotten was a founding member of the Mercury Theatre. His breakout role, playing the part that Cary Grant would later make famous in the movie, was that of C. K. Dexter Haven in *The Philadelphia Story* on Broadway opposite Katharine Hepburn. He then played Jedediah Leland in *Citizen Kane* (1941), and went on to have a long and varied career in Hollywood. He played Eugene in *The Magnificent Ambersons* (1942), and appeared in Hitchcock's *Shadow of a Doubt* (1943), as well as *Gaslight* (1944), and four movies with Jennifer Jones, including *Duel in the Sun* (1946). He also played Marilyn Monroe's husband in *Niagara* (1953), and even showed up in Michael Cimino's notorious *Heaven's Gate* (1980).

Samuel Goldwyn formed Samuel Goldwyn Pictures in 1916. In 1924, it was folded into Metro-Goldwyn-Mayer. (Roaring Leo the lion, the MGM trademark, was originally his.) He subsequently became a successful independent producer. William Wyler made his best films for Goldwyn, including *Wuthering Heights* (1939), *The Little Foxes* (1941), and *The Best Years of Our Lives* (1948). Many of Hollywood's finest writers worked for him, including Ben Hecht, Dorothy Parker, and Lillian Hellman. He was also notorious for mangling the English language, coming up with locutions affectionately known as "Goldwynisms." Trying to cheer up Billy Wilder after a flop, he once said, "You gotta take the sour with the bitter."

Charles Higham, a prolific biographer, published two books on Welles, *The Films of Orson Welles* and *Orson Welles: The Rise and Fall of an American Genius*. Welles and his admirers detested Higham for perpetuating the view that Welles was a failure. Welles delighted in mispronouncing his name "Higgam."

Lena Horne was Hollywood's Jackie Robinson, so to speak, the first black movie star, in an era when most black performers were relegated to the roles of butlers, nannies, cooks, or cannibals. She began her career in the chorus line of the legendary Cotton Club in 1933 when she was sixteen. She was known for her silken voice, and eventually replaced Dinah Shore on NBC's jazz show *The Chamber*

Music Society of Lower Basin Street. She signed with MGM, becoming the first black star under a long-term contract. Horne appeared in numerous films, but her scenes were excised in states that banned movies with black performers. She gained considerable fame for playing Georgia Brown in the all-black musical *Cabin in the Sky* (1943), and for singing the title song in *Stormy Weather* (1943). She was an outspoken civil rights activist. She worked closely with Paul Robeson in the 1930s; and during the war, entertaining the troops, she refused to perform before segregated audiences or those in which black GI's were seated behind German POWs, as was sometimes the case. Her later career, in the 1950s, was blighted by the blacklist that forced her out of Hollywood into clubs and television.

Garson Kanin wrote and directed for the stage and screen. He is best known for *Born Yesterday* (1950). With his wife, actress Ruth Gordon, he wrote two Tracy-Hepburn comedies, *Adam's Rib* (1949) and *Pat and Mike* (1952).

Elia Kazan was a towering figure of the American stage and screen. He was closely associated with "the Method" school of acting, and cofounded the Actors Studio in 1947. He directed its most famous graduate, Marlon Brando, in three films, *A Streetcar Named Desire* (1951), the risible *Viva Zapata!* (1952), and the brilliant *On the Waterfront* (1954), in which the actor gave the greatest performance of his career. Even Kazan's lesser works, like *Panic in the Streets* (1950), *Baby Doll* (1956), *A Face in the Crowd* (1957), and *Wild River* (1960) are compelling. The director also gave Warren Beatty his first starring role in *Splendor in the Grass* (1961). But Kazan was an old lefty from the Group Theatre, and in 1952 he sullied his reputation forever by naming names, that is, throwing his old friends and colleagues to the wolves by testifying against them before the House Committee on Un-American Activities. Many of his associates never forgave him.

Alexander Korda was a Hungarian-born producer and director. After his career floundered in several countries—Hungary, Austria, Germany, and the United States—he relocated to England, where he had immediate success directing Charles Laughton in *The Private Life of Henry VIII* (1933). He went on to direct many more films, including *Four Feathers* (1939) and *The Thief of Bagdad* (1940). He bought into British Lion Films, and entered a coproduction deal with David O. Selznick in 1948. A good friend of Welles's, he hired him for *The Third Man*, released in 1949.

Irving "Swifty" Lazar, one of the first so-called superagents, was reportedly so nicknamed by Humphrey Bogart when he put together three deals for him in one day on a bet. Separated at birth from Mr. Magoo, he was tiny, bald, and wore thick glasses in heavy black frames. But he was an immaculate dresser, and despite his unprepossessing appearance, counted among his clients, at one time or another, Lauren Bacall, Moss Hart, Ernest Hemingway, Cole Porter, and even Madonna. He was known for his abrupt phone manner, called everybody "kiddo," and even the biggest stars killed for invitations to his Oscar parties.

Charles Lederer was the writer, cowriter, or contributor to several classic comedies, including *The Front Page* (1931), *His Girl Friday* (1940), *I Was a Male War Bride* (1949), *Gentlemen Prefer Blondes* (1953), and *Monkey Business* (1952), as well as Richard Widmark's chilling debut film, *Kiss of Death* (1947), and Howard Hawks's sci-fi landmark, *The Thing* (1951). Even more precocious than Welles, Lederer entered college at the age of thirteen, and was entangled with Welles throughout his life. Lederer was raised by Marion Davies, his aunt, who was, of course, Hearst's mistress and one of Welles's ostensible targets in *Kane*. He married Welles's first wife, Virginia Nicholson, at Hearst Castle. Lederer and Welles became great friends. After Rita Hayworth threw Welles out, he lived next door to the Davies estate, where Lederer and Nicholson were living, and dined with them nearly every night. Occasionally, when Davies joined the couple, Welles was barred from the table, and stood outside the window watching them eat. Both he and Lederer were fond of practical jokes.

In 1924, **Louis B. Mayer** became head of the combined Metro Pictures, Goldwyn Pictures, and Mayer Pictures—soon to be Metro-Goldwyn-Mayer. Mayer reported to Nicholas Schenk in New York, whom he disliked and resented, invariably referring to him as "Mr. Skunk," but he ran the lot, located in Los Angeles, like his own fiefdom. Mayer built MGM into the most successful studio in Hollywood, the crown jewel of the golden age of movies, and he is credited, if that's the right word, for inventing the star system. MGM was home to Greta Garbo, Clark Gable, Carole Lombard, Jean Harlow, Judy Garland, John Barrymore, Joan Crawford, and a host of other stars, all of whom the studio held in virtual thralldom. Mayer was extremely conservative and a lifelong Republican.

Louella Parsons and **Hedda Hopper**. Parsons was a preternaturally powerful Hollywood gossip columnist who went to work for William Randolph Hearst in 1923. Before long she was syndicated in more than six hundred papers worldwide, and was read by an estimated 20 million people. Parsons reigned supreme until Hedda Hopper emerged as an equally if not more powerful rival in 1937, writing for competing newspapers. Hopper called her Beverly Hills house "the house that fear built." Long before Bob Dylan mocked Jackie Kennedy's "leopard-skin pill-box hat," Hopper was famous for her flamboyant headgear. An avid supporter of HUAC, Joe McCarthy, and the blacklist, her relentless attacks on Charlie Chaplin for his lefty politics and predilection for young women is at least partially responsible for driving him into exile in Switzerland. She was rumored to have tried to out Cary Grant and Randolph Scott as a couple, and one Valentine's Day she was the recipient of a skunk, courtesy of actress Joan Bennett. Both Parsons and Hopper attacked *Kane*, even before it opened in 1941. Parsons was particularly vituperative, and took an active part in her boss's campaign to block the release of the film, even smuggling one of Hearst's lawyers into a private screening.

David O. Selznick became head of production at RKO in 1931. It was there that he produced *King Kong* (1933). He moved to MGM in 1933. Production head Irving Thalberg's health was failing, and Louis B. Mayer gave Selznick his own production unit. But Selznick, who married Mayer's daughter Irene, had grander ambitions. Two years later he left to start his own company, Selznick International Pictures. He produced *A Star Is Born*, *Nothing Sacred*, and, in conjunction with MGM, *Gone With the Wind*. He brought Alfred Hitchcock from England to America, and produced *Rebecca*, for which Hitchcock won an Oscar, as well as *Spellbound* and *Duel in the Sun*, among other films.

Erich von Stroheim was regarded as one of the greatest directors of the silent era. When he landed on Ellis Island in 1909, he claimed that his name was Count Erich Oswald Hans Carl Maria von Stroheim und Nordenwall, and that he was descended from Austrian royalty, although in reality he was the son of a hat maker. He did some acting and writing, and directed himself in *Blind Husbands* (1919). Three years later, he clashed with Thalberg over the length of *Foolish Wives*. Von Stroheim will always be mentioned in the same breath as his most notorious film, *Greed* (1924), an eight-hour epic based on Frank Norris's novel *McTeague*. Eventually, he edited it down to six hours, then four, and offered to reduce it further, to three, but Thalberg took it away from him, and it was hacked to pieces, becoming a symbol of studio stupidity, to which Welles could all too strongly relate. Von Stroheim went on to direct *The Merry*

Widow (1925) and *The Wedding March* (1928), and eventually devoted the remainder of his career to acting. Although it was no more than a footnote to a great directing career, he will always be remembered for playing Gloria Swanson's butler in Billy Wilder's *Sunset Boulevard* (1950).

Louis B. Mayer's masterpiece was not a movie but the sickly "boy wonder" **Irving Thalberg**. He was already vice president in charge of production at Mayer Pictures when three companies merged to form MGM. Still under twenty-five, he quickly became a legend in his own right. Thalberg innovated in several areas, introducing story conferences, previews, and reshoots. MGM produced four hundred pictures during his tenure, and he was credited with making the studio the powerhouse it became with pictures such as *Ben Hur* (1959), *Grand Hotel* (1932), *Camille* (1936), *Mutiny on the Bounty* (1935), and *The Good Earth* (1937). He suffered from congenital heart disease and was told as a child that he would die before he was thirty. He in fact died in 1936 at the age of thirty-seven, and was survived by his wife, actress Norma Shearer.

Gregg Toland, a legendary Hollywood cinematographer, was under a long-term contract to Sam Goldwyn, who lent him to Welles for *Citizen Kane*. His name is invariably associated with the deep-focus cinematography for which *Kane* is famous, where objects in the foreground and background are equally sharp.

Darryl Zanuck headed what would become Twentieth Century Fox from 1933 until he left in 1956 to shoot in Europe. In his heyday, he was known for prestige films that tackled social issues, including *The Grapes of Wrath* (1940), *How Green Was My Valley* (1941), and *Gentleman's Agreement* (1947). Once in Europe, his films became vehicles for a succession of girlfriends, including Bella

Darvi, Irina Demick, Geneviève Gilles, and Juliette Gréco. He returned to Fox—sinking fast under the weight of *Cleopatra* (1963)—riding the success of *The Longest Day* (1962). He made his son, Richard, head of production, but was ousted by him, with the help of the board, and left for good in 1971.

Acknowledgments

First and foremost, I would like to thank Henry Jaglom for making his conversations with Orson Welles available to me, and for doing so without any thought of benefitting financially from his close friendship with him. I would also like to acknowledge Eugene Corey, the heroic transcriber, who put in countless hours over many months, transforming what were sometimes no more than barely intelligible grunts recorded in a noisy restaurant into coherent transcripts. My sharp-as-a-tack agent, Kathy Robbins, helped me in more ways than I can count, while my good friend and genius editor Sara Bershtel steadfastly refused to let anything slip by her. Thanks also to transcript wranglers Sharon Lester Kohn and Courtney Kirkpatrick, in Jaglom's office. And finally, to my wife, Elizabeth Hess, for her forbearance while I shut myself away to finish the manuscript, coming out of my office only to bore her with Orson stories that I had already told her.

Notes

Introduction: How Henry Met Orson

2 "Everyone will always owe": Jean-Luc Godard, quoted by Michel Ciment, "Les Enfants Terribles," *American Film*, December 1984, p. 42.

6 "crushing ego": Chris Welles Feder, *In My Father's Shadow: A Daughter Remembers Orson Welles* (New York: Algonquin, 2009), p. 27.

9 "We used to talk": Henry Jaglom, author interview (hereafter AI), July 23, 1993.

10 "He won't do it": Peter Bogdanovich, quoted by Jaglom, AI, March 5, 2012.

11 "You're the arrogant kid": Orson Welles, quoted by Jaglom, AI, March 5, 2012.

13 "Yeah, I'm very moved": Bert Schneider, quoted by Jaglom, AI, March 5, 2012.

13 "Jack was ready": Schneider, AI, February 19, 1995.

14 "I had begun to think": Jaglom, AI, no date.

14 "I've lost my girlish enthusiasm": Jaglom, e-mail, June 26, 2012.

15 "It's not that he didn't": Jaglom, AI, March 5, 2012.

16 "Orson couldn't get a movie done": Jaglom, AI, July 23, 1993.

16 "three weeks later": Jaglom, AI, July 23, 1993.

17 "is a man who has": Welles, quoted by Jaglom in a memo to Jack Nicholson, May 20, 1982.

17 "*The Big Brass Ring* was about": Jaglom, AI, July 23, 1993.

17 "if I got one of six": AI, July 23, 1993.

18 "he needed to bring": Jaglom, e-mail, June 8, 2012.

18 "Then he made me": Jaglom, AI, March 5, 2012.

19 "shower curtain": Patrick Terrail, *A Taste of Hollywood: The Story of Ma Maison* (New York: Lebhar-Friedman, 1999), p. 46.

19 "the fanciest French restaurant": Charles Perry, "Ma Maison, the Sequel," *Los Angeles Times*, October 25, 2001.

19 "The restaurant had become": Terrail, AI, June 2012.

20 "They'll fly you": Terrail, AI, June 2012.

20 "crotch": Terrail, AI, June 2012.

20 "I am flattered": Terrail, AI, June 2012.

20 "HELLO, HOW ARE YOU?!": Jaglom, AI, March 7, 2012.

20 "People would say": Jaglom, AI, March 7, 2012.

20 "You have to do something": Jaglom, AI, March 7, 2012.

20 "was often surreal": Gore Vidal, "Remembering Orson Welles," *The New York Review of Books*, June 1, 1989.

21 "that's the only thing": *My Lunches with Orson*, p. 79.

21 "Underrated": *My Lunches with Orson*, p. 186.

21 "Ruined by all the French chefs": *My Lunches with Orson*, p. 250.

21 "Everyone treated Orson badly": Jaglom, AI, May 10, 1995.

22 "single most destructive enemy": Welles and Bogdanovich, *This Is Orson Welles*, New York, 1998, p. xxi.

22 "Houseman started out": Barbara Leaming, *Orson Welles: A Biography* (New York: Viking, 1989), p. 81.

22 "two dishes of flaming": Simon Callow, *Orson Welles: The Road to Xanadu* (New York: Viking, 1995), p. 477.

23 "Are you OK?": Jaglom, AI, March 7, 2012.

23 "Even Orson was shocked": Jaglom, AI, March 7, 2012.

23 "It just shows me": Barbara Leaming, "Orson Welles: The Unfulfilled Promise," *The New York Times*, July 14, 1985.

25 "Orson is an enigmatic figure": Jaglom, "Who was that masked man?" *Los Angeles Times Book Review*, February 29, 2004, p. 3.

25 "The final scene of *The Lady from Shanghai*": Jaglom, "Who was that masked man?" *Los Angeles Times Book Review*, February 29, 2004, p. 3.

25 "Wait till I die": Jaglom, "Who was that masked man?" Ibid.

26 "I gave him": Jaglom, AI, March 7, 2012.

Part I

119   "Unless we made a 35 millimeter blimp": A blimp is an enclosure that surrounds the camera for the purposes of deadening the sound the camera makes when running.

143   "So a check came": According to a document cited by Simon Callow in the second volume of his biography of Welles, the sum was $5,000. Cf. Simon Callow, *Orson Welles: Hello Americans* (New York: Viking, 2006), p. 8.

Part II

253   **"balling Deanna Durbin":** According to Samantha Barbas, in her book *The First Lady of Hollywood: A Biography of Louella Parsons*, Hopper "falsely" accused Cotton of having an affair with Durbin.

264   **"Susan Smith":** a pseudonym.

272   "But this fellow Carringer found the smoking gun": Nowhere in his memoir, *Unfinished Business*, does Houseman flat-out deny there was a second Welles script, but nowhere does he mention it, either, and gives full writing credit to Mankiewicz. I could not find a reference in Carringer's book to finding a telegram from Houseman to Welles favoring Welles's script over Mankiewicz's, although there is a footnote referring to a telegram Houseman sent to Mankiewicz in which the former wrote that he "liked most of Orson's new scenes" (p. 153).

272   "He has a description of me": I have not been able to find a passage that states that Welles put his arms around Carringer. Carringer himself has not responded to queries.

272   "use of the word *collaborative*": Welles misremembers, slightly. The passage in question appears in Carringer's essay "Orson Welles and Gregg Toland: Their Collaboration on 'Citizen Kane,'" not in his book on *Kane*. It reads: ". . . the very mention of the term collaboration at a wrong moment can be enough to send him into a rage."

283   "this producer *wants* me to say no": It may very well be that the "bad Welles legend" poisoned Mitterand, whom Welles considered his ace in the hole. In a telegram he sent to Kodar on the occasion of Welles's death, he wrote that Welles "may not have been able or may not have wanted to have followed to an end this film." The implication, bizarre at best, is that by *not* financing the film, France was fulfilling Welles's

conscious or unconscious desire. Quoted in Jonathan Rosenbaum, *Discovering Orson Welles* (Berkeley: University of California Press, 2007), p. 86.

287 "terrible wine again": Henry Jaglom, "Orson Welles: Last Take," *Los Angeles Times*, October 14, 1995.

Appendix

292 "It's an essay on Spain": Mary Blume, *International Herald Tribune*, 1983.

292 "Up to now": Mary Blume, Ibid.

294 "You gotta take the sour with the bitter": A. Scott Berg, *Goldwyn: A Biography* (New York: Riverhead, 1998), p. 396.

297 "Mr. Skunk": Edward Baron Turk, *Hollywood Diva: A Biography of Jeanette MacDonald* (Berkeley: University of California Press, 2000), p. 219.

About the Editor

Peter Biskind is the acclaimed author of *Easy Riders, Raging Bulls, Down and Dirty Pictures, Seeing is Believing,* and *Star,* among other books. His work has appeared in *The New York Times, The Los Angeles Times, The Washington Post, Newsweek, The Nation, Rolling Stone,* and many other publications. He is the former executive editor of *Premiere* and the former editor-in-chief of *American Film,* and is a contributing editor to *Vanity Fair.* He lives in the Hudson Valley.